Visual Reference Basics

Microsoft® Access 2000

Diana Rain

MOUS

Microsoft® initiated the **MOUS (Microsoft® Office User Specialist) program** to provide Office users a means of demonstrating their level of proficiency in each application in the Office suite. After the successful completion of the certification test in an application, users receive a certificate that reflects their level of proficiency.

The **MOUS program** establishes the criteria for both proficient and expert levels in Word, Excel, PowerPoint, FrontPage, and Access, and proficient skill levels in Outlook.

Tests are given at Authorized Testing Centers around the country. Each test takes about 45 minutes to complete.

For more information on how you can become MOUS certified, visit our Web site!

www.ddcpub.com

Acknowledgements

Managing Editor
Jennifer Frew

Project Manager
David Lott

Technical Editors
Frank Dauenhauer
John Ralston

English Editors
Ellen Falk
Emily Hay

Editorial Assistant
Jacinta O'Halloran

Layout and Design
Shawn Morningstar
Elsa Johannesson

Cover Design
Amy Capuano

Published by DDC Publishing, Inc.

For information, address:
DDC Publishing, Inc
275 Madison Avenue
New York, NY 10016.
Internet address: http://www.ddcpub.com

ISBN: 1-56243-631-7
Catalog Number: G43

First DDC Publishing, Inc. Printing

10 9 8 7 6 5 4 3 2 1

Printed in the United States of America.

Table of Contents

Introduction vii

Visual Reference Index xi

Databases 1

Display Objects in the Database Window 2
Create a Group in the Database Window 4
Disable the Startup Dialog Box 6
Change the Default Database Folder. 7
Personalized Menus 8
Show or Hide a Toolbar. 10
Add a Toolbar Button That Opens a Web Page 12
Create a Database Using a Wizard 14
Open a Database. 18
Add or Edit Table Relationships 20
Link to a Table in Another Access Database 24

Tables 27

Create a Table Using a Wizard 28
Open a Table. 30
Add a Field to a Table 32
Add a Lookup Field to a Table 34
Set the Default Field Value. 36
Require a Field Value. 37
Apply a Validation Rule to a Field. 38
Move a Field in a Table 40
Delete a Field from a Table. 42
Set the Primary Key for a Table 44
Index a Table. 46

Queries 49

Create a Find Duplicates Query Using a Wizard 50
Create a Find Unmatched Query Using a Wizard. 52
Create a Crosstab Query Using a Wizard 54
Create a Make-Table Query 56
Create an Update Query. 58
Create an Append Query 60
Create a Simple Select Query. 64
Add or Remove a Table in a Query. 66
Add or Remove a Field in a Query 68
Display All Fields in Query Results. 70
Exclude Duplicate Records in a Query 72

Enter Data 73

Adjust Datasheet Column Width and Row Height 74
Hide or Show Datasheet Gridlines 76
Hide a Column in a Datasheet 78
Enter Data in a Datasheet, Form, or Page. 80
Copy and Move Data in Forms, Datasheets, and Pages. 82
Navigate in a Datasheet, Form, or Page 84
Find Data in a Form or Datasheet. 86
Replace Data in a Form or Datasheet 88
Filter Records in a Datasheet or Form 90
Sort the Data in a Datasheet or Form 94

Forms 97

Create a Form Using a Wizard 98
Create a Form Using AutoForm 100
Create a Multiple-Tab Form 102
Open a Form 104
Apply an AutoFormat to a Form 106
Create a Subform and Add It to a Form 108
Edit a Subform 110
Set the Tab Order in a Form. 112
Add a Form Header and Footer 114
Change the Form Window Title 116
Show the Result of a Calculation on a Form. 117
Apply an Input Mask to a Field on a Form 118
Add a Field to a Form or Report. 120

Reports 123

Create a Report Using a Wizard 124
Create an AutoReport 126
Apply an AutoFormat to a Report 127
Create Mailing Labels Using a Wizard 128
Open a Report 130
Set Report Page Margins and Orientation 132
Add a Header and Footer to a Report 134
Add Page Numbers to a Report 136
Insert the Date/Time in a Report 138
Group a Report 140
Preview a Report 142
Print a Report 144
Create a Report Snapshot 146

Data Access Pages 149

Create a Data Access Page Using a Wizard 150
Create a Data Access Page Using AutoPage 152
Apply a Theme to a Data Access Page 154
Create a Hotspot Control That Opens a Web Page 156
Open a Data Access Page 158

Design View 161

Control Basics 162
Properties 164
Copy Control Formatting 166
Set Default Properties for Controls 167
Expressions 168
Use the Grid in Design View 170
Draw a Line on a Form, Report, or Page 172
Add Borders to a Form, Report, or Page 174
Add a Command Button to a Form 176
Add a Label to a Form, Report, or Page 178
Change the Font of Text in a Label 179
Add a Graphic to a Form or Report 180
Create a Tip for a Control 182
Change the Record Source for a Form or Report 184

Import/Export Data 185

Import from Another Access Database 186
Import Data from a Non-Access Database 188
Export to a Word Mail Merge Data Source 190
Output Report Data to Microsoft Excel 191

Get Help 193

Get Help Using the Answer Wizard 194
Get Help Using the Office Assistant 196
Customize the Office Assistant 198
Change the Office Assistant Character 200
Disable the Office Assistant 201
Get Help Using the Table of Contents 202
Get Help from Office on the Web 203
Get Help in the Office Update Search Page 204

Glossary 207

Index 211

Introduction

What Is a Database?

A database is a collection of related information. For example, a telephone book is an example of a database; it contains related information about each person listed in it: his or her name, address, and telephone number.

A database contains records and fields. A record is a collection of different types of information about the same subject. In the case of the telephone book, each person (listing) is a record. A field is a category of information; in the case of the telephone book, the category "Address" is a field.

Field ↓

Name	John Smith
Address	123 Main Street ← **Record**
City	Willowbrook
Tel. No.	630-222-5555

One of the useful things about a database is that, unlike a telephone book, it not only stores data, it allows you to sort and organize it. You can easily find records that have common characteristics. For example, you could sort out and list all the people who live on Main Street whose telephone number begins with 222.

What Is Access?

Access is a *relational* database. A relational database utilizes two or more tables (covered in more detail on the next page), containing data arranged in rows and columns, to cross-reference and define *relationships* between the data. In contrast, a *flat-file* database is limited to a single table.

A relational database breaks the "big picture" into smaller, more manageable pieces. For example, if you were gathering information about a new product line, each type of information—product, seller, and distributor—would be stored in its own, related table, rather than in one large, all-inclusive table. This unique ability to store data in smaller, related groups gives a relational database much more efficiency, speed, and flexibility in locating and reporting information.

Elements of a Database

A *table* is a collection of data about a specific topic, such as business contacts or a book collection. The table is the basic element of the database. Tables organize data into *rows*, called *records,* and *columns*, called *fields.* Records and fields, combined, make up the table.

Each *record* (row) contains information about one item or entity and is a complete record of the item. For example, in a table called "Books," all the information about one book is in one row.

Each *field* (column) contains information of a certain type for all records. A field consists of a name or category such as "Publisher," and an entry such as "Ramona Publishing." The field "Publisher" contains the title of the publisher of each book in the "Books" table.

The Database Window

In addition to tables, Access 2000 has many features that enable you to manage data in meaningful ways. You can view the data from different perspectives using forms, extract data based on certain conditions using queries, analyze the data in different ways using reports, and utilize various automatic procedures, such as macros and modules.

The *database window* is where all elements of an Access database are brought together. Each time you open a database, the database window displays information about the database and each type of object it contains. All information associated with a given project is available with a few clicks of the mouse. This organizational concept allows you to work effectively and creatively by dealing with the pieces of the big picture individually.

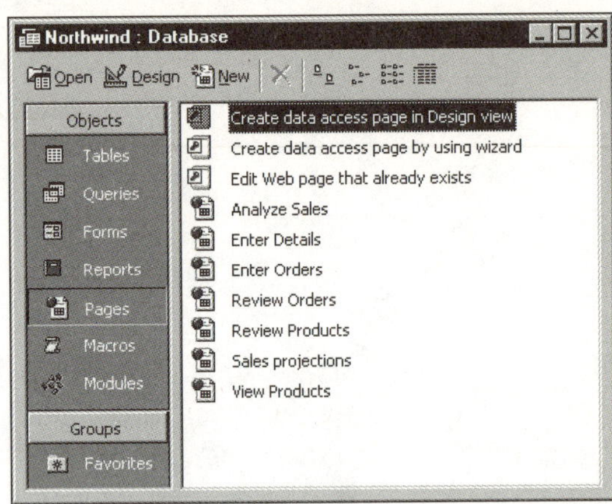

Use the database window to access database objects in a database as follows:

Tables Click **Tables** to list the tables in the current database. A table stores data. You can open the table in Datasheet view to enter data in it. Or, you can create a data entry form for the table.

Queries Click this button to show the queries in the current database. A query is either a question about the data stored in your tables or a request to perform an action on the data.

Forms Use **Forms** to create a custom interface for data entry. You can use a single form to enter and display data from multiple record sources (tables and/or queries). Examples of forms are sales summaries, phone lists, and mailing labels.

Reports Click the **Reports** button to display the reports in your database. You can create reports using queries and tables as the data source for the report.

Pages Click **Pages** to show the data access pages in the database. Data access pages are used for entering and/or viewing data from a Web site or intranet. The data access page is the user interface for the database.

Macros/Modules Macros are small programs used to automate a repetitive task or set the database startup and exit code. A module stores program code.

A Note to the New Access User

Microsoft Access 2000 is an extremely complex program. This guide is written for the user who has some familiarity with the concepts involved with creating a new database—either flat-file databases or relational databases. If you would like help with fundamental database concepts, the following books are available from DDC Publishing: *Learning Microsoft Office 2000 and Microsoft Access 2000 Short Course.*

Visual Reference Index

Databases

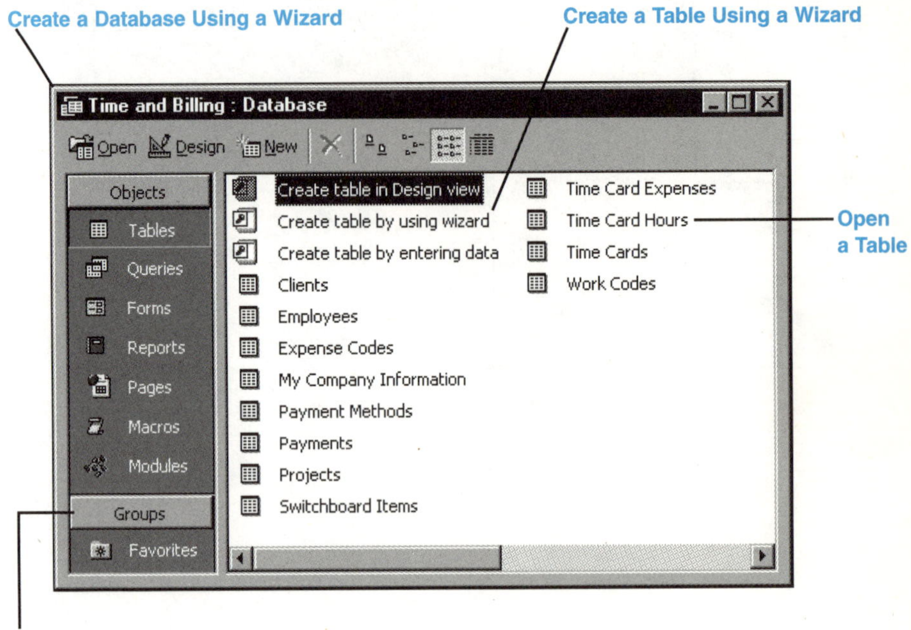

Databases *(continued...)*

Add or Edit Table Relationships

Create a Database Using a Wizard
The Database Wizard sets up all table relationships for you.

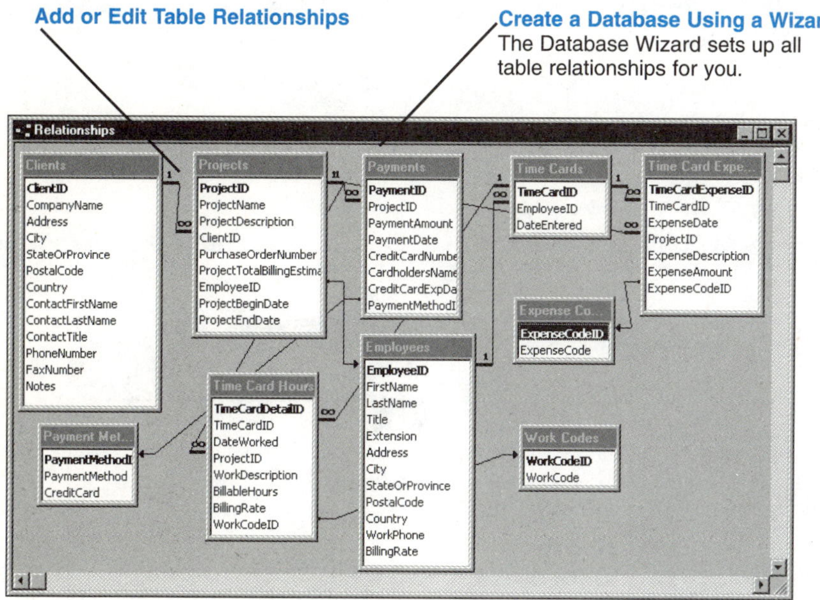

Combine Information from Multiple Tables

Show the information stored in several tables in a separate table and save the new table.

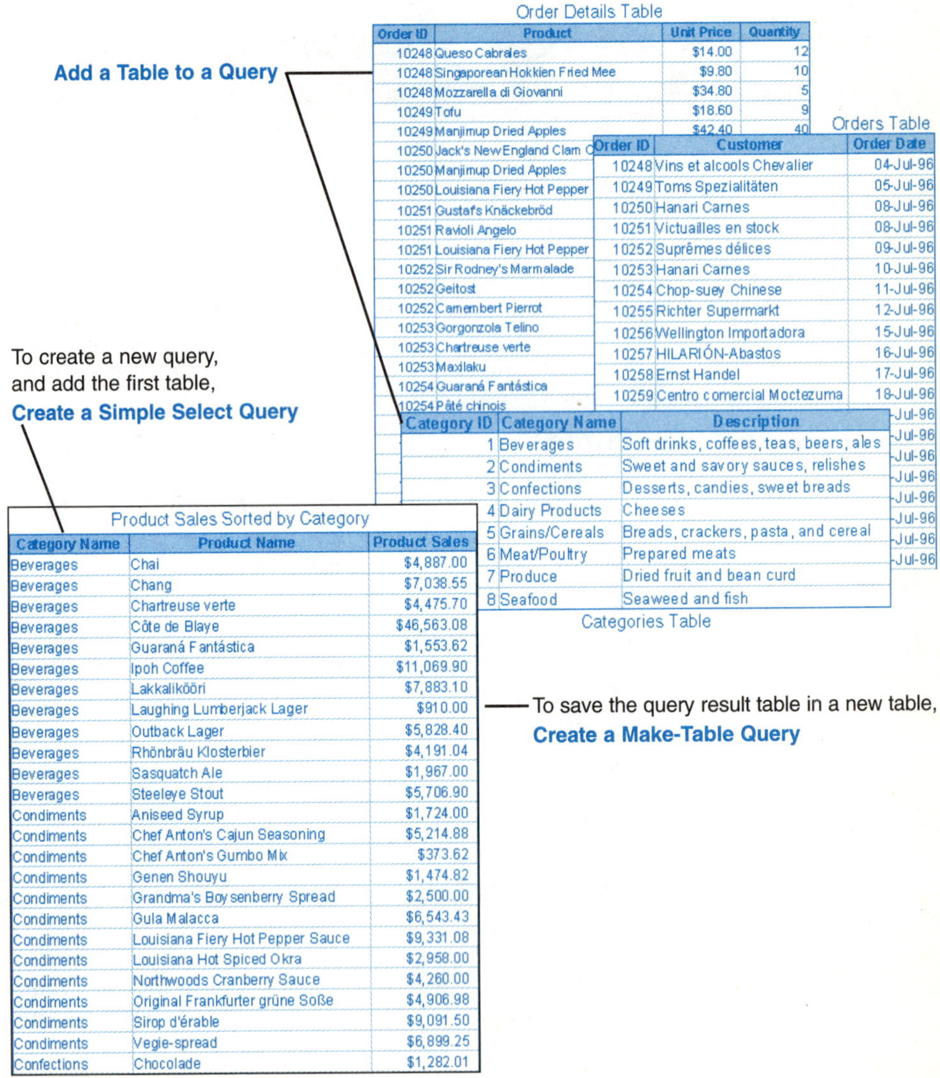

Add a Table to a Query

To create a new query, and add the first table, **Create a Simple Select Query**

To save the query result table in a new table, **Create a Make-Table Query**

Order Details Table

Order ID	Product	Unit Price	Quantity
10248	Queso Cabrales	$14.00	12
10248	Singaporean Hokkien Fried Mee	$9.80	10
10248	Mozzarella di Giovanni	$34.80	5
10249	Tofu	$18.60	9
10249	Manjimup Dried Apples	$42.40	40
10250	Jack's New England Clam C		
10250	Manjimup Dried Apples		
10250	Louisiana Fiery Hot Pepper		
10251	Gustaf's Knäckebröd		
10251	Ravioli Angelo		
10251	Louisiana Fiery Hot Pepper		
10252	Sir Rodney's Marmalade		
10252	Geitost		
10252	Camembert Pierrot		
10253	Gorgonzola Telino		
10253	Chartreuse verte		
10253	Maxilaku		
10254	Guaraná Fantástica		
10254	Pâté chinois		

Orders Table

Order ID	Customer	Order Date
10248	Vins et alcools Chevalier	04-Jul-96
10249	Toms Spezialitäten	05-Jul-96
10250	Hanari Carnes	08-Jul-96
10251	Victuailles en stock	08-Jul-96
10252	Suprêmes délices	09-Jul-96
10253	Hanari Carnes	10-Jul-96
10254	Chop-suey Chinese	11-Jul-96
10255	Richter Supermarkt	12-Jul-96
10256	Wellington Importadora	15-Jul-96
10257	HILARIÓN-Abastos	16-Jul-96
10258	Ernst Handel	17-Jul-96
10259	Centro comercial Moctezuma	18-Jul-96

Category ID	Category Name	Description
1	Beverages	Soft drinks, coffees, teas, beers, ales
2	Condiments	Sweet and savory sauces, relishes
3	Confections	Desserts, candies, sweet breads
4	Dairy Products	Cheeses
5	Grains/Cereals	Breads, crackers, pasta, and cereal
6	Meat/Poultry	Prepared meats
7	Produce	Dried fruit and bean curd
8	Seafood	Seaweed and fish

Categories Table

Product Sales Sorted by Category

Category Name	Product Name	Product Sales
Beverages	Chai	$4,887.00
Beverages	Chang	$7,038.55
Beverages	Chartreuse verte	$4,475.70
Beverages	Côte de Blaye	$46,563.08
Beverages	Guaraná Fantástica	$1,553.62
Beverages	Ipoh Coffee	$11,069.90
Beverages	Lakkaliköõri	$7,883.10
Beverages	Laughing Lumberjack Lager	$910.00
Beverages	Outback Lager	$5,828.40
Beverages	Rhönbräu Klosterbier	$4,191.04
Beverages	Sasquatch Ale	$1,967.00
Beverages	Steeleye Stout	$5,706.90
Condiments	Aniseed Syrup	$1,724.00
Condiments	Chef Anton's Cajun Seasoning	$5,214.88
Condiments	Chef Anton's Gumbo Mix	$373.62
Condiments	Genen Shouyu	$1,474.82
Condiments	Grandma's Boysenberry Spread	$2,500.00
Condiments	Gula Malacca	$6,543.43
Condiments	Louisiana Fiery Hot Pepper Sauce	$9,331.08
Condiments	Louisiana Hot Spiced Okra	$2,958.00
Condiments	Northwoods Cranberry Sauce	$4,260.00
Condiments	Original Frankfurter grüne Soße	$4,906.98
Condiments	Sirop d'érable	$9,091.50
Condiments	Vegie-spread	$6,899.25
Confections	Chocolade	$1,282.01

Web Pages

To see how the page will look in your Web browser.

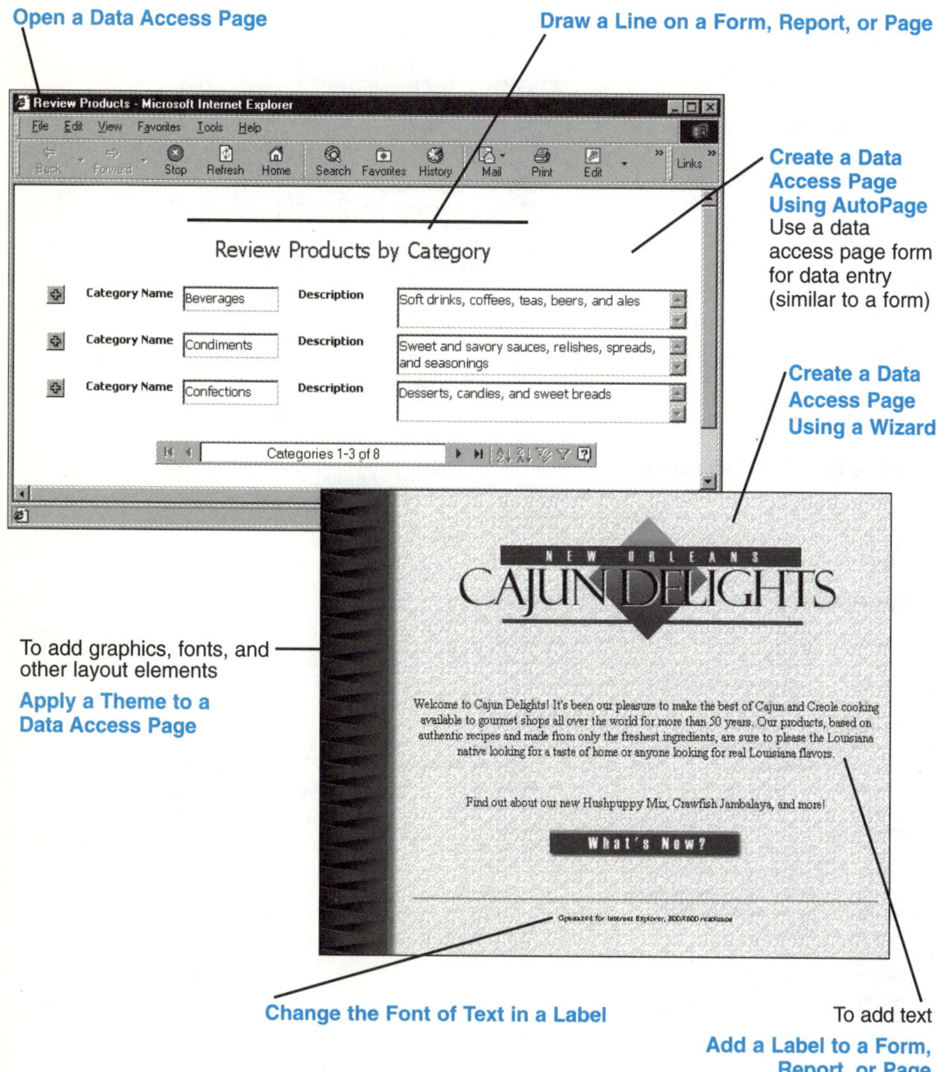

Filter Data

Product Name	Category	Unit Price	Units In Stock
Chai	Beverages	$18.00	39
Chang	Beverages	$19.00	17
Aniseed Syrup	Condiments	$10.00	13
Chef Anton's Cajun Seasoning	Condiments	$22.00	53
Chef Anton's Gumbo Mix	Condiments	$21.35	0
Grandma's Boysenberry Spread	Condiments	$25.00	120
Uncle Bob's Organic Dried Pears	Produce	$30.00	15
Northwoods Cranberry Sauce	Condiments	$40.00	6
Mishi Kobe Niku	Meat/Poultry	$97.00	29
Ikura	Seafood	$31.00	31
Queso Cabrales	Dairy Products	$21.00	22
Queso Manchego La Pastora	Dairy Products	$38.00	86
Konbu	Seafood	$6.00	24
Tofu	Produce	$23.25	35
Genen Shouyu	Condiments	$15.50	39
Pavlova	Confections	$17.45	29
Alice Mutton	Meat/Poultry	$39.00	0
Carnarvon Tigers	Seafood	$62.50	42
Teatime Chocolate Biscuits	Confections	$9.20	25
Sir Rodney's Marmalade	Confections	$81.00	40
Sir Rodney's Scones	Confections	$10.00	3
Gustaf's Knäckebröd			
Tunnbröd			
Guaraná Fantástica			

To show only particular records, **Filter Records in a Datasheet or Form**

Product Name	Category	Unit Price	Units In Stock
Aniseed Syrup	Condiments	$10.00	13
Chef Anton's Cajun Seasoning	Condiments	$22.00	53
Chef Anton's Gumbo Mix	Condiments	$21.35	0
Grandma's Boysenberry Spread	Condiments	$25.00	120
Northwoods Cranberry Sauce	Condiments	$40.00	6
Genen Shouyu	Condiments	$15.50	39
Gula Malacca	Condiments	$19.45	27
Sirop d'érable	Condiments	$28.50	113
Vegie-spread	Condiments	$43.90	24
Louisiana Fiery Hot Pepper Sauce	Condiments	$21.05	76
Louisiana Hot Spiced Okra	Condiments	$17.00	4
Original Frankfurter grüne Soße	Condiments	$13.00	32

This example filters out all records that do not have Condiments in the Category field.

Edit in Datasheet View

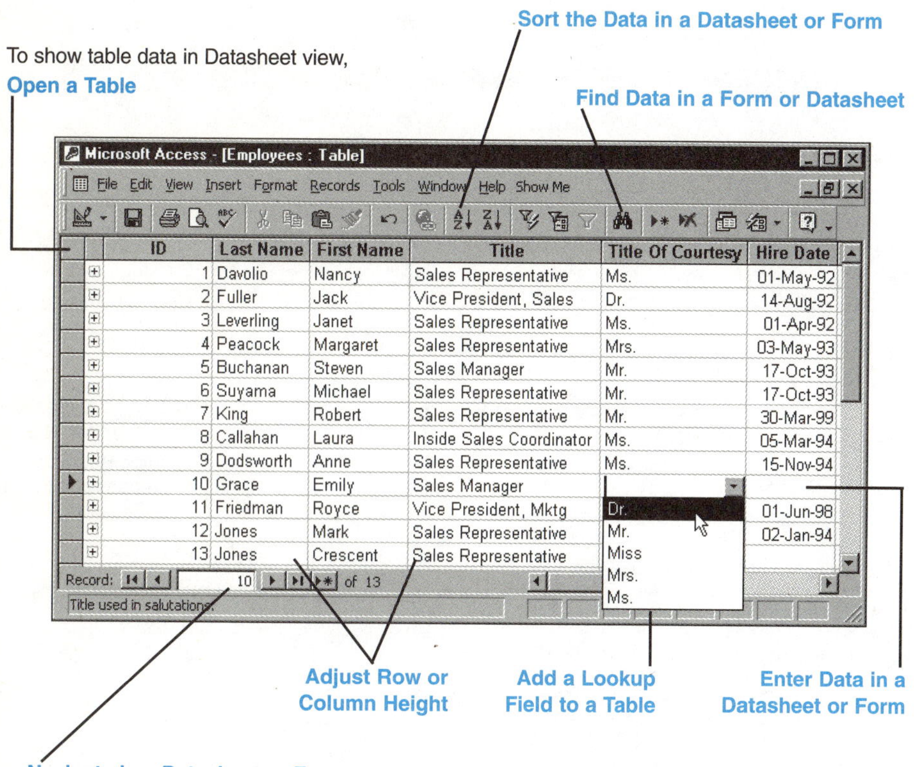

Export Data

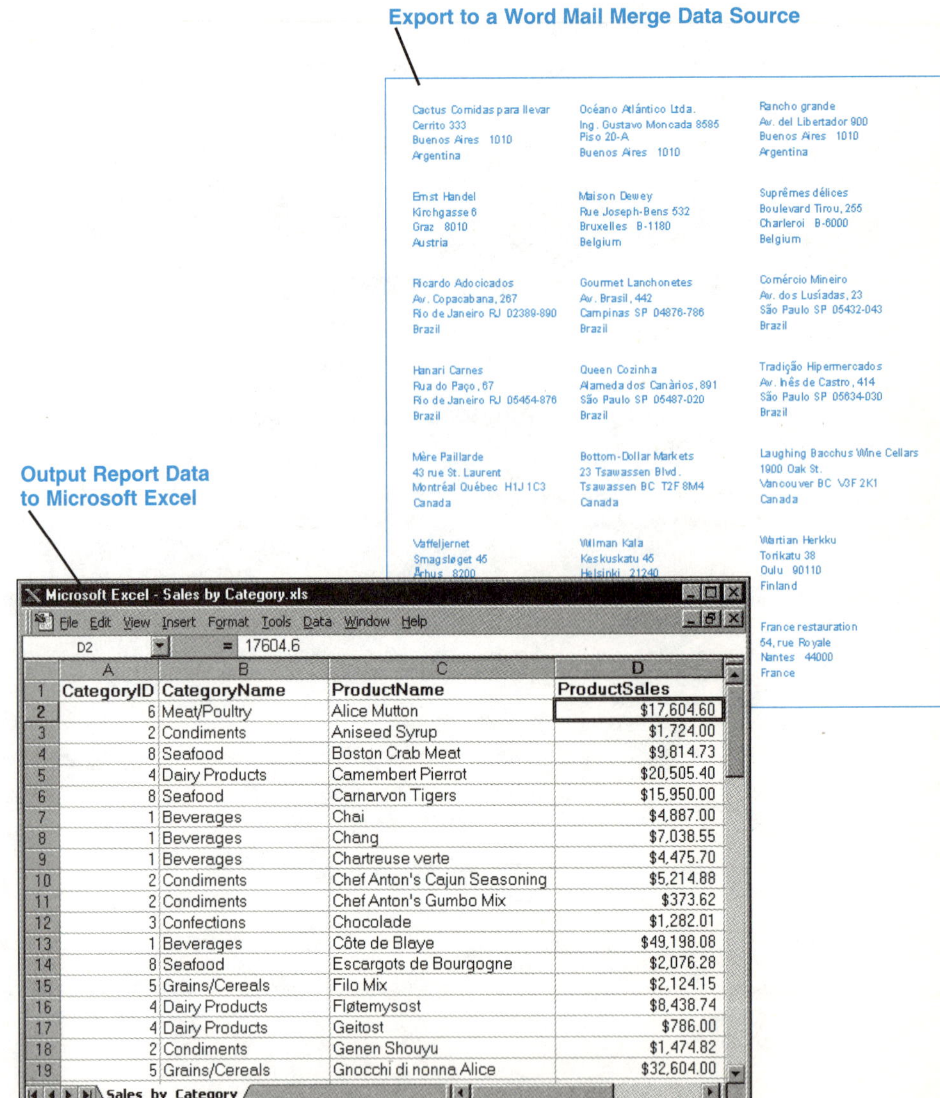
Export to a Word Mail Merge Data Source
Cactus Comidas para llevar
Cerrito 333
Buenos Aires 1010
Argentina
Océano Atlántico Ltda.
Ing. Gustavo Moncada 8585
Piso 20-A
Buenos Aires 1010
Rancho grande
Av. del Libertador 900
Buenos Aires 1010
Argentina
Ernst Handel
Kirchgasse 6
Graz 8010
Austria
Maison Dewey
Rue Joseph-Bens 532
Bruxelles B-1180
Belgium
Suprêmes délices
Boulevard Tirou, 255
Charleroi B-6000
Belgium
Ricardo Adocicados
Av. Copacabana, 267
Rio de Janeiro RJ 02389-890
Brazil
Gourmet Lanchonetes
Av. Brasil, 442
Campinas SP 04876-786
Brazil
Comércio Mineiro
Av. dos Lusíadas, 23
São Paulo SP 05432-043
Brazil
Hanari Carnes
Rua do Paço, 67
Rio de Janeiro RJ 05454-876
Brazil
Queen Cozinha
Alameda dos Canàrios, 891
São Paulo SP 05487-020
Brazil
Tradição Hipermercados
Av. Inês de Castro, 414
São Paulo SP 05634-030
Brazil
Mère Paillarde
43 rue St. Laurent
Montréal Québec H1J 1C3
Canada
Bottom-Dollar Markets
23 Tsawassen Blvd.
Tsawassen BC T2F 8M4
Canada
Laughing Bacchus Wine Cellars
1900 Oak St.
Vancouver BC V3F 2K1
Canada
Vaffeljernet
Smagsløget 45
Århus 8200
Wilman Kala
Keskuskatu 45
Helsinki 21240
Wartian Herkku
Torikatu 38
Oulu 90110
Finland
France restauration
54, rue Royale
Nantes 44000
France
Output Report Data to Microsoft Excel
Microsoft Excel - Sales by Category.xls
File Edit View Insert Format Tools Data Window Help
D2 = 17604.6
A B C D
1 CategoryID CategoryName ProductName ProductSales
2 6 Meat/Poultry Alice Mutton $17,604.60
3 2 Condiments Aniseed Syrup $1,724.00
4 8 Seafood Boston Crab Meat $9,814.73
5 4 Dairy Products Camembert Pierrot $20,505.40
6 8 Seafood Carnarvon Tigers $15,950.00
7 1 Beverages Chai $4,887.00
8 1 Beverages Chang $7,038.55
9 1 Beverages Chartreuse verte $4,475.70
10 2 Condiments Chef Anton's Cajun Seasoning $5,214.88
11 2 Condiments Chef Anton's Gumbo Mix $373.62
12 3 Confections Chocolade $1,282.01
13 1 Beverages Côte de Blaye $49,198.08
14 8 Seafood Escargots de Bourgogne $2,076.28
15 5 Grains/Cereals Filo Mix $2,124.15
16 4 Dairy Products Fløtemysost $8,438.74
17 4 Dairy Products Geitost $786.00
18 2 Condiments Genen Shouyu $1,474.82
19 5 Grains/Cereals Gnocchi di nonna Alice $32,604.00
Sales_by_Category

Reports

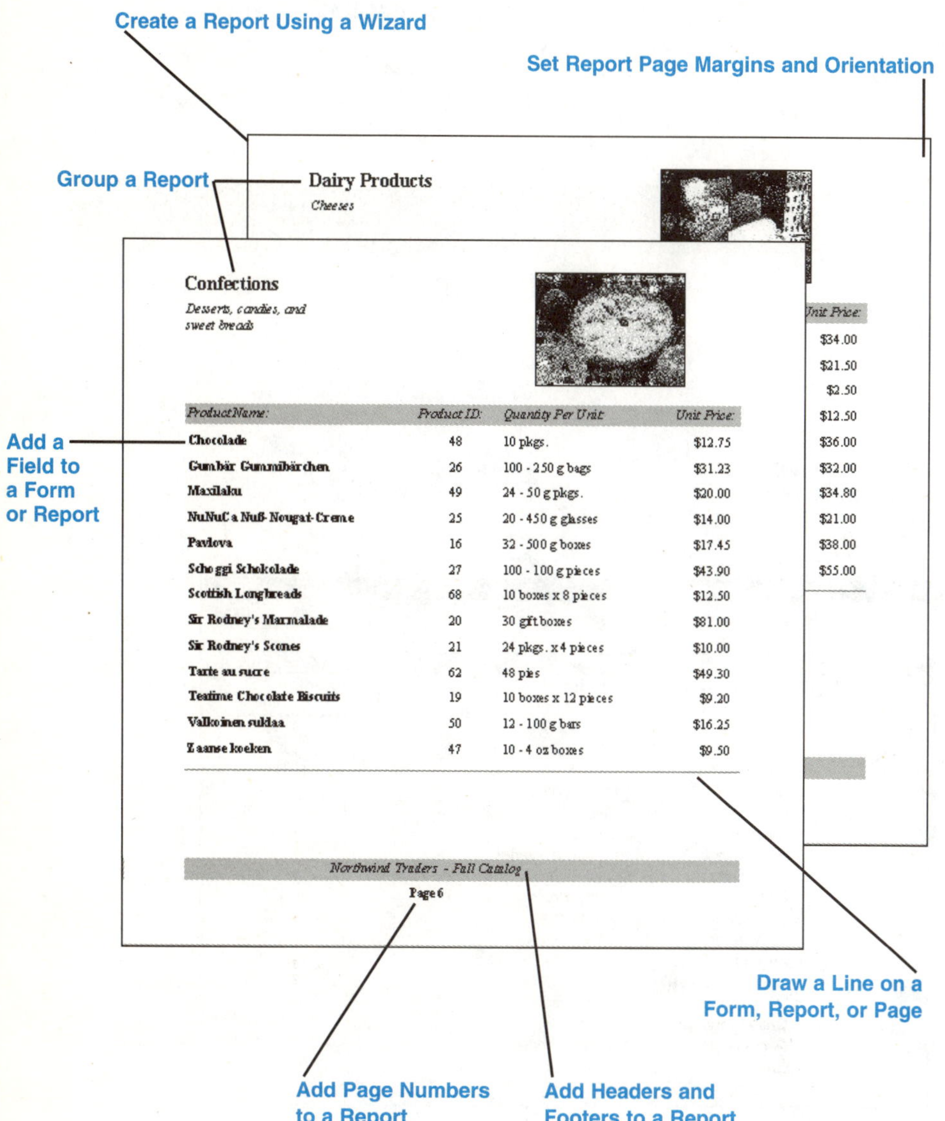

Create a Report Using a Wizard
Set Report Page Margins and Orientation
Group a Report
Dairy Products
Cheeses
Unit Price:
$34.00
$21.50
$2.50
$12.50
$36.00
$32.00
$34.80
$21.00
$38.00
$55.00
Confections
Desserts, candies, and sweet breads
Product Name:
Product ID:
Quantity Per Unit:
Unit Price:
Chocolade 48 10 pkgs. $12.75
Gumbär Gummibärchen 26 100 - 250 g bags $31.23
Maxilaku 49 24 - 50 g pkgs. $20.00
NuNuCa Nuß-Nougat-Creme 25 20 - 450 g glasses $14.00
Pavlova 16 32 - 500 g boxes $17.45
Schoggi Schokolade 27 100 - 100 g pieces $43.90
Scottish Longbreads 68 10 boxes x 8 pieces $12.50
Sir Rodney's Marmalade 20 30 gift boxes $81.00
Sir Rodney's Scones 21 24 pkgs. x 4 pieces $10.00
Tarte au sucre 62 48 pies $49.30
Teatime Chocolate Biscuits 19 10 boxes x 12 pieces $9.20
Valkoinen suklaa 50 12 - 100 g bars $16.25
Zaanse koeken 47 10 - 4 oz boxes $9.50
Add a Field to a Form or Report
Northwind Traders - Fall Catalog
Page 6
Draw a Line on a Form, Report, or Page
Add Page Numbers to a Report
Add Headers and Footers to a Report

Forms

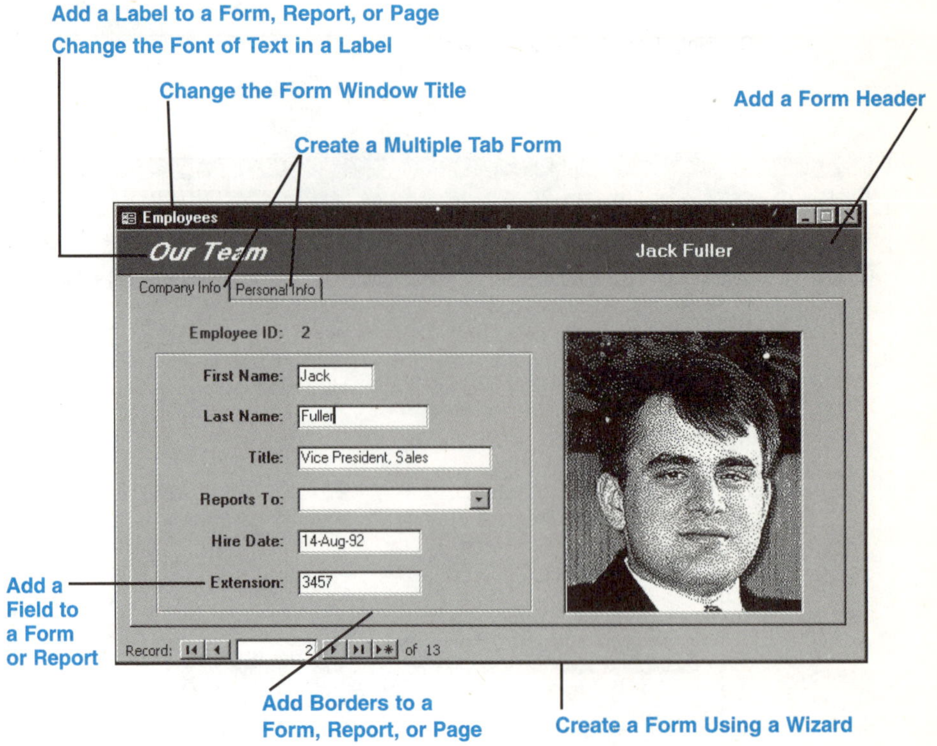

Add a Label to a Form, Report, or Page
Change the Font of Text in a Label
Change the Form Window Title
Create a Multiple Tab Form
Add a Form Header
Employees
Our Team
Jack Fuller
Company Info
Personal Info
Employee ID: 2
First Name: Jack
Last Name: Fuller
Title: Vice President, Sales
Reports To:
Hire Date: 14-Aug-92
Extension: 3457
Record: 2 of 13
Add a Field to a Form or Report
Add Borders to a Form, Report, or Page
Create a Form Using a Wizard

Create a Subform and Add it to a Form
Add a Field to a Form or Report
Quarterly Orders
Customer ID ERNSH
City Graz
Company Name Ernst Handel
Country Austria
Product Name
Qtr 1
Qtr 2
Qtr 3
Qtr 4
Alice Mutton $1,123 $2,607
Aniseed Syrup $180
Chartreuse verte $2,106
Chocolade $607
Fløtemysost $241 $344
Totals $10,260 $9,174 $11,772 $16,890
Grand Total for 1998: $48,096
Record: 19 of 86
Show the Result of a Calculation on a Form

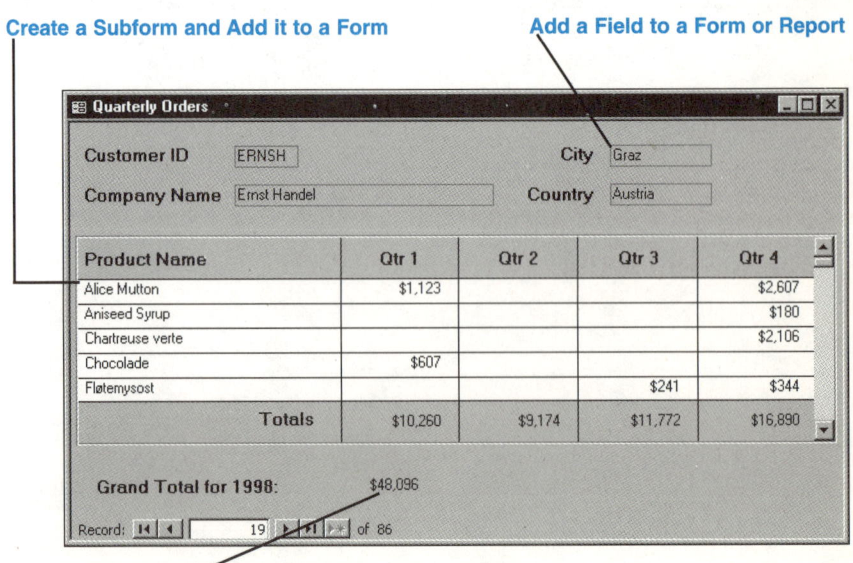

Visit the Office Update Web Site

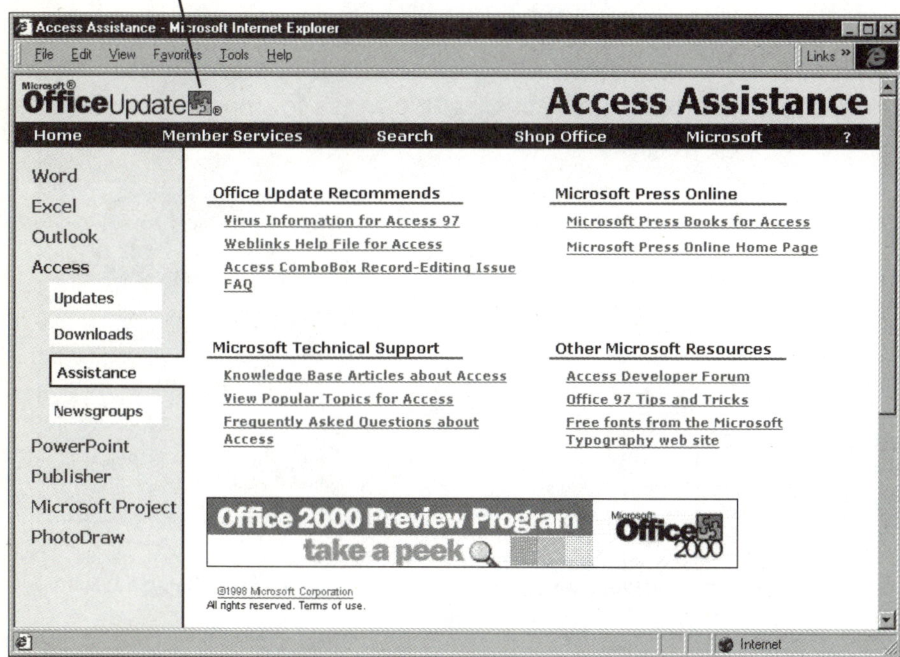

Databases

A database consists of one or more tables that store related data. In addition to tables, a database can include other database objects, such as reports for analyzing data, queries for manipulating the data, and forms used to enter data into tables.

The Database window, shown below, displays the database objects in the current database. You can only open one Access database at a time.

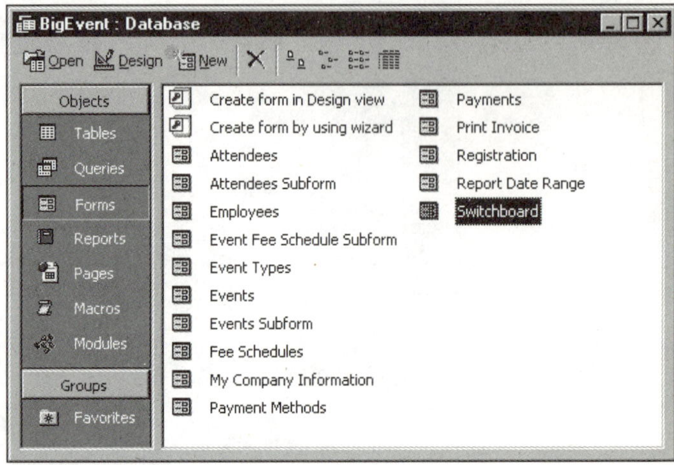

The Database Wizard includes a number of design templates that you can use to create databases for various applications. For example, you can create a Ledger, an Order Entry, or a Time and Billing database from templates in the Wizard. For a description of Database Wizard templates, see the Appendix.

Display Objects in the Database Window

Each database has a Database window that displays the objects (such as forms, reports, tables, etc.) in the currently open database. You can customize how Access displays objects in the window.

Notes:

- The Database window is always open when you are working in a database. However, it might be minimized or hidden behind other open windows. Press **F11** to display it.
- Access menus are context-sensitive. This means that the options on menus vary depending on what you are working on. For example, the View menu contains one set of options when the Database window is active and another set when, for example, a table or Switchboard is open.

1 If the Database window is not on your screen, press **F11**

or click  to display it.

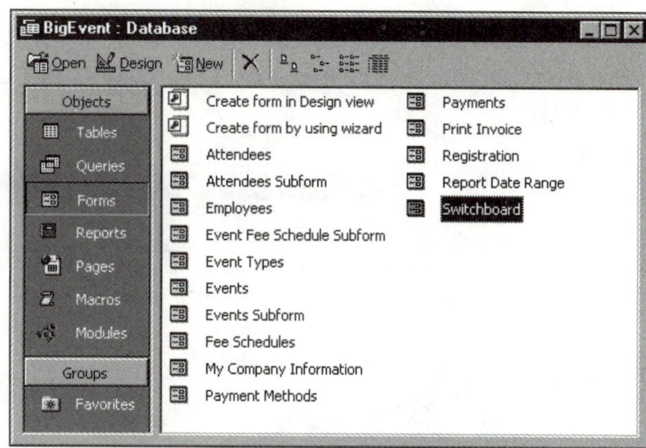

2 To change the icon size if desired:

- Click **Small Icons** .
- Click **Large Icons** .

Note: *This changes the size of both the icons representing database objects and the buttons in the Database window.*

Notes:

- Database objects can be arranged alphabetically by name, or by type, date created, or date last modified.

3 To hide or show extra information about each database object if desired:

- To show only the object name, click **List** .
- To display additional information about each database object, click **Details** . The following illustration shows the Database window in Details view.

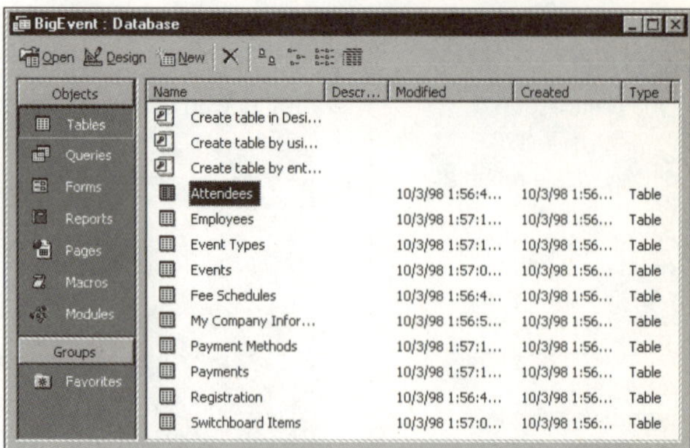

4 To arrange the database icons in a different order if desired:

a. Right-click the background of the window pane to open the shortcut menu.

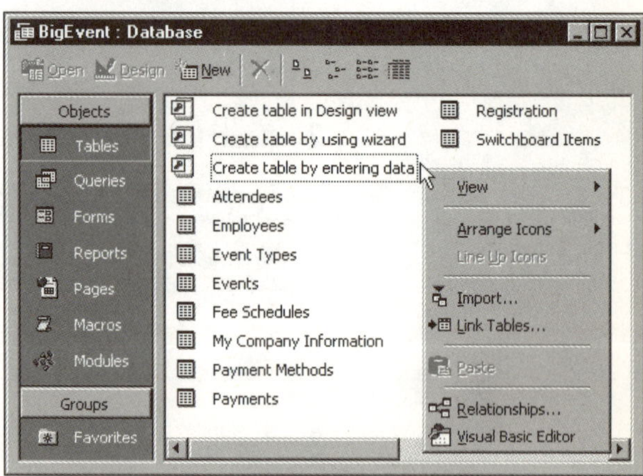

b. Click **Arrange Icons**.

c. Select a sort order from the menu. For example, to sort objects alphabetically according to their names, you would click **By Name**.

Create a Group in the Database Window

Use groups to organize database objects such as tables, forms, reports, and queries in the Database window. A group is a collection of shortcuts to database objects in the current database.

Notes:

- Use groups to categorize and quickly locate related database objects. For example, you could create a group with shortcuts to all tables, queries, forms, and reports relating to a particular project. To list the database objects in the group, click the group icon in the Database window.
- Adding database objects to a group does not remove them from their original location in the Database window. For example, if you add the Movies query to a group, it will still be in the list of queries in the database window.

1 Right-click beneath the **Groups** button in the Database window to open the shortcut menu.

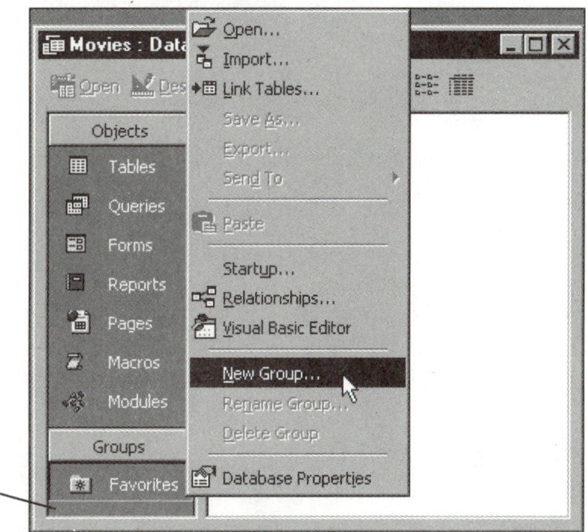

2 Select **New Group**. The New Group dialog box displays.

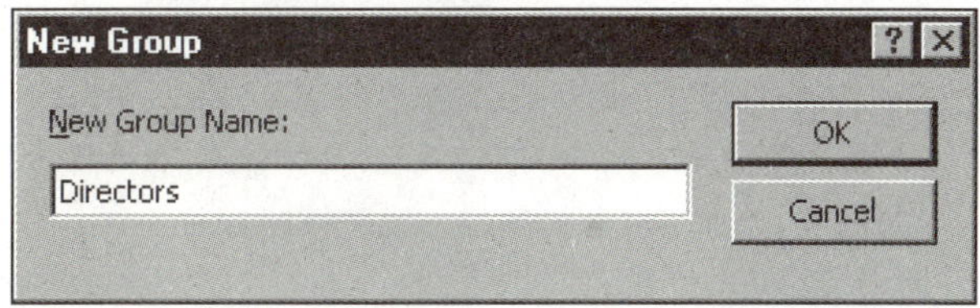

3 Type a name for the new group and click OK.

Notes:

- When you install Access, the Favorites group is added to the Database window by default. You cannot delete the Favorites group. To add shortcuts to files in the Favorites group, you add them to the Favorites folder on your hard disk. For example, if you place a shortcut to a different database in the Favorites folder, you can open the database from the Database window by clicking the shortcut icon in the Favorites group.
- To delete a group, right-click the group and select **Delete Group**.

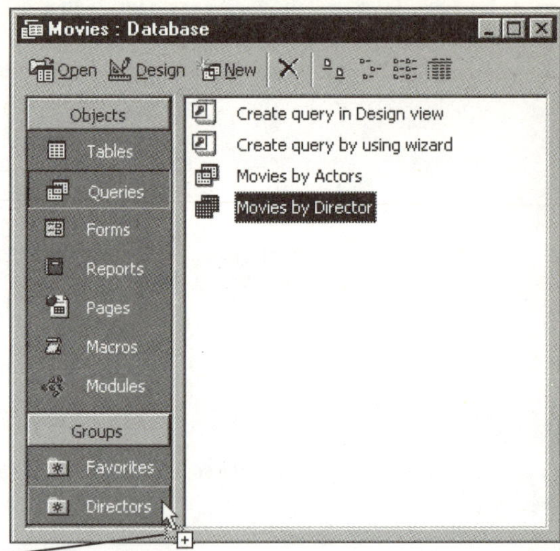

4 Drag the objects to add to the group from the window to group icon.

5 To view the database objects in the group, click the group icon in the Database window. The following illustration shows database objects added to the Directors group in the Movies database.

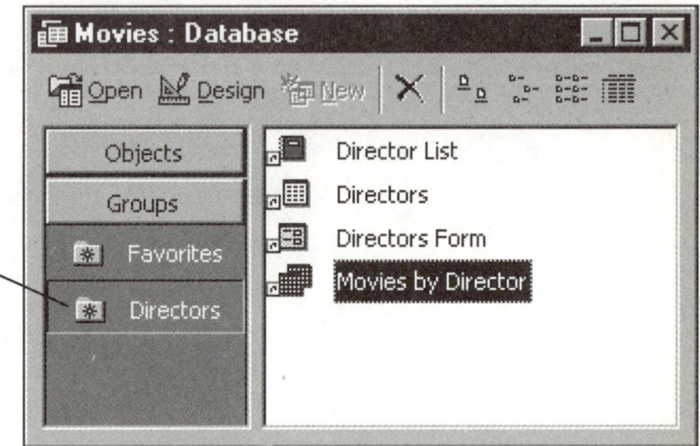

Disable the Startup Dialog Box

By default, every time you start Access, the Startup dialog box displays. You can disable the Startup dialog box so that it does not display.

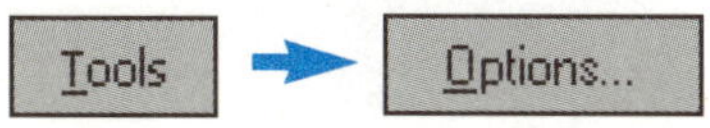

Notes:

- The Startup dialog box is handy when you are first learning Access. After that it may slow you down because you must either select a file from the dialog box or else close it before you can work in Access.
- To show the Startup dialog box whenever you start Access, repeat the procedure.

1 Select **Tools**, **Options**. The Options dialog box displays.

Note: You can do this only if a database is open.

2 Click the **View** tab.

3 Click the **Startup dialog box** option to cancel the selection.

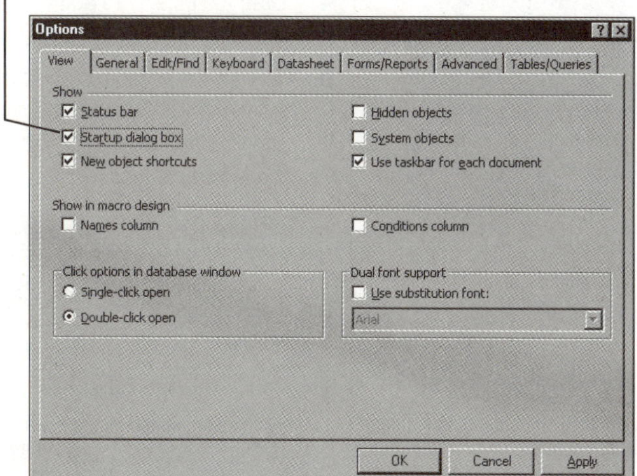

4 Click OK.

Change the Default Database Folder

Specify the folder in which Access will save new databases that you create.

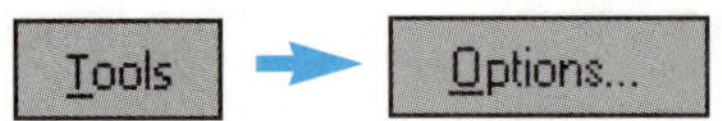

Notes:

- When you save a new database, Access assumes that you want to save it in the default database folder. Whenever you open a database, Access looks for it in the default folder.
- This setting applies to all Access databases.

1 Select **Tools**, **Options**. The Options dialog box displays.

Note: You can do this only if a database is open.

2 Click the **General** tab.

3 Type the pathname of the default folder.

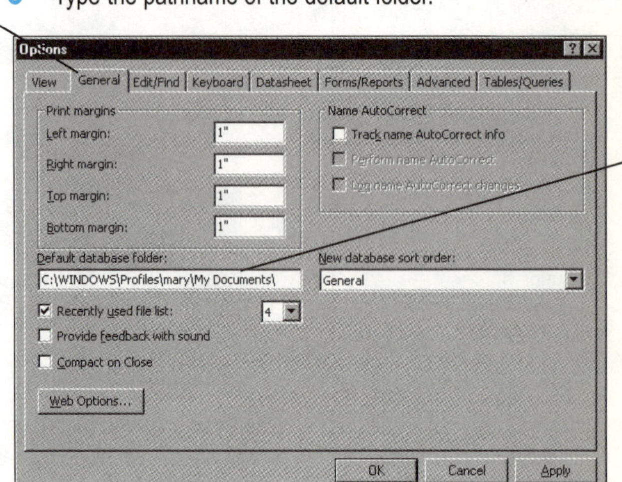

4 Click OK.

Personalized Menus

The personalized menus feature places the commands you use most at the top of each menu and hides the commands that you do not use as often.

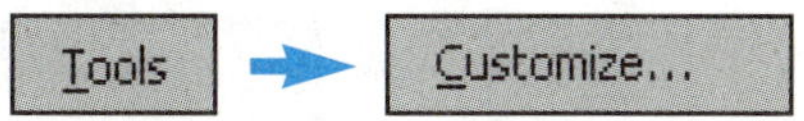

Notes:

- Access continually rearranges menu items by moving commands closer to the top of the menu and hiding commands that you do not use often. Because of this, when you open a menu, the command you are looking for might have been moved or hidden.
- When a menu contains hidden commands, an arrow symbol appears at the bottom of the menu. To unhide commands, click the arrow or pause the mouse pointer on the menu until the full menu is displayed.

- When menu commands are hidden, an arrow symbol appears at the bottom of the menu. Click the arrow to open the full menu.

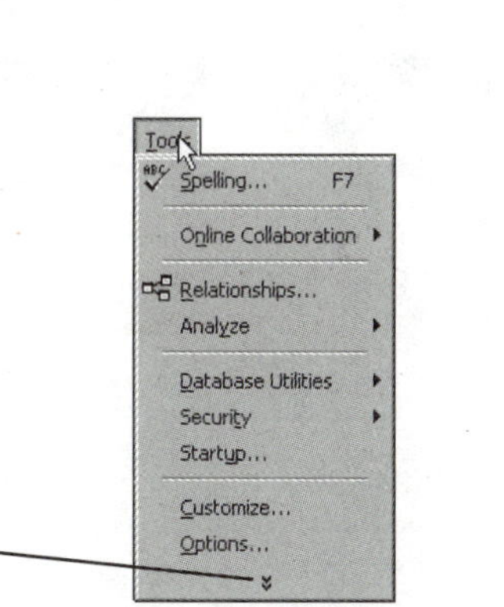

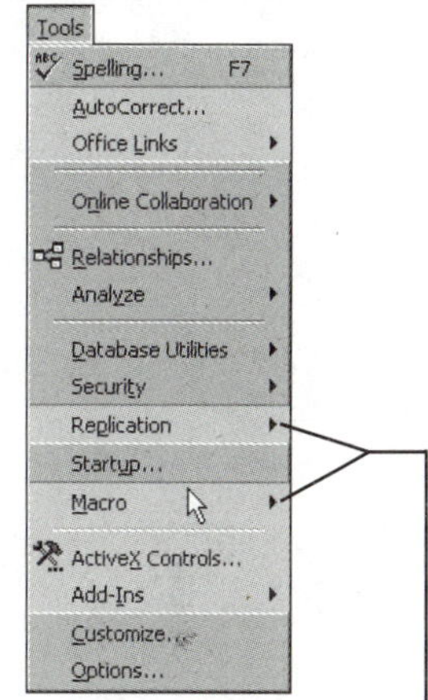

- When you open the menu, commands that were formerly hidden are shown using lighter shading.

Notes:

- If you want menu commands to remain where they are, disable personalized menus.
- You enable or disable personalized menus for each individual database.

Disable or Enable Personalized Menus

1 Select **Tools**, **Customize**. The Customize dialog box displays.

2 Click the **Options** tab.

3 To return all menus to their original state before commands were moved (does not remove menu customizations you have made yourself) if desired:

a. Click Reset my usage data. A prompt displays.

b. Click Yes.

4 To disable personalized menus, deselect **Menus show recently used commands first**.

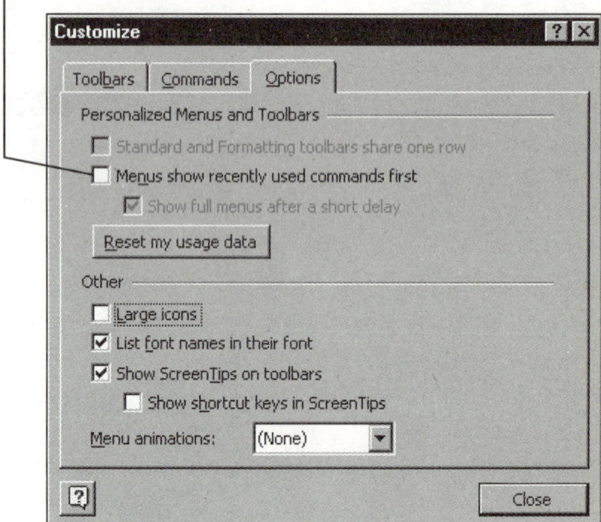

5 Click Close.

Show or Hide a Toolbar

The toolbars that are displayed depend on the database object you are working on (such as a form or report) and the current view (such as Page view or Design view). You can display any toolbar you want, including toolbars that you have created.

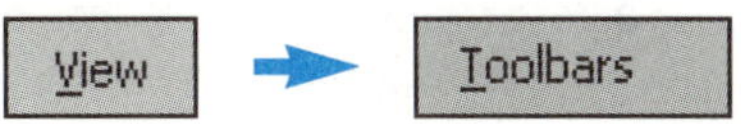

Notes:

- If personalized menus are enabled, the buttons that you use most often remain on the toolbars. Buttons that you do not use over a period of time do not remain on the toolbar. See **Personalized Menus** to disable this feature.

1. Select **View**, **Toolbars**, **Customize**. The Customize dialog box displays.
2. Click the **Toolbars** tab.
3. Select the toolbar(s) to show or hide. Toolbars with a check mark will be displayed.

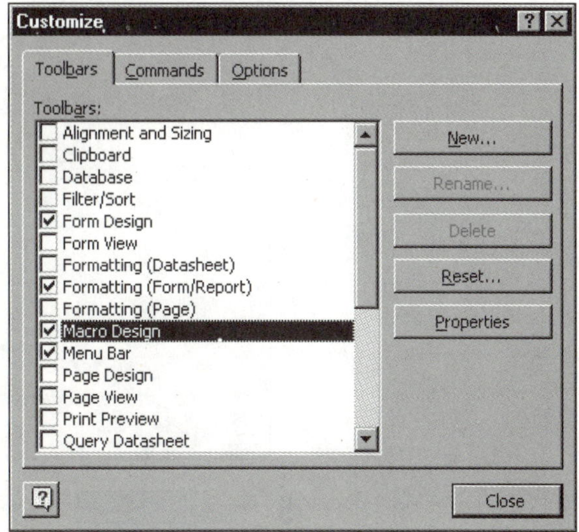

4. Click Close or press **Esc**.

Notes:

- If you have toolbars positioned next to each other or if you have resized the window so that not all buttons display, use the **More Buttons** button to show buttons that do not fit in the window.

Show Hidden Toolbar Buttons

Note: *When more buttons are on a toolbar than can be shown, a **More Buttons** symbol appears at the right side of the toolbar.*

1 Click **More Buttons** (located at the right side of the toolbar). Hidden buttons display in a pop-up window as in the following illustration:

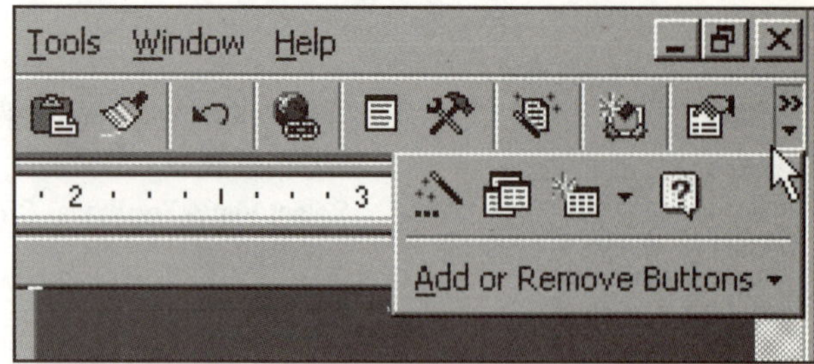

2 Click the desired toolbar button.

Note: *You can use the **Add or Remove Buttons** command to open a list of toolbar buttons and add buttons to and remove buttons from the toolbar.*

Notes:

* You can place toolbars next to each other in the window. Just drag a toolbar to the position next to a displayed toolbar.
- You can remove a toolbar from the top of the window and place it anywhere on the screen. Toolbars that appear at the top, bottom, and sides of the window are called "docked toolbars." Toolbars that you have moved to other locations are called "floating toolbars."

Move a Toolbar

1 Drag the symbol (located on the left side of the toolbar).

2 When the toolbar is where you want it, release the mouse button.

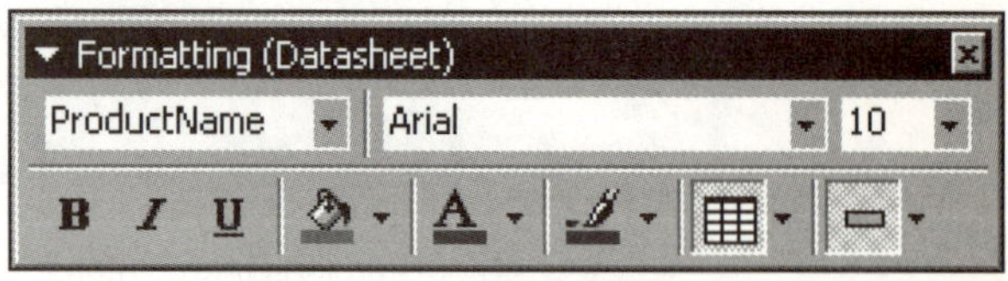

Add a Toolbar Button That Opens a Web Page

This type of toolbar button starts your Web browser and displays a Web page that you specify.

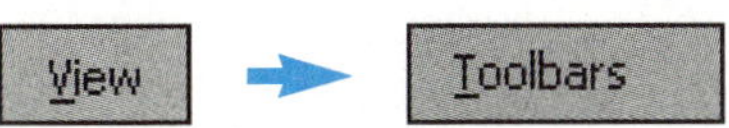

Notes:

- By default, when you hover the mouse pointer over the button, the hyperlink destination address displays. You can change the pop-up tip text (also known as a ScreenTip) so that it displays text that you specify, such as the name of the Web page.

1. Display the toolbar to which you will add the button. See **Show or Hide a Toolbar**.
2. Select **View**, **Toolbars**, **Customize**. The Customize dialog box displays.
3. Click the **Commands** tab.
4. Scroll down in the **Categories** list and select **Web**.

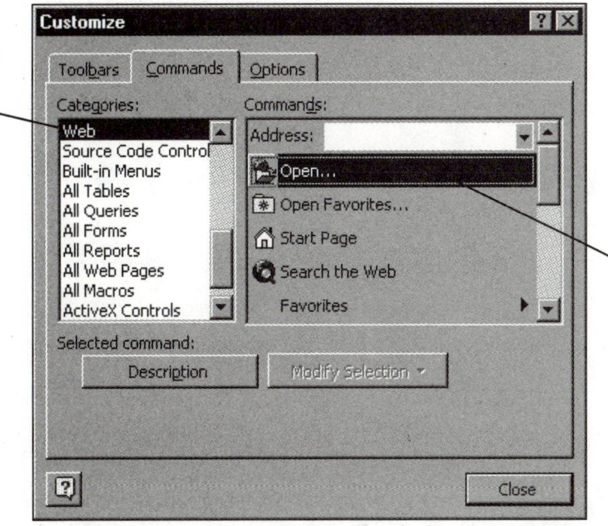

5. Drag the **Open** button from the Customize dialog box to the toolbar displayed on the screen. The button: is added to the toolbar.
6. Click .

7. Select **Assign Hyperlink**, **Open**. The Assign Hyperlink: Open dialog box displays.

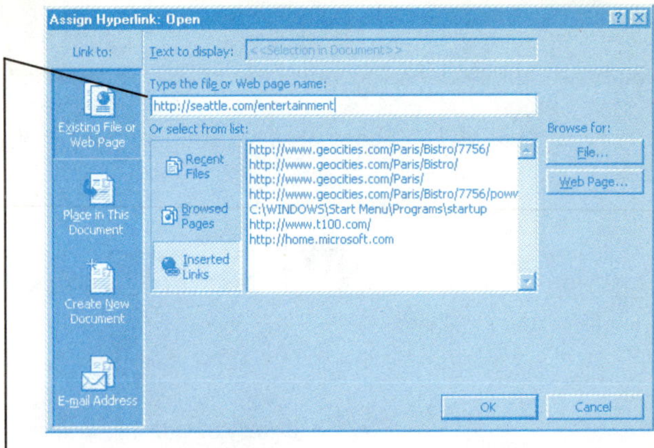

8 Type the destination address of the button.

Note: *You can use the buttons on the left side of the dialog box to browse Web pages that you have recently visited.*

9 Click OK. The Assign Hyperlink: Open dialog box closes.

10 To change the ScreenTip text if desired:

a. Click Modify Selection ▾ and select **Properties**. The Database Control Properties dialog box opens.

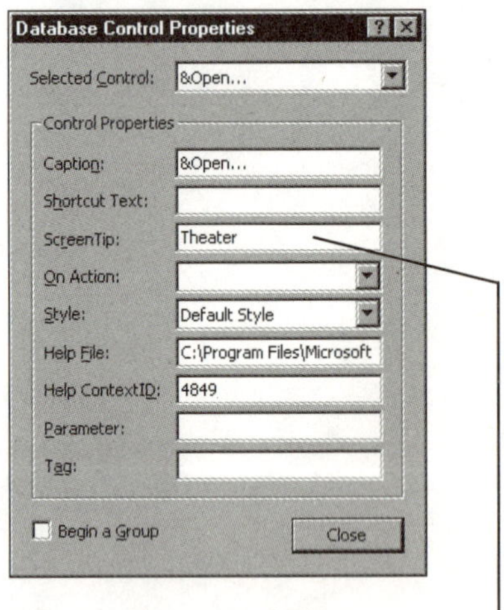

b. Type the **ScreenTip** text to display.

c. Click Close.

11 Click Close to close the Customize dialog box.

Create a Database Using a Wizard

A database contains tables, queries, forms, reports, and code modules. Office 2000 provides a number of database designs that you can use to create a database. Using the Database Wizard and database designs, you can quickly create a complete database.

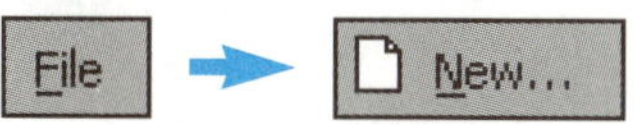

Notes:

- The Database Wizard creates either a generic database or a database based on a design that you choose.
- When you use the Database Wizard to create a database based on a design, the wizard creates the database objects that you need. This includes tables, reports, forms, switchboards, and other database objects.

1 If you just launched Access, click **Access database wizards, pages, and projects** at the startup Microsoft Access dialog box and click **OK**.

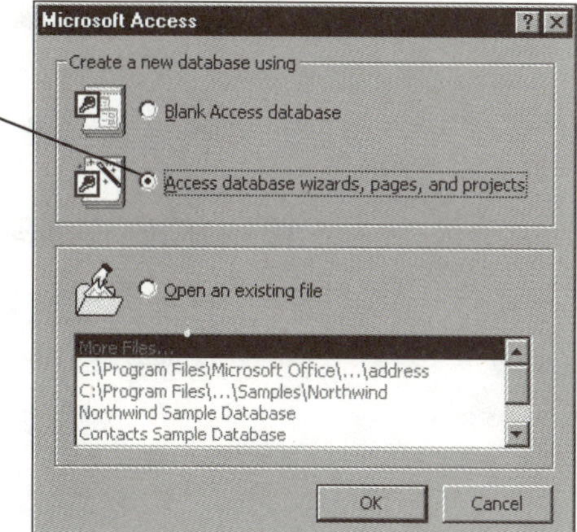

OR

If the above dialog box is not on your screen, press **Ctrl+N**.

2 To create a database based on a design, click the **Databases** tab and double-click an icon.

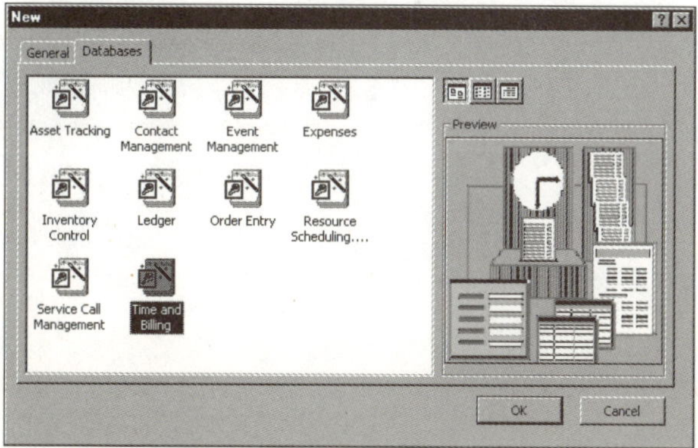

Notes:

- See the Appendix for a list of some of the available database designs. Not all available designs are installed when you install using Typical installation. If a particular design does not appear in your version of Access, run Setup to install it. See Access online Help for information on running Setup to add Access components.

OR

To create a database not based on a design, click the **General** tab and double-click the **Database** icon.

Note: If you use this option, you won't get the Database Wizard.

3 Select a folder in the **Save in** list or click a button representing a folder to specify the folder in which to save the database.

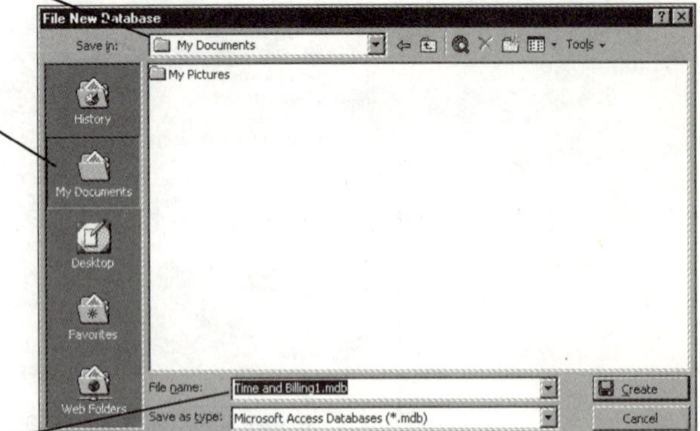

4 Type a file name for the database.

5 Click Create. The Database Wizard starts and displays the first Database Wizard dialog box which describes the database.

6 Click Next > to display the next dialog box.

The contents of the Database Wizard screens vary depending on the database design that you chose in step 2. The remainder of this procedure shows you the dialog boxes for creating a database used for Time and Billing data.

7 Select fields to include in the database in the **Fields in the table** list. Clear the fields that you do not want to include.

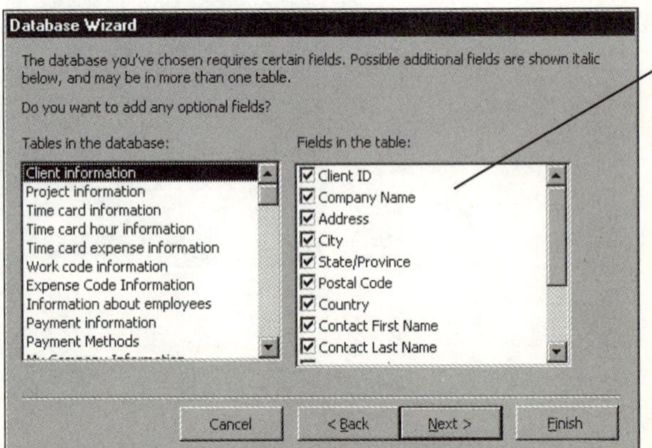

Create a Database Using a Wizard

(continued)

Notes:

- After you use the Database Wizard to create a database, you can modify the database objects in Design view to customize it.

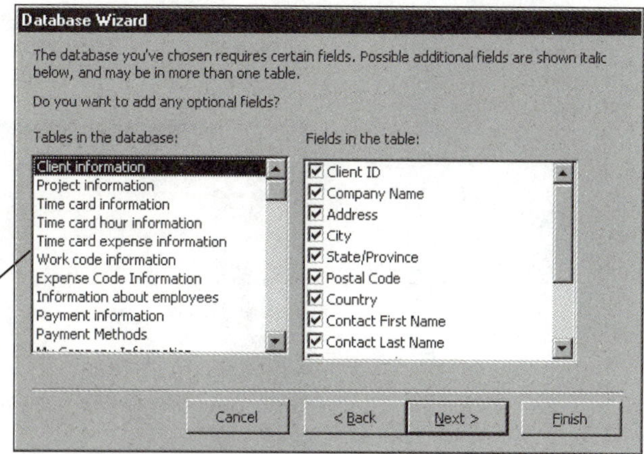

To view fields in another table, select a table in the **Tables in the database** list. The right pane shows fields in the selected table.

8 Click Next >.

9 Select a format for screen displays. A sample of the selected format displays in the preview pane.

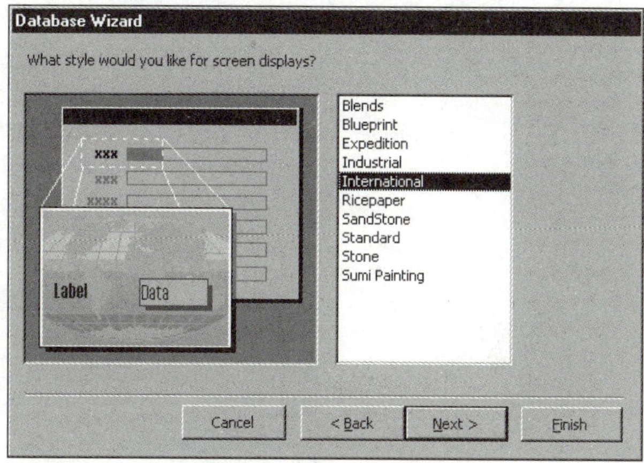

10 Click Next >.

Notes:

- The Database Wizard dialog boxes vary depending on the database design that you choose. This procedure shows the dialog boxes for creating a database based on the Time and Billing design.

11 Select a report style.

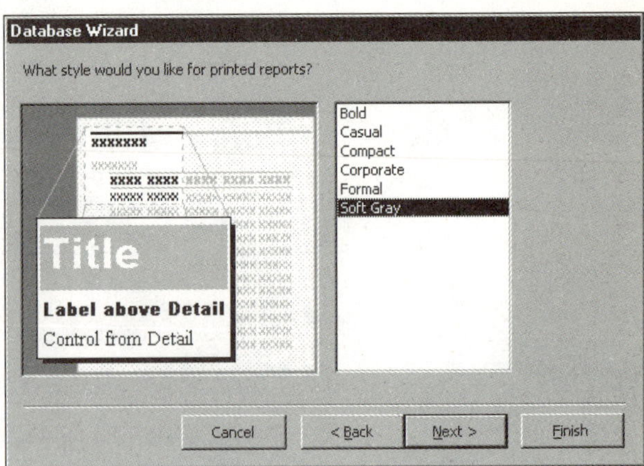

12 Click Next >.

13 Type a name for the database (does not have to be the same as the file name that you entered in step 4).

14 Click Next >.

15 To open the new database, click Finish at the last Database Wizard dialog box.

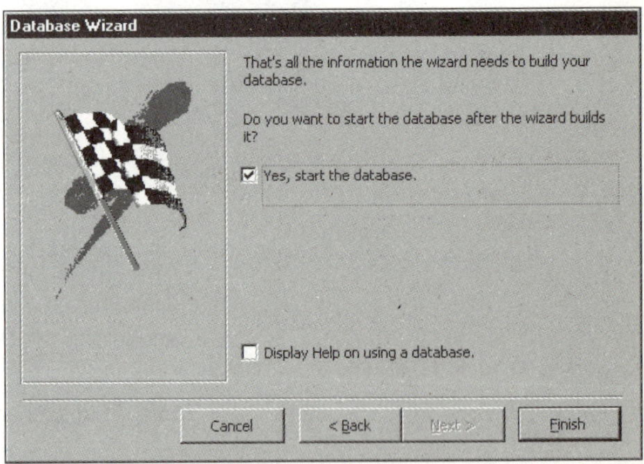

The Wizard creates the database.

Open a Database

Opens an existing database and displays the objects (such as tables, reports, forms, etc.) in the database in the Database window.

Notes:

- Only one database can be open at a time in Access.
- In Access 2000 you can search for a file from the Open dialog box. You do not need to use a separate utility to locate a file.
- By default, Access saves new databases in the My Documents folder.

If You Are Already in Access:

1 Press **Ctrl+O**. The Open dialog box displays.

2 To display the file to open if necessary:

- Click a button corresponding to the folder.
- Select a different folder from the **Look in** list.

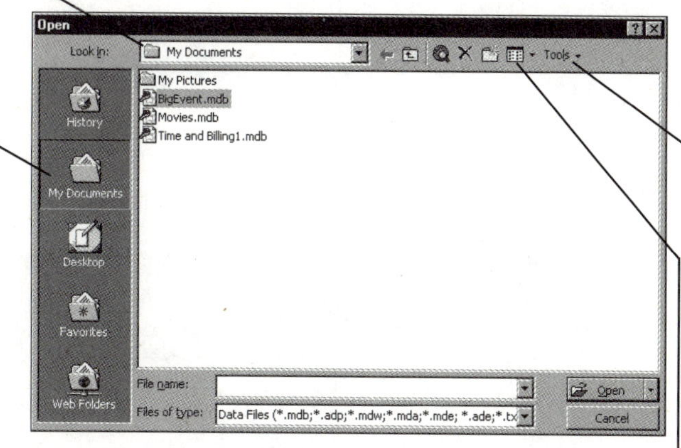

- Click **Views** and select an option to display different information about files in the Open dialog box (for example, click the **Details** option to view information such as the file size).
- Click **Tools**, **Find** to search for a filename.

3 Double-click the file to open.

Notes:

- How you open the database depends on whether you have just started Access, in which case the Startup dialog box is on the screen, or whether you are already working in the program.
- The Microsoft Access Startup dialog box appears each time you start Access unless you disable it (See **Disable the Startup Dialog Box**).

If You Just Launched Access:

1 Select **Open an existing file** in the Microsoft Access startup dialog box.

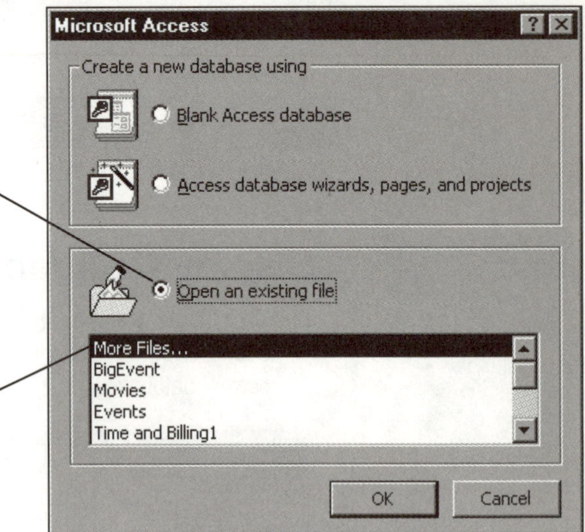

2 Double-click a database to open.

OR

3 Double-click **More Files** to display the Open dialog box. See step 2 on the previous page ("If you are already in Access") for a description of this dialog box.

Add or Edit Table Relationships

Relationships link information stored in separate tables in a database. Data in one table can be matched up or linked with data in the related table using a field that is present in both tables.

Display Relationships

1 Click **Tools**, **Relationships**. The Relationships window opens, showing relationships between the tables in the current database.

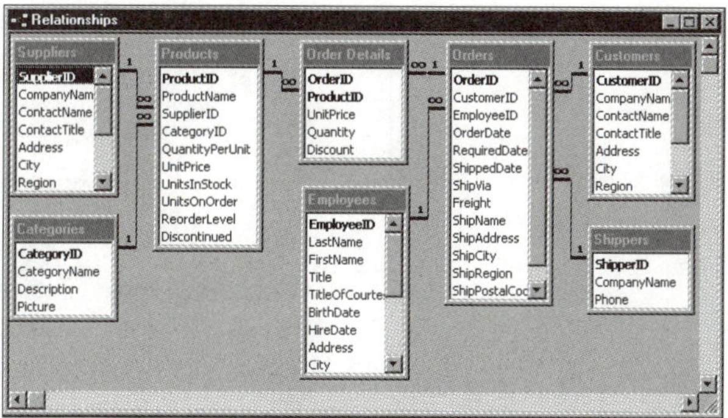

2 To close the Relationships window when finished viewing, adding, or editing relationships, click .

Notes:

- In order to open the Relationships window, all tables in the database must be closed.
- If the database does not have any table relationships defined, the Show Table dialog box displays. Follow **Add a Relationship** procedure.

Notes:

- A database is like a family. Tables are family members linked by relationships. Some tables are parent tables; others are child tables. Some are both a parent to child tables and a child of other parent tables. A well-designed relational database consists of two or more tables related by one or more common fields.

Notes:

- When you have defined relationships, you can display data from multiple tables on the same form or printed in the same report. For example, say the EmployeeNumber field exists in both the Benefits table and the Employee table. These two tables are related through the EmployeeNumber field. You could create a report that includes employee information stored in the Employee table and work benefit information for each employee located in the Benefits table.
- When you create a database using the Database Wizard, the wizard automatically sets up the relationships between tables.
- Each join line in the Relationships window represents a relationship between the two tables it connects.
- Enforcing referential integrity preserves the relationships between tables. When you change the data in a field that links two tables, the new value must be updated in all the linked records so that they will stay linked. Also, if you delete a record in a parent table, Access asks you whether or not it should delete related records in child tables.

Add a Relationship

1 If table(s) to relate are not displayed in the Relationships window:

a. Click **Show Table** . The Show Table dialog box displays.

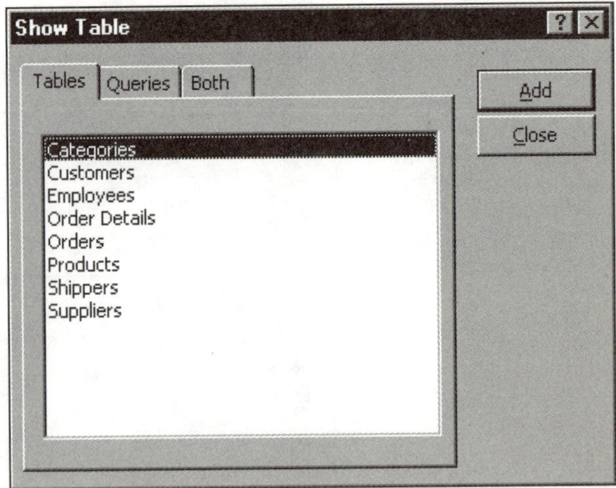

b. Select each table to add to the Relationships window (press **Ctrl** and click each table to select multiple tables).

*Note: Or, you can add queries by clicking the **Queries** tab and selecting queries.*

c. Click Add. Selected table(s) are added to the Relationships window.

d. Click Close.

*Note: To remove a table from the Relationships window, click the table in the Relationships window and press the **Del** key.*

2 Drag the field name for the common field shared by both tables from one table to the linking field name in the related table. This adds a join line representing the join.

Add or Edit Table Relationships

(continued)

Notes:

- Use the Cascade Update Related Fields option to ensure that whenever the value of the linked field changes, the value in the related field in other tables also changes.

When you release the mouse button, the Edit Relationships dialog box displays.

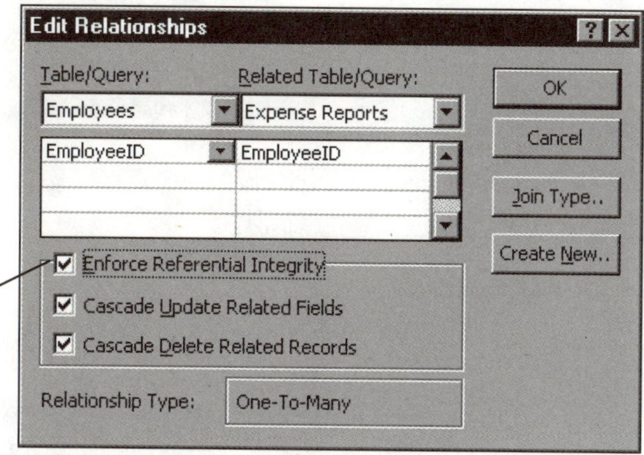

3 Turn on the option to **Enforce Referential Integrity** if desired. Enabling referential integrity causes the Cascade options to be available.

4 Select **Cascade Update Related Fields** and/or **Cascade Delete Related Records** if desired.

5 Click OK.

Notes:

- Use the Cascade Deleted Related Records option to ensure that whenever a parent record is deleted, all child records in linked tables are also deleted. For example, if you delete an order for a customer, not only will the order be deleted from the Orders table, but all order items will be deleted from the Order Items table for that particular order.

Edit a Relationship

1 Double-click the line segment (called a join line) connecting two tables to display the Edit Relationships dialog box.

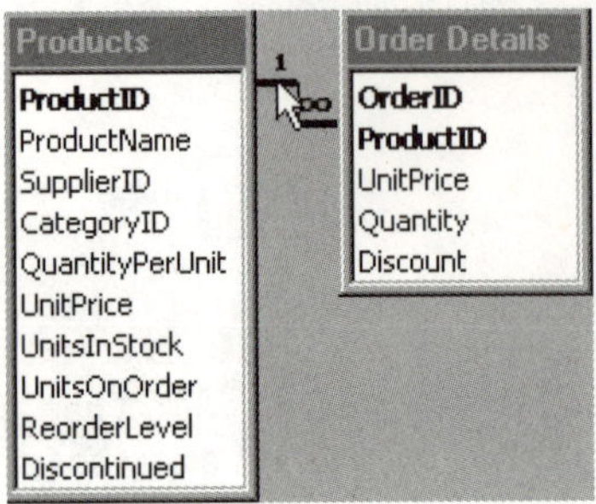

OR

Right-click the join line of the relationship to edit and select **Edit Relationship**.

2 Make changes as desired in the Edit Relationships dialog box.

3 Click OK.

Link to a Table in Another Access Database

Linking allows you to use the data located in a table in another Access database. For example, you could include the data from the external table in a report created in the current database. Note: a database must be open.

Notes:

- When you link a table, you do not have to recreate and maintain separate tables with identical data in two databases. For example, you might need to use information from an Employee table in both the Employee database and the Sales database.
- When tables are stored on a network server, you need to link them in order to access them.
- You can edit the data in the linked table either from the current database or from the database in which it was created.
- You cannot edit the underlying structure of a linked table. For example, you cannot add or delete a field from a linked table. You must open it in the original database to modify the structure.

1 Select **File**, **Get External Data**, **Link Tables**. The Link dialog box displays.

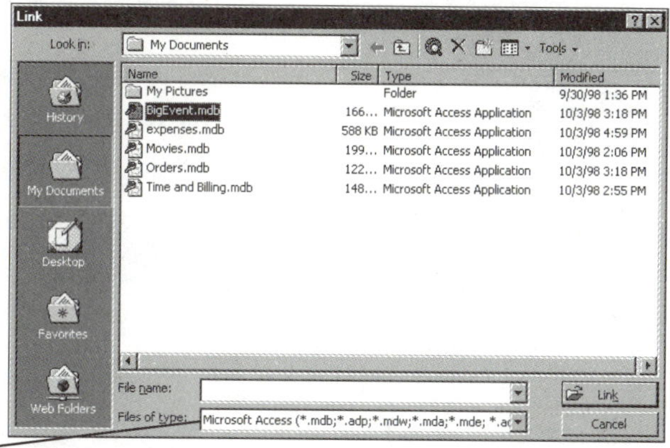

2 Select **Microsoft Access** in the **Files of type** list.

3 Select the database containing the table to link.

4 Click Link. The Link Tables dialog box displays.

Notes:

- This arrow appears only in the database in which you created the link, not in the database in which the table was created.

5 Select the table to link and click OK.

6 In the Database window, the icon for a link to a table has an arrow next to it.

Customers

Notes:

- Removing the link does not delete the linked table. To access the table, open it in the database in which it was created.

Remove the Link to a Table

1 Open the database containing the link.

2 Select the link icon in the Database window.

3 Press **Delete**.

4 At the prompt, click **Yes**.

Tables

A table is the basic unit of a database. Each database must contain at least one table. A table stores data such as contact names and addresses, employee information, or information about orders placed with your company.

You create and edit the structure of a table in Design view. For example, you can add a field to a table, delete a field, or change the size of a field.

You can edit the data in a table in Datasheet view or you can use a form for entering data in a table.

Create a Table Using a Wizard

Tables contain the data that you enter into a database. The Table Wizard walks you through each step of creating a table.

Notes:

- You can create a table using the Table Wizard and then open it in Design view to customize the table structure if necessary.
- Create a separate table for each type of information that will be stored in a database. For example, create one table to store product information and another to store information about companies that supply the products.
- One field in every table should identify each record in the table as unique. This field is called the primary key. Often this is an AutoNumber field, which automatically adds a sequential number to each record when it is created. You can also create a primary key from multiple fields if one field alone will not uniquely identify records.

1. Open or create a database.
2. Press **F11** to display the Database window.
3. Click **Insert**, **Table**. The New Table dialog box displays.

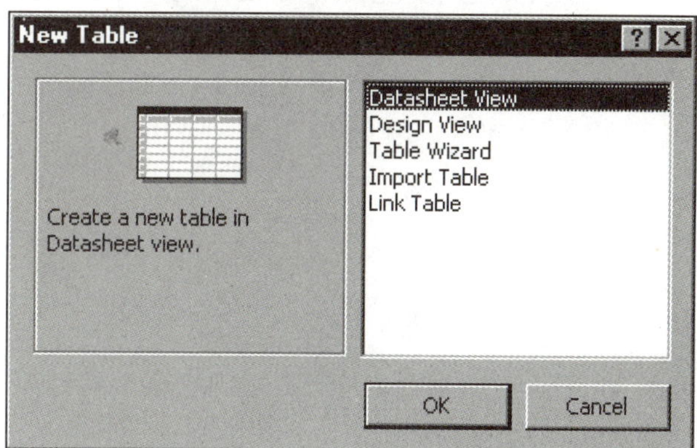

4. Double-click **Table Wizard**. The Table Wizard starts.
5. Select one of the Sample Tables on which to model your table. The list of Sample Fields changes depending on the selected Sample Table.

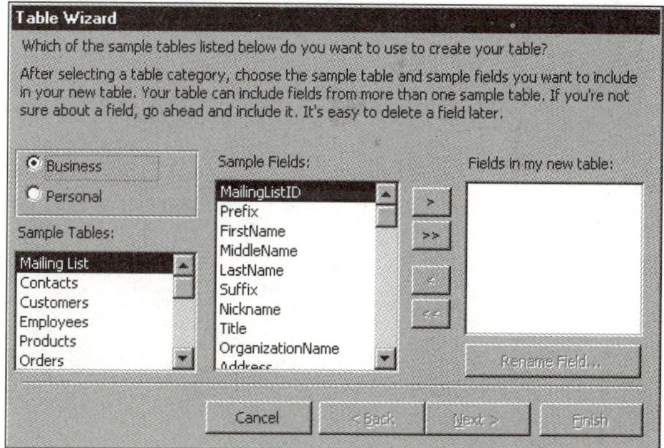

Notes:

- These instructions assume that this table is the first added to a new database. If you are adding a table to a database that already has at least one table, an additional dialog box displays, allowing you to define relationships between the new and existing tables (see **Add or Edit Table Relationships**).

6 Select a field to add to your new table, then click [>]. Repeat until all fields that you want to include are listed in the **Fields in my new table** pane.

Tip: *To add all of the fields in the Sample Fields list to the table, click* [>>].

7 To rename a field in your table if desired:

a. Click the field to rename.

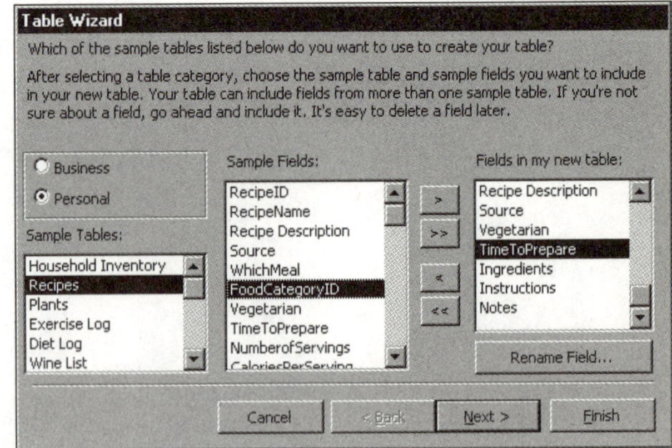

b. Click [Rename Field...].

c. Type the new field name and press **Enter**.

8 Click [Next >].

9 Type a name for the table and click [Next >].

10 The final step in the Table Wizard allows you to choose what happens next. Select an option and then click

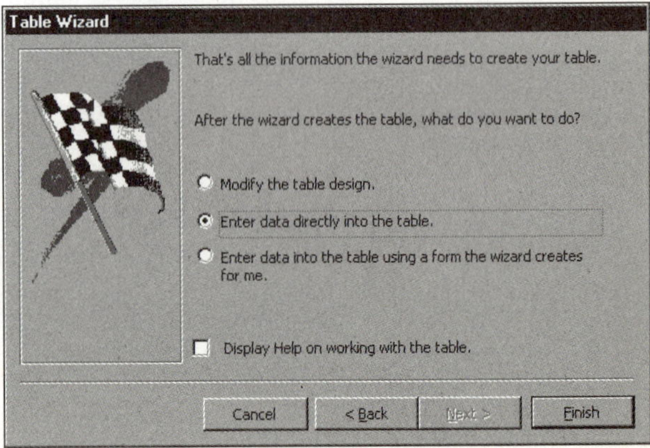

Open a Table

Open a table in Design view to work with the underlying table structure. Open it in Datasheet view to enter data in the table.

Notes:

- In Design view, you can add, edit, and delete fields in a table. You can add field descriptions and set field properties.
- The top of the table Design window lists the fields in the table and their data types. The bottom of the window shows field properties for the currently selected field (the field at the top of the window containing the cursor).

Open a Table in Design View

1 Click **Tables** in the Database window. The right pane displays the tables in the current database.

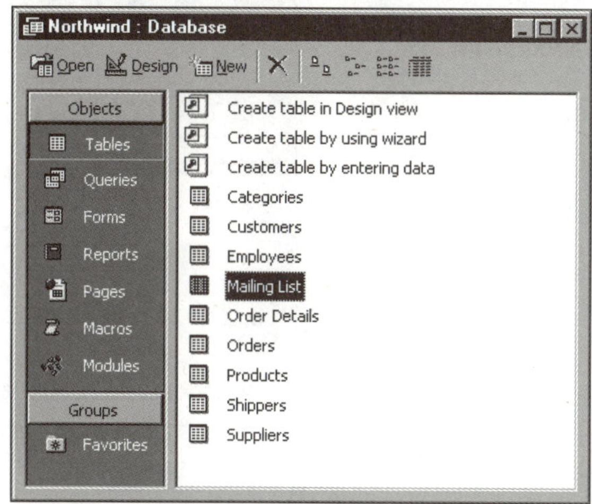

*Note: To switch to the Database window, press **F11**.*

2 Select the table to open.

3 Click Design or press **Ctrl+Enter**. The table opens in Design view.

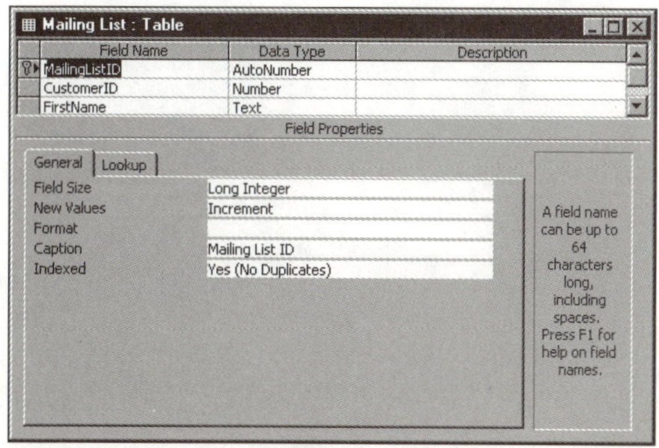

4 When finished editing, adding, or deleting fields, click ☒ to close the window.

Open a Table in Datasheet View

Notes:

- In Datasheet view, the data in the table is displayed in a datasheet.
- Each column in the datasheet is a field. Each row is a record.

1 Click **Tables** in the Database window. The right pane displays the tables in the current database.

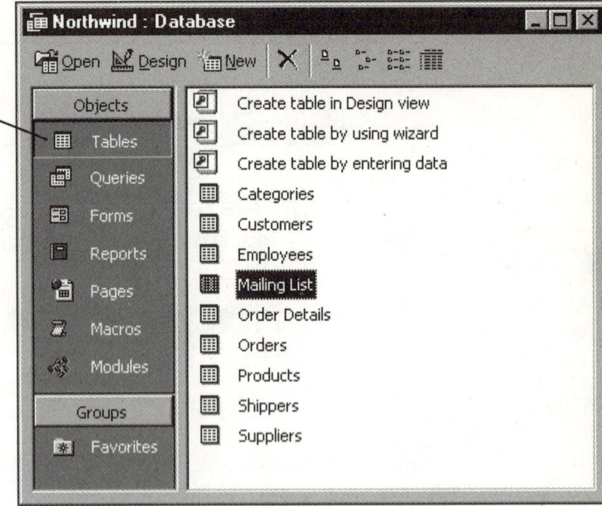

2 Select the table to open.

3 Press **Enter**. The table opens in Datasheet view.

4 When finished editing data, click [X] to close the table.

Switch Between Design and Datasheet Views

Notes:

- Use the **View** button, located in the Database toolbar, to switch between the different views of a table.

If the table is open in Datasheet view, click **View** to switch to Design view.

OR

If the table is open in Design view, click **View** to switch to Datasheet view.

Add a Field to a Table

Modify the structure of a table by adding a new field.

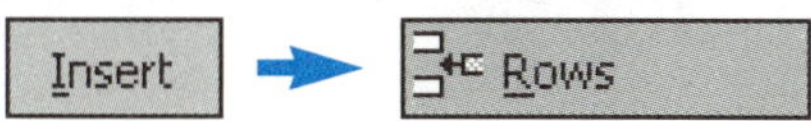

Notes:

- When you add a new field to a table, the new field is not automatically added to forms and reports that you have created. If you want the field to appear in forms and reports, open the form or report in Design view and add the field.
- Use field properties to customize fields. (See **Apply a Validation Rule to a Field** and **Set the Default Field Value** for a description of some of these properties.)

1 Open the table in Design view (see **Open a Table**).

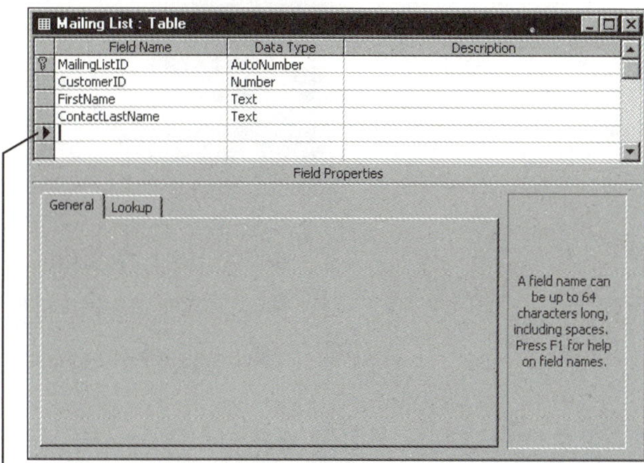

2 Click the first available blank row in the field list. An arrow appears next to the field.

OR

To insert a new field above an existing field, click the field that will be directly below the new field and select **Insert**, **Rows**.

3 Type a field name in the **Field Name** column.

4 Press the **Enter** or **Tab** key to move to the **Data Type** column.

Note: *You can also use arrow keys to move from column to column and field to field.*

Notes:

- See also **Add a Lookup Field to a Table** (following page) to add a field that displays a list of values when you enter data in the field. With a lookup field, you select from a list of available values to enter data in the field.

5 Click [icon] to open the list of data types (by default, new fields are Text type) and select the data type for the new field.

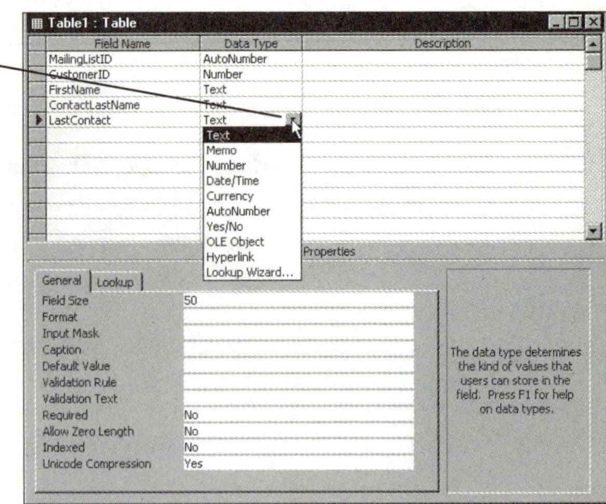

6 Press **Enter** or **Tab** to move to the **Description** column and type a description of the field if desired.

Note: The Description is optional. You can leave it blank.

7 Press **F6** to switch to the Field Properties pane.

8 Type the number of characters for the field in the **Field Size** property.

9 Set other properties if desired.

10 Click **Save** [icon] on the Database toolbar to save your changes.

11 Click [icon] to close the table design when you have finished modifying it.

Add a Lookup Field to a Table

A lookup field displays a list of the values that can be entered into a field when you enter data in a table. Instead of typing a value for the field, select the data from the lookup list.

Notes:

- The lookup list will appear when you enter data in a table using either a form or Datasheet view.
- Before you create the lookup field, you must first create the table that contains the values that will appear in the lookup list.
- You can create two kinds of lookup fields in Access. This procedure shows you how to create a lookup field that displays the values in an existing table in the lookup list. For example, if you have a Category table, you could have the lookup list display all of the available categories.

1 Open the table in Design view (see **Open a Table**).

2 Type a name for the new field in the first blank row in the **Field Name** column.

*Note: See **Add a Field to a Table** for an illustration.*

3 Click ▼ in the Data Type field and select **Lookup Wizard**. The Lookup Wizard starts.

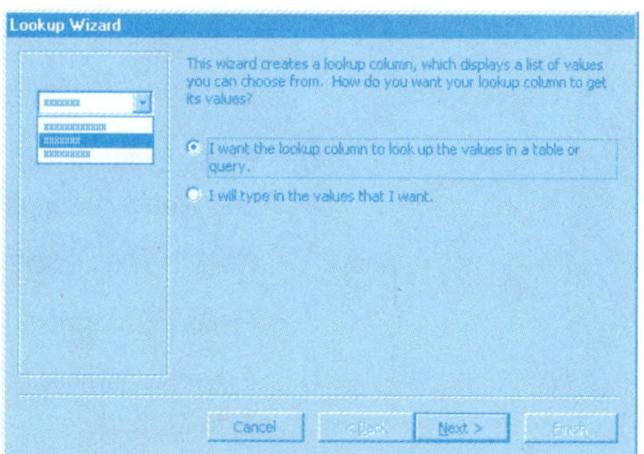

4 Select **I want the lookup column to look up the values in a table or query** and click Next >.

*Note: This procedure shows you how to create a lookup field using a set of values in an existing table in the database. You can also create a lookup field and type the values that will be in the lookup list by selecting **I will type in the values that I want** and following the Lookup Wizard prompts.*

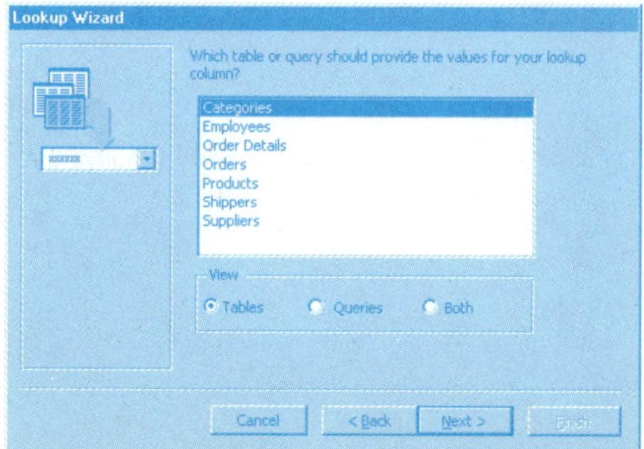

Notes:

- The other kind of lookup field does not rely on an existing table. Create the lookup list by typing in the values that you want to appear in the list. This procedure does not show you how to create that type of lookup field, but you can use this procedure to start the Lookup Wizard and then follow the wizard prompts to create the field.

5 Select the table or query containing the values that will appear in the lookup list and click [Next >].

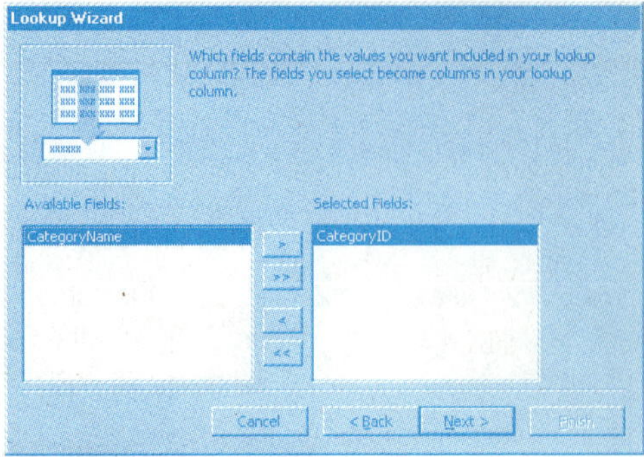

6 Select the field containing the values to appear in the lookup list and click [>]. Repeat to add more fields if desired.

7 Click [Next >].

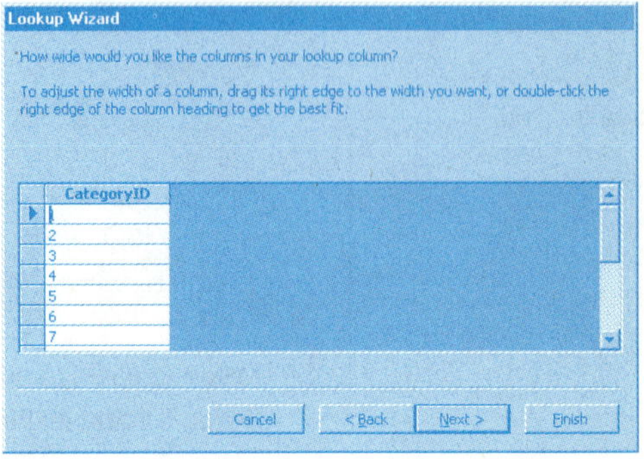

8 Adjust the width of the lookup column as desired.

9 Click [Finish]. The Wizard closes.

A prompt (message box) asking you to save your changes appears automatically. Click [Yes] to save your table.

10 Click [X] to close the table design when you have finished modifying it.

Set the Default Field Value

Save data entry time by having Access automatically enter a value in a particular field. When you add a new record, the field already contains the default value.

Notes:

- Set the default value for a field if the field usually contains a particular entry. For example, if a date field in an order entry usually contains the current date, you can use a function to always add the current date to the field. The field data can be changed during data entry to enter a different date when necessary.
- To enter a different value in the field when entering data, simply type over the default field value.

1 Open the table in Design view (see **Open a Table**).

2 Position the cursor in the field to modify. The field properties for the field display at the bottom of the Design window.

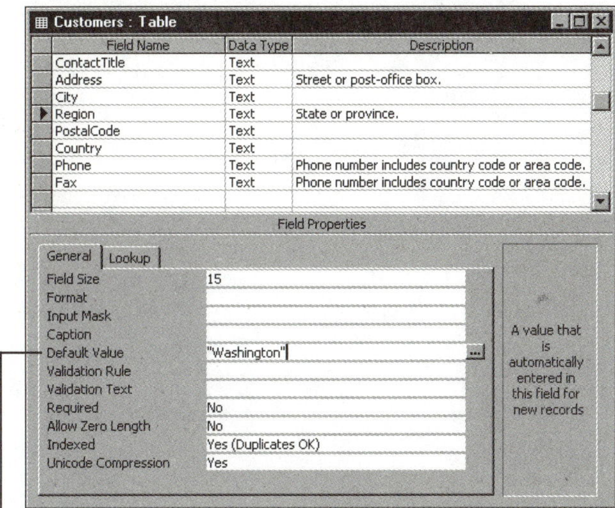

3 Type the value to automatically enter in the field in the **Default Value** text box.

Note: *Access automatically adds quotation marks around a text default value. The quotation marks will not appear in the datasheet.*

4 Click **Save** on the database toolbar to save changes to the table design.

5 Click to close the table design when you have finished modifying it.

Require a Field Value

When you require a value in a field, the field cannot be left blank when you enter data in the table. You must enter something in the field.

Notes:

- Require a field value when a record is not usable if it does not contain information in the field. For example, if entering new clients, you can require that a value be entered in the ClientID field since other data in your database are dependent on this field.
- Access will display an error message if you try to save the record without entering data in the field.

1 Open the table in Design view (see **Open a Table**).

2 Position the cursor in the field to modify. The field properties for the field display at the bottom of the Design window.

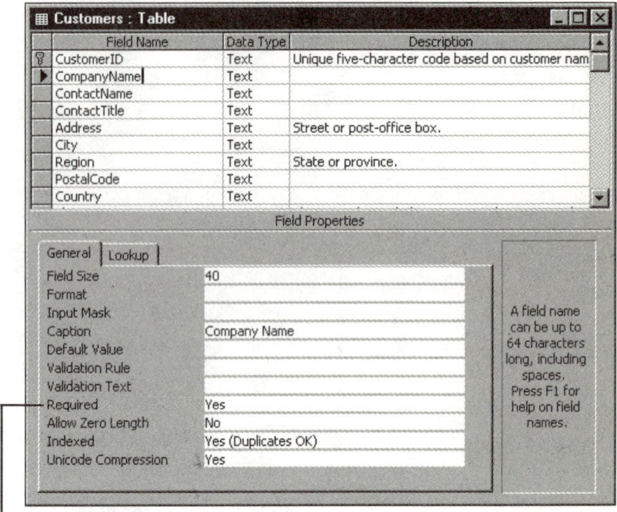

3 Place your cursor in the **Required** field.

4 Select **Yes**.

5 Click **Save** on the database toolbar to save changes to the table design.

6 Click to close the table design when you have finished modifying it.

Apply a Validation Rule to a Field

Apply a validation rule when you want the data in the field to meet specific criteria. For example, you might require that a date entry fall between a range of dates.

Notes:

- When data is entered into a field that has a validation rule, Access compares the data to the rule to make sure that it meets the criteria. If the data does not conform to the rule, an error message is displayed. The entry will not be accepted until valid data is entered into the field.

1. Open the table in Design view (see **Open a Table**).
2. Click the field to which the validation rule will be added.

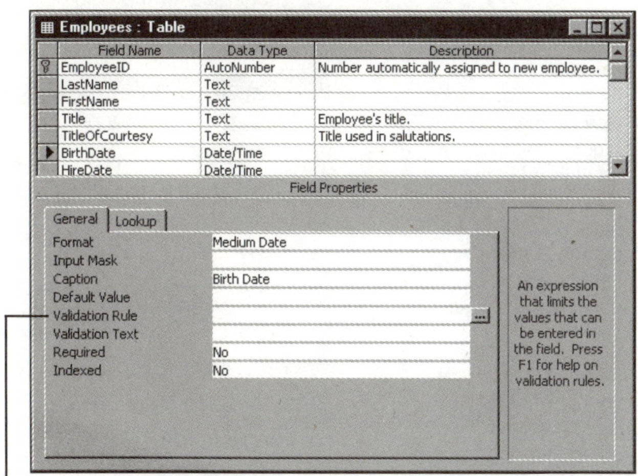

3. Click the **Validation Rule** field in the Field Properties pane at the bottom of the window.
4. Click the Expression Builder button to open the Expression Builder dialog box.

   Note: If you are familiar with expressions, you can type one into the Validation Rule field property directly without using the Expression Builder.

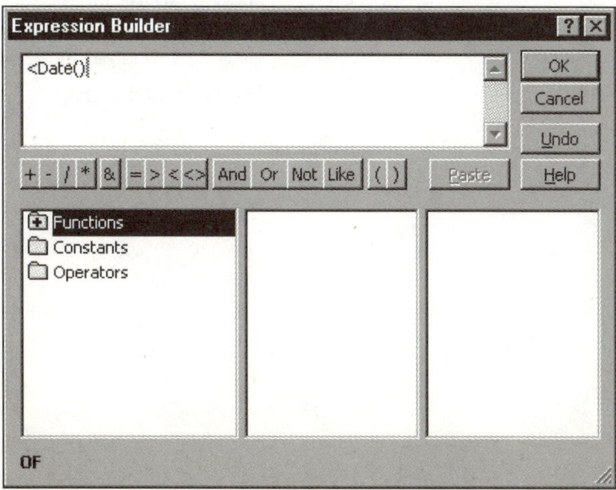

Notes:

- Certain data types cannot be validated. In this case, the Validation Rule property will not be available.

5 Type or build an expression against which entered values will be validated.

6 Click OK to close the Expression Builder.

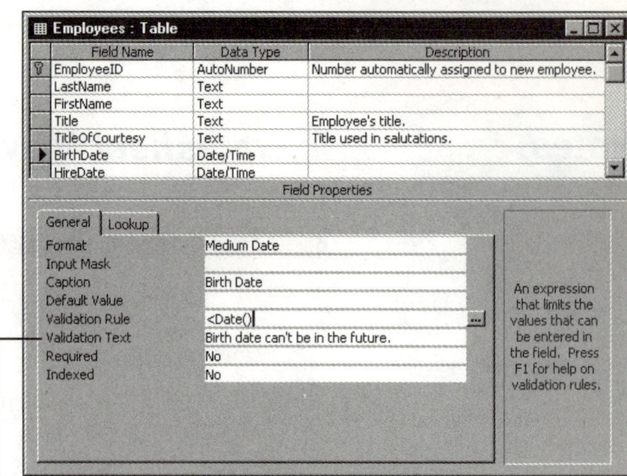

7 Type the text of the message that will display if you attempt to enter invalid data in the field in the **Validation Text** box.

8 Click **Save** on the database toolbar to save changes to the table design.

9 Click to close the table design when you have finished modifying it.

Move a Field in a Table

Although it makes no difference to Access where fields are located in a table, it is much easier for you to work with them when they are organized in a logical order.

Notes:

- Moving a field in Datasheet view does not change the structure of the table.
- You can select multiple fields in Datasheet view by pressing the **Ctrl** key while clicking another column heading.

In Datasheet View:

1 Open the table in Datasheet view (see **Open a Table**).

2 Click the column heading of the field you want to move to select it.

3 Drag the column heading of the selected column to the desired location.

When you drag the column heading, the mouse pointer changes to an arrow with a transparent rectangle under it (see illustration below). This indicates that the selected column will be moved.

The column will not move until you release the mouse button. As you drag the mouse past a column border, a dark line appears down the border. This line indicates where the column will be placed when you release the mouse button (see illustration, below).

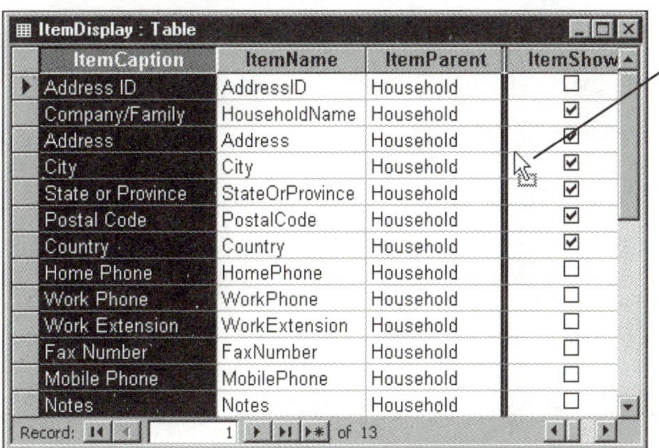

ItemDisplay : Table

ItemCaption	ItemName	ItemParent	ItemShow
Address ID	AddressID	Household	☐
Company/Family	HouseholdName	Household	☑
Address	Address	Household	☑
City	City	Household	☑
State or Province	StateOrProvince	Household	☑
Postal Code	PostalCode	Household	☑
Country	Country	Household	☑
Home Phone	HomePhone	Household	☐
Work Phone	WorkPhone	Household	☐
Work Extension	WorkExtension	Household	☐
Fax Number	FaxNumber	Household	☐
Mobile Phone	MobilePhone	Household	☐
Notes	Notes	Household	☐

Record: 1 of 13

4 Release the mouse button. Access moves the column.

Notes:

- When you move a field in Design view, the field will be moved in Datasheet view.
- Moving a field in Design view does not affect the order in which fields appear on the form for the table if you have already created it. To move a field on a form, open the form in Design view.

In Design View:

1 Open the table in Design view (see **Open a Table**).

2 Click the record selector next to the field to move to select it.

3 Drag the record (row) to the new position.

The row will not move until you release the mouse button. As you drag past a row border, a dark line appears across the border. This line indicates where the record will be placed when you release the mouse button (see illustration, below).

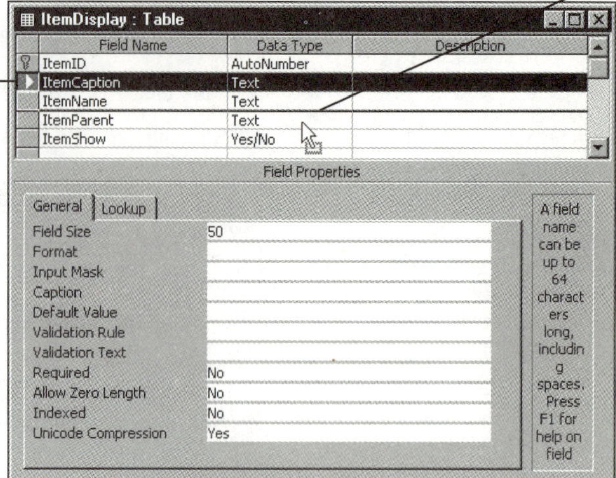

4 Release the mouse button.

5 Press **Ctrl+S** to save changes.

6 Click ☒ to close the table design when you have finished modifying it.

Delete a Field from a Table

When you delete a field from a table, all the data in that field is deleted with it. Be absolutely sure you won't need the data before deleting any fields.

Notes:

- Fields deleted from a table are not automatically deleted from forms and reports. You must open the form or report in Design view and remove the field. References to deleted fields in expressions must also be deleted manually.
- Access won't allow you to delete a primary key field or a field that is part of a relationship. You must delete any relationships to this field or remove the primary key before you can delete the field.

In Datasheet View:

1 Open the table in Datasheet view (see **Open a Table**).

2 Right-click the column heading of the field to delete.

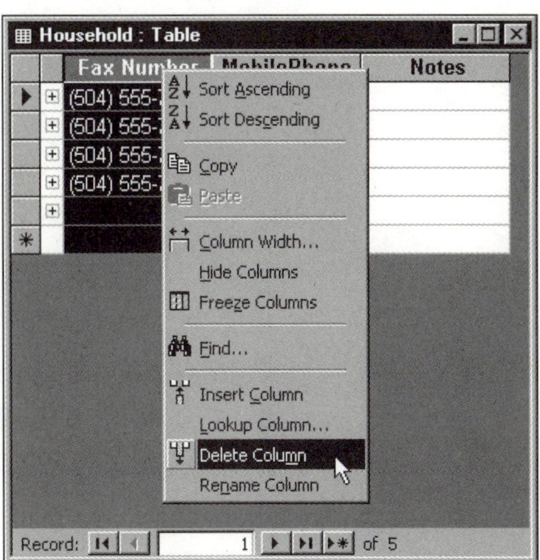

3 Click **Delete Column**. A prompt displays, confirming that you want to delete the field.

4 Click Yes.

Notes:

- Deleting a field deletes all the data in the field.
- Before deleting a field you might want to create a backup copy of the table from which you will delete the field in case you need the data in the future.

In Design View:

1. Open the table in Design view (see **Open a Table**).
2. Click the record selector to the left of the field to delete it.
3. Select **Edit**, **Delete**. Access displays a confirmation prompt.

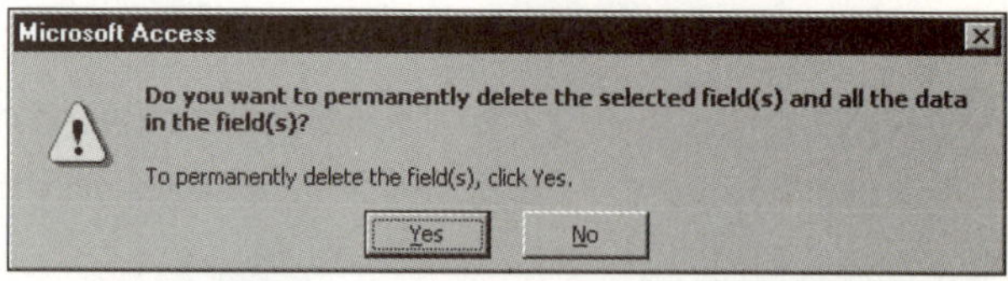

4. Click Yes.
5. Press **Ctrl+S** to save changes.
6. Click [X] to close the table design when you have finished modifying it.

Set the Primary Key for a Table

A primary key is a field that contains unique data for each record. No two records can have the same entry in a primary key field.

Notes:

- The primary key field is used to identify each record in the table. For example, in a list of customers, the CustomerID field would be unique for each customer record. You would not have the same Customer IDs for multiple customers.
- Often, AutoNumber fields are used as the primary key. An AutoNumber field numbers each record sequentially. The number can be used to identify each record. To create this type of field, set the data type to AutoNumber.

1 Open the table in Design view (see **Open a Table**).

2 For a single-field primary key, position the cursor in the field name.

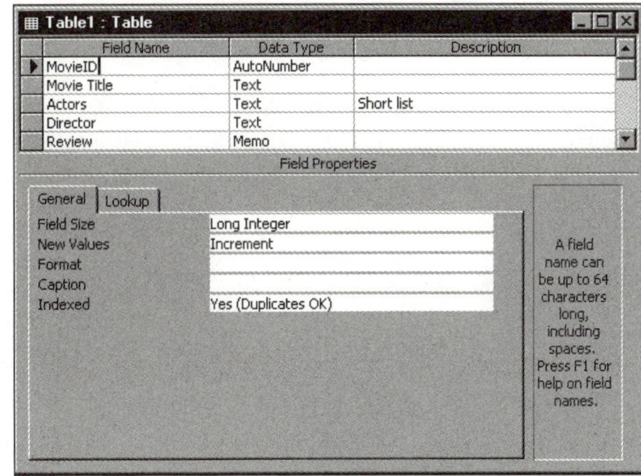

For a multiple-field primary key, hold down **Ctrl** and click the record selector next to each field.

Notes:

- You cannot enter duplicate values in a primary key field as Access uses the field to uniquely identify each record. An error message displays if you attempt to enter a value already stored in the field.
- To remove a primary key, repeat the procedure. Removing the primary key does not delete the field.

3 Click **Primary Key** .

A key indicator appears next to primary key field(s).

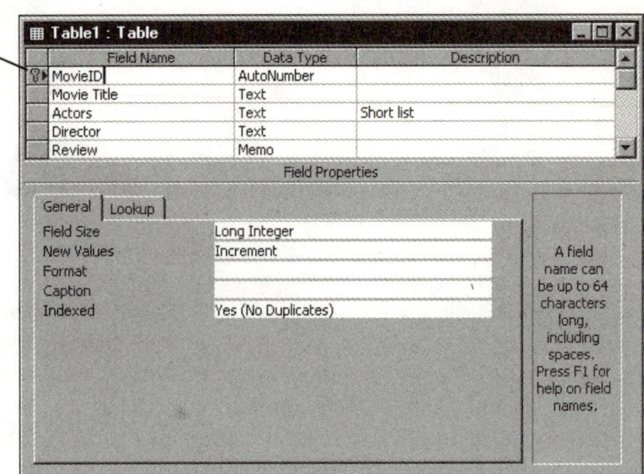

4 Press **Ctrl+S** to save changes.

5 Click to close the table design when you have finished modifying it.

Index a Table

Like a card catalog in a library, an index helps Access find and sort records very quickly.

Notes:

- Index the fields on which you frequently sort the table or search for data. For example, if you often sort a table on the City field, you would index the City field. If you frequently search for clients by state, you would index the State field.
- A single-field index indexes the table on only one field, such as just the City field or just the State field. You can create multiple single-field indexes in a table.
- Removing a field from the index does not delete the field from the table.

Add a Single-Field Index

1 Open the table in Design view (see **Open a Table**).

2 Click in the field to index. The field properties display in the bottom of the window.

3 Click the **Indexed** property and then click ▼.

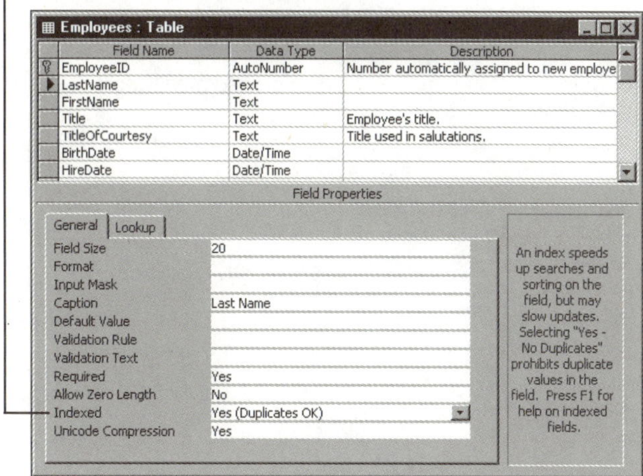

4 Select **Yes (No Duplicates)** to prevent entering duplicate values in this field.

OR

Select **Yes (Duplicates OK)** to allow multiple records with the same data in the field.

Note: To remove an index, select ***No*** *in the indexed field.*

5 Close the table when finished.

Notes:

- Add an index that indexes more than one field when you often sort or search for table data in multiple fields. For example, if you often sort the table on both the State field and the City field (alphabetizes by state and then by city within the state), create a multiple-field index. Add the State and the City fields to the index.
- The Indexes dialog box lists both single-field and multiple-field indexes. You can tell them apart by their name. A multiple-field index shows only one name for each of the fields included in the index. For example, the illustration shows a table with one multiple-field index (called StateCityZip) and a number of single-field indexes.

Add a Multiple-Field Index

1 Open the table in Design view (see **Open a Table**).

2 Click **Indexes** in the toolbar. The Indexes dialog box, listing all of the indexes in the current table, displays.

3 Type a name for the index. You can use a field name or type a name that describes the index.

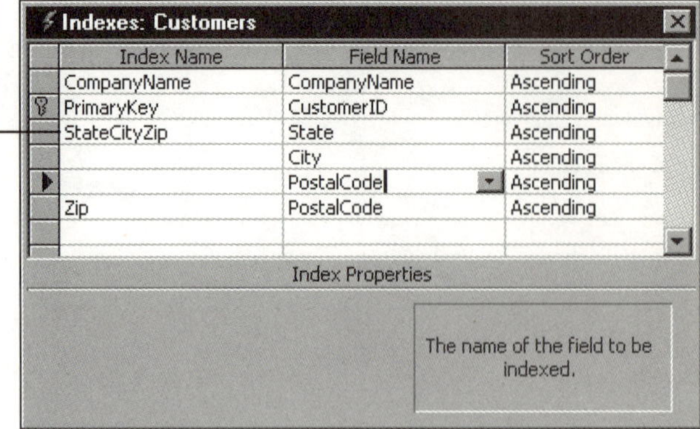

4 Click under Field Name, and select the first field to index on.

5 Select whether you want to sort in **Ascending** or **Descending** order.

6 Under Field Name, select the next field to index on.

7 Repeat step 6 for each field to add to the index.

Note: To remove a field from a multiple-field index, select the row containing the field and press ***Delete****.*

8 Click to close the Indexes dialog box.

9 Press **Ctrl+S** to save changes.

10 Close the table when finished.

Queries

Access queries are used to perform operations and manipulate data. For example, you can use a Find Duplicates query to have Access locate duplicate records in a table. Use a simple select query to select data that meets certain criteria that you specify. For example, you could create a query to select all records in a table where the date in the Due Date field is older than 60 days.

You can save data selected by a query in a separate table by creating a make-table query. This creates a new table containing the data.

Create a Find Duplicates Query Using a Wizard

A Find Duplicates query searches for duplicate values in one or more fields that you specify.

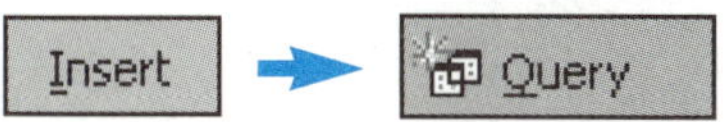

Notes:

- A Find Duplicates query returns a result table that lists all records with duplicate values in one or more fields that you specify.
- Use a Find Duplicates query to make sure you do not have duplicate records in tables where that would be harmful. You can also use it to determine information about your data such as which customers have the same zip code.

1 Click **Queries** in the Database window.

2 Click New.

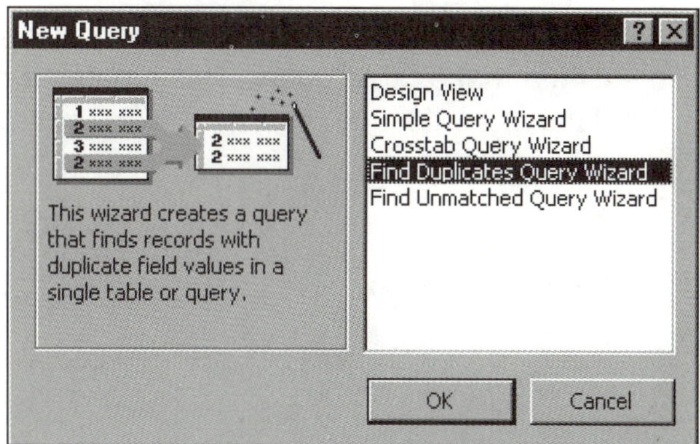

3 Double-click **Find Duplicates Query Wizard**.

4 Select the table or query to search for duplicate values.

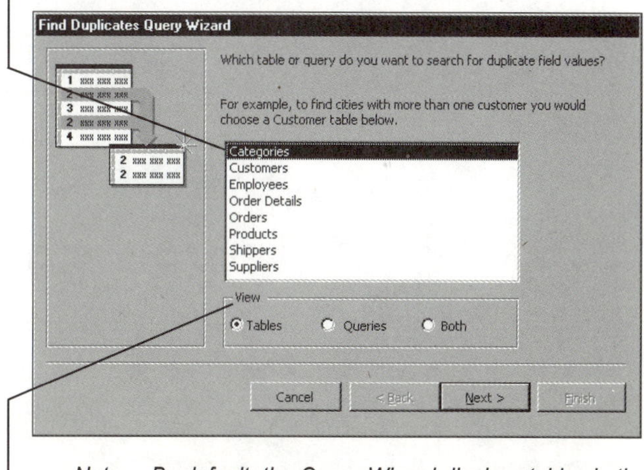

Note: By default, the Query Wizard displays tables in the current database. You can also view ***Queries*** *only or* ***Both*** *tables and queries in the dialog box.*

Notes:

- Using the wizard, you query one record source at a time. To search multiple record sources, run the wizard again for the next record source.
- A Find Duplicates query does not delete duplicate values. You must either do this manually or create a Delete query (see **Create a Delete Query**).

5 Click Next >.

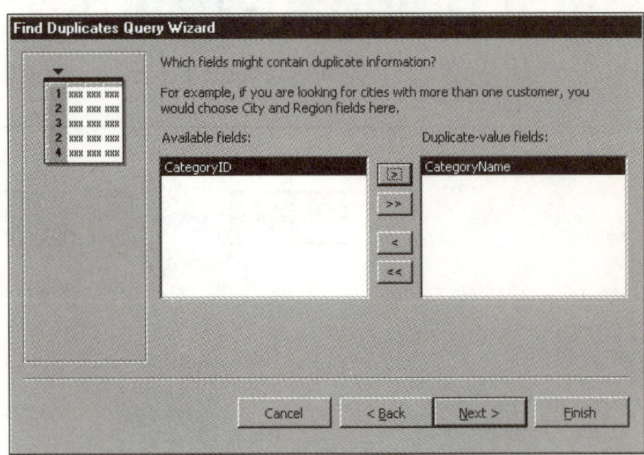

6 Select the field(s) in the record source to search for duplicate values. Click >, or click >> to search all fields.

7 Click Next >.

8 The query result table will show all of the fields that you searched for duplicate values. To display additional fields from the record source in the query result table, select field(s) to include and click >, or click >> to include all fields.

Note: The Find Duplicates query will not search these additional fields for duplicate values. It will simply include them in the query results table.

9 Click Next >.

10 Type a name for the new query.

11 Select what you want to do next: **View the query** (runs the query and displays the crosstab table) or **Modify the design** (opens the query in Design view).

12 Click Finish.

13 The Select Query window appears showing duplicate values, if any.

14 Close the Query window.

Create a Find Unmatched Query Using a Wizard

Use a Find Unmatched query to produce a list of records from one table that do not have related records in another table.

Notes:

- A common use for a Find Unmatched query is to find customers who have never placed an order. You could also find products that have never been ordered, or that have not been ordered recently.

1 Click **Queries** in the Database window.

2 Click New.

3 Double-click **Find Unmatched Query Wizard**.

4 Double-click a record source in the list. The next Query Wizard screen displays.

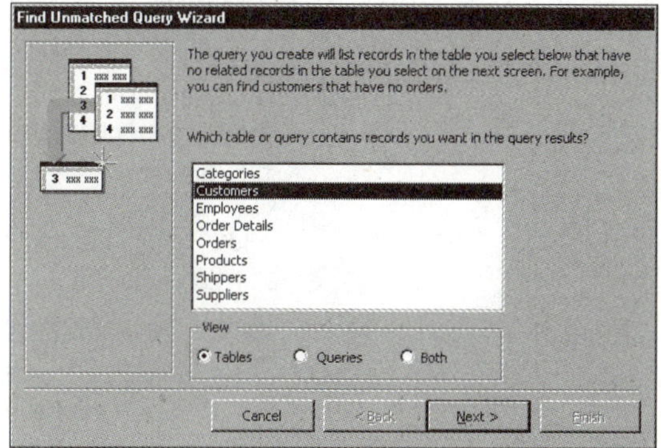

Note: *The Query Wizard assumes that you want to check tables in the current database. You can also select from* ***Queries*** *only or* ***Both*** *tables and queries in the dialog box.*

5 Double-click the record source to check for the presence of related records.

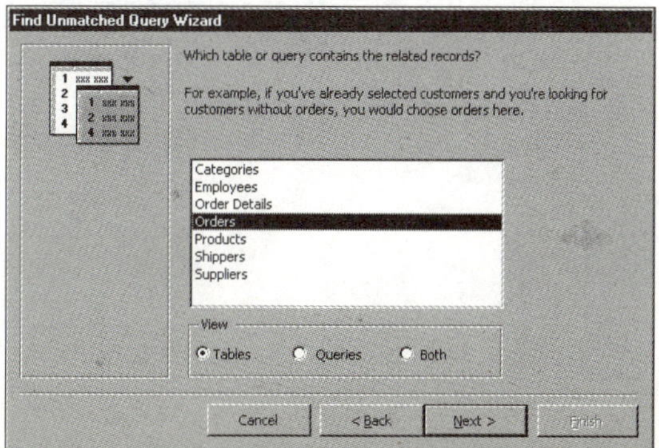

Notes:

- Access allows you to select field names that do not work in the query. For example, you could select the City field in one table and match it to the CustomerID in another table if the data types are the same. Access will accept this but the query results will not be useful. Make sure that you specify related fields in each record source.

6 To specify the related field in the record sources:

a. Select the field common to both record sources in the left column.

b. Select the common field also in the right column.

Note: The matching fields can have different names but must have the same data type. For example, the field might be named CustomerID in one table but CustID in the other.

c. Click <=> to tell the wizard how the record sources are related.

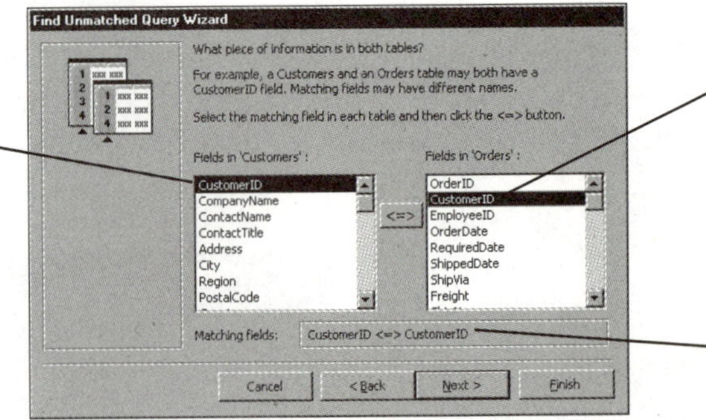

Note: Matching fields are displayed in the dialog box.

7 Click Next >.

8 Specify the fields to display in the query result table.

Select field(s) to include and click >, or click >> to include all fields.

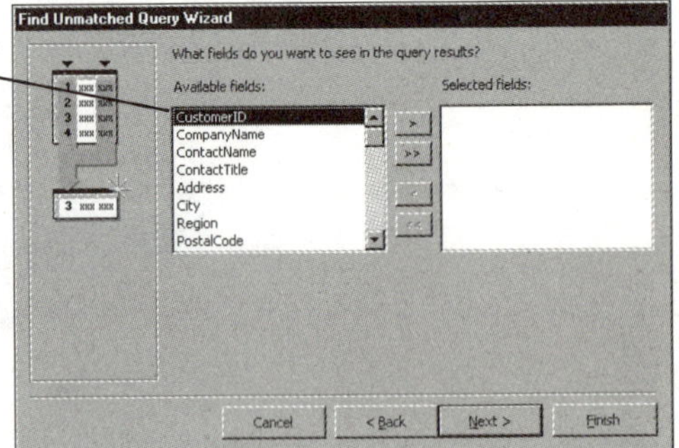

9 Click Next >.

10 Type a name for the new query.

11 Select what you want to do next: **View the query** (runs the query and displays the crosstab table) or **Modify the design** (opens the query in Design view).

12 Click Finish.

Create a Crosstab Query Using a Wizard

A crosstab query summarizes and groups data in both rows and columns. For instance, to know how many orders you filled for customers in each state grouped by product, you would use a crosstab query to display each state in a different column and a different product in each row, with a count for each.

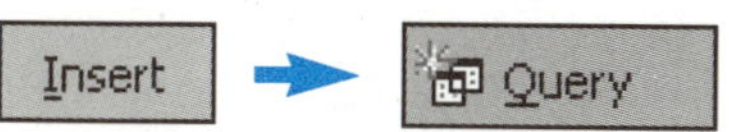

Notes:

- When you use the Crosstab Query Wizard, the crosstab query can use only one data source. The data source can be a table or another query. To use data from multiple tables, create the query in Design view and add the tables to include.

1. Select **Insert**, **Query**. The New Query dialog box opens.
2. Double-click **Crosstab Query Wizard**. The Crosstab Query Wizard starts.
3. Select a data source for the query.

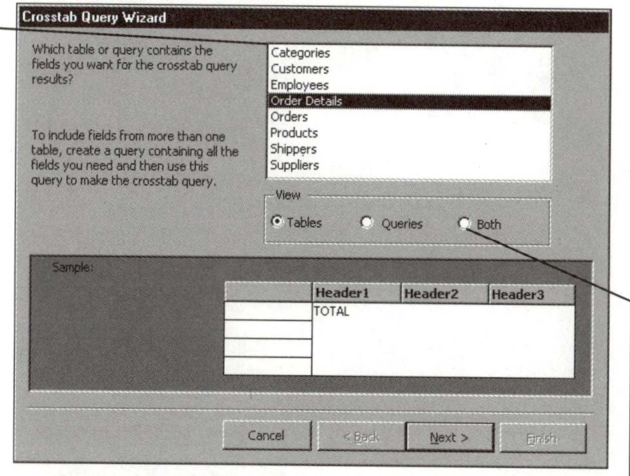

Note: *You can view tables, queries, or both in the dialog box.*

4. Click Next >. The next Crosstab Query Wizard dialog box displays.

Notes:

- Access can also create PivotTables in forms and PivotTable List controls in data access pages. See Access online Help.

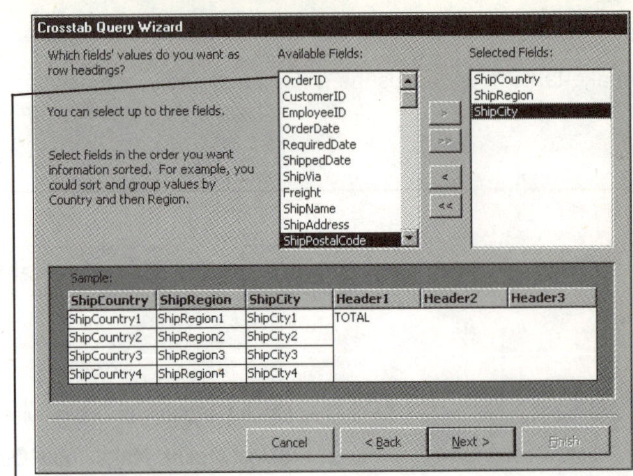

5 Select a field to use as a row heading and click [>] to add it to the query.

6 Repeat step 5 to add up to three row heading fields.

7 Click [Next >].

8 Double-click a field to use for column headings. The next Crosstab Query Wizard dialog box displays.

9 Select a field on which to calculate a value for the column/row intersections of the crosstab.

10 Access assumes that you want to summarize each row. To omit row summaries, clear **Yes, include row sums**.

11 Click [Next >].

12 Type a name for the new query.

13 Select what you want to do next: **View the query** (runs the query and displays the crosstab table) or **Modify the design** (opens the query in Design view).

14 Click [Finish].

Create a Make-Table Query

A make-table query saves the query result table in a new table.

Notes:

- Create a make-table from an existing query by changing its query type to make-table. The make-table query creates a new table for the results when you run it.
- You can create a make-table query from any query that selects records from one or more data sources.
- One common use for a make-table query is to create a copy of a table to be used in another database. You can have the query create the table in another Access database.

1 Open the query in Design view.

2 Select **Query**, **Make-Table Query**.

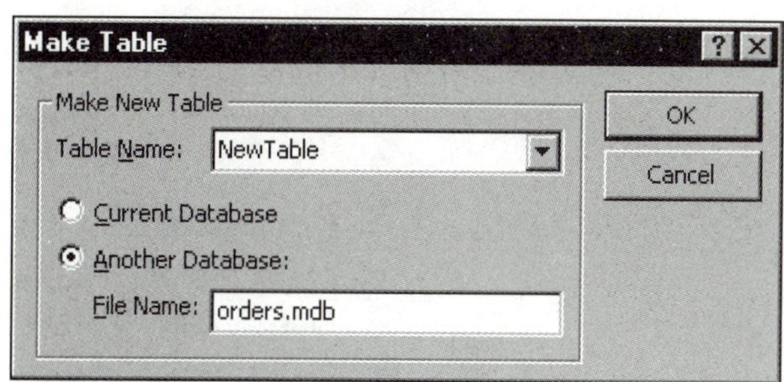

3 Type a name for the new table.

4 To create the table in another Access database if desired:

a. Select **Another Database**.

b. Type the name of the database in which to create the table.

5 Click OK.

6 To run the query, click **Run** ! in the toolbar. Access calculates the number of records that will be created in the new table and displays a prompt.

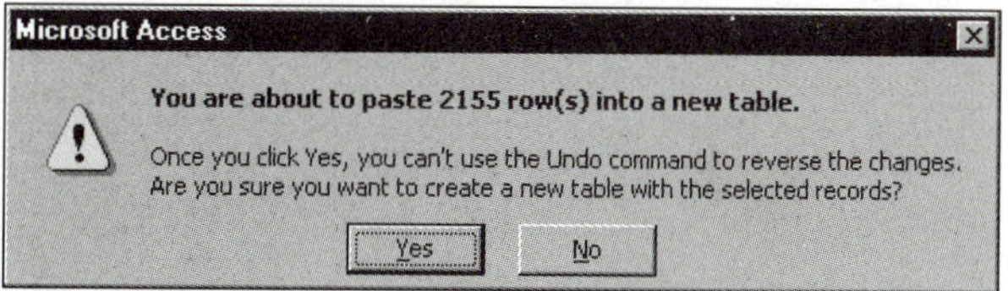

Microsoft Access
You are about to paste 2155 row(s) into a new table.
Once you click Yes, you can't use the Undo command to reverse the changes.
Are you sure you want to create a new table with the selected records?
Yes
No

7 Press **Enter**. Access creates the table.

8 Close the Make Table Query window.

Answer Yes to the prompt when asked if you want to save changes.

Continue

Create an Update Query

An update query changes data in a table. This is useful when you need to make the same change to all or a group of records.

Notes:

- Use an update query to replace values in a table, even when the replacement value is based on a calculation. For example, you could decrease the price of all products by 5% or increase the price of only particular products by 7%.
- To replace a specific value with another specific value, see also **Replace Values in a Table**. Although you can use an update query to make this type of replacement, when you use the find and replace feature, you can have Access prompt you before replacing each value.

1. Select **Insert**, **Query**. The New Query dialog box opens.
2. Double-click **Design View**.
3. Add the table containing the data to update. See **Add or Remove a Table in a Query**.
4. Add all fields that either contain data that you want to change or that you will use for criteria to the criteria grid. To add a field, drag the field name from the field list to the grid or double-click it.
5. Select **Query**, **Update Query**.
6. In the **Criteria** field, enter criteria to specify which records to replace if desired. For example, the criteria in the following illustration updates records only for customers located in Sweden or UK.

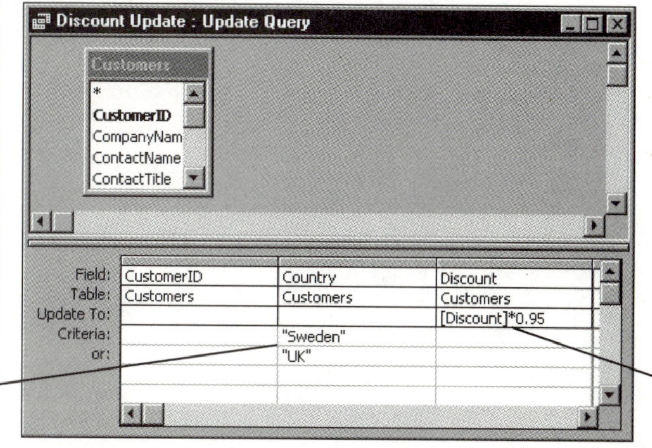

7. In the **Update To** field, enter either the new value or the expression that calculates the new value. For example, in the above illustration, the expression decreases the discount amount by 5%.

Notes:

- Add all the fields that you want to update from the source table to the query grid. Also add fields that you will use to enter criteria specifying which data to update. For example, if you want to change the bonus amount of all employees located in Florida, you would add both the Bonus field and the Location field to the query.
- It is a good idea to preview the records that the query will change before you actually run it. That way you can tell if your query is going to modify the records that you expect it to. Previewing a query enables you to find errors before you change your data.

8 Click **Save** to save the query design.

9 To preview the records that will be changed when you run the update query:

a. Select **View**, **Datasheet View**. Access displays a datasheet with the records that will be updated.

b. Select **View**, **Design View** to return to the query design.

10 To run the query, click **Run** in the toolbar. Access displays a prompt telling you how many rows (records) in the data source will be changed by the query.

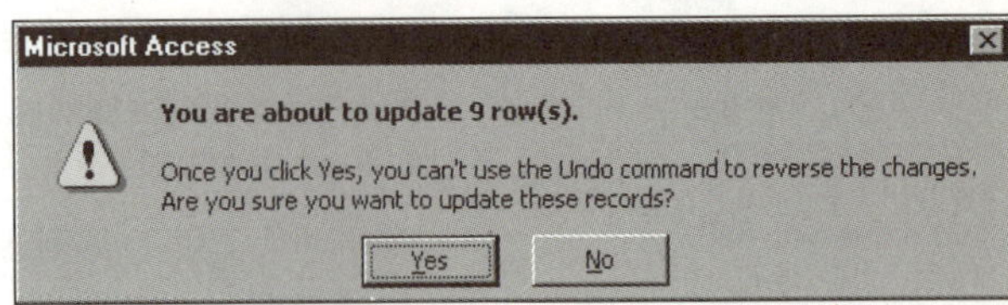
Microsoft Access
You are about to update 9 row(s).
Once you click Yes, you can't use the Undo command to reverse the changes.
Are you sure you want to update these records?
Yes
No

11 Click Yes to update the table.

Create an Append Query

An append query adds records from one table to another table.

Notes:

- The structure of the two tables must be the same although field names do not have to be identical. However, the field types and lengths should match up. For example, if one table has an LName field and the other a LastName field, you can still append records as long as they are both text fields of the same length and in the same field order in both tables. You cannot append records from a table that has a different structure.

1. Click **Tables** in the Database window.
2. Select the table containing the records that you wish to add to another table.

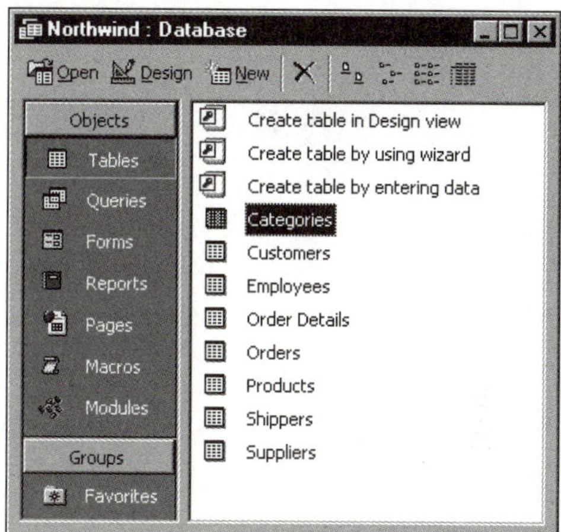

3. Select **Insert**, **Query**. The New Query dialog box displays.
4. Select **Design View** and click OK. Access creates a new query. The field list for the table that you selected in step 2 appears above the query grid.
5. Select **Query**, **Append Query**. The Append dialog box displays.
6. Type the name of the table to which you will append the records.

   *Note: If the table is in the currently open database, you can select it from the **Table Name** drop-down list.*

Notes:

- You can specify criteria to determine which records to append. For example, you could append only categories with a category ID number that starts with 7. Or, you could append all contacts except for the ABC Company. This procedure shows an example of this type of criteria. See also **Create a Simple Select Query** and **Add or Remove a Field in a Query** for more examples.

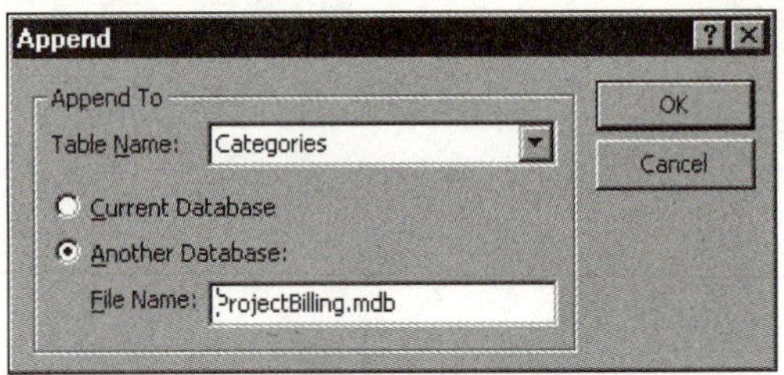

7 If the table is in another Access database:

a. Select **Another database**.

b. Type the name of the database file containing the table.

8 Click OK.

9 Add fields from the field list by dragging them from the field list to the query grid.

OR

If all fields in both tables have the same name and you are going to append all records in the table, drag the asterisk (*) from the field list to the first column in the grid. This adds all fields in the table to the query, as shown in the following illustration.

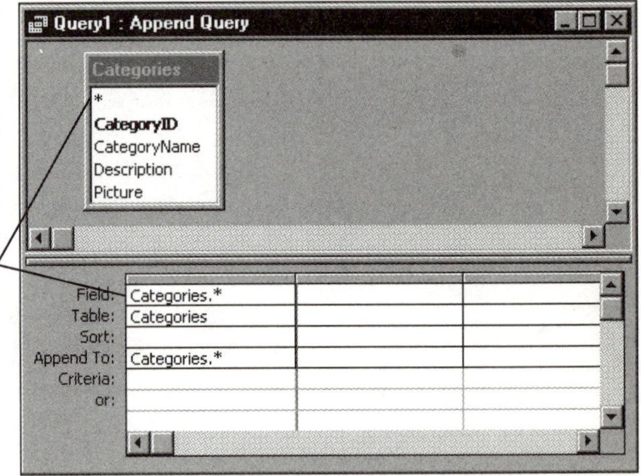

Create an Append Query

(continued)

Notes:

- It is a good idea to preview the records that the query will append before you actually run it. That way you can tell if your query is going to add the records that you expect it to. Preview a query to find errors before you change your data.

10 Add criteria to specify which records will be appended if desired. The following illustration shows criteria that limit the records appended based on a range of category numbers.

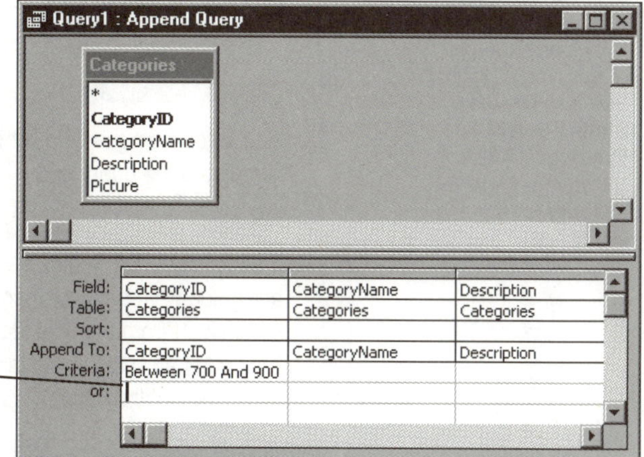

11 To preview the records that will be changed when you run the update query:

a. Select **View**, **Datasheet View**. Access displays all of the records that will be updated in a datasheet.

b. Select **View**, **Design View** to return to the query design.

12 To run the query, click **Run** [!] in the toolbar. Access displays a prompt telling you how many rows (records) in the source table will be added to the destination table.

13 Click [Yes] at the prompt to append the records.

14 Close the Append Query window.

Continue

Create a Simple Select Query

A simple select query returns a subset of the data in a table.

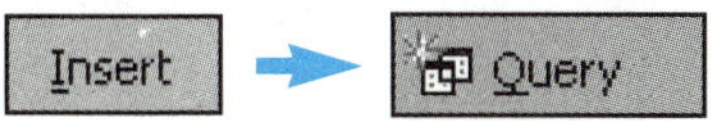

Notes:

- You can create a simple select query to show only a subset of the fields in a table. For example, you could create a query that shows only the company name and region and does not display the company address.
- A simple select query can also display a subset of the records in a table. For example, you could create a query that retrieves all contacts in a particular zip code.

1 Select **Queries** in the Database window.

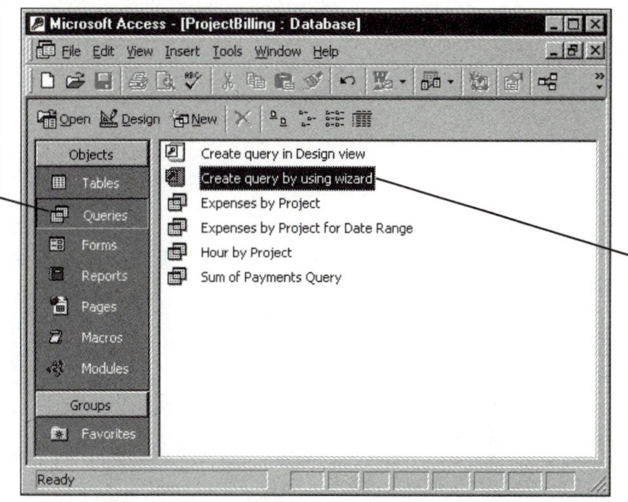

2 Double-click **Create query by using wizard**. The first Simple Query Wizard dialog box displays.

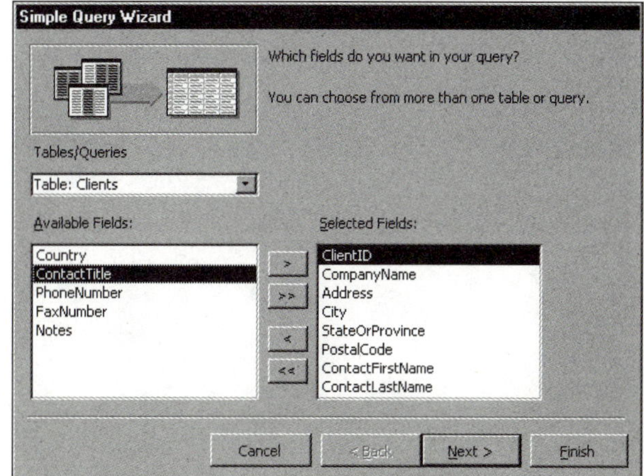

Notes:

- Using the Simple Query Wizard to create the query allows you to create a select query with only one data source. The data source can be a table or another query. To add another data source, see **Add or Remove a Table in a Query**.

3 Select a data source for the query.

4 Select the fields to include in the result table.

5 Click Next >.

6 Follow the wizard dialog boxes. The dialog boxes that display depend on the data source that you choose.

7 Type a name for the query.

8 To enter criteria to select only records from the data source that meet the criteria, select **Modify the query design**.

9 Click Finish. The query opens in Design view.

10 Type the criteria for the records to include in the result table in the Criteria row for the field. For help on entering criteria you can:

- Press **Shift+F2** to open the zoom box to give you more room to type long expressions, or
- Right-click in the Criteria field and select **Build** to start the Expression Builder.

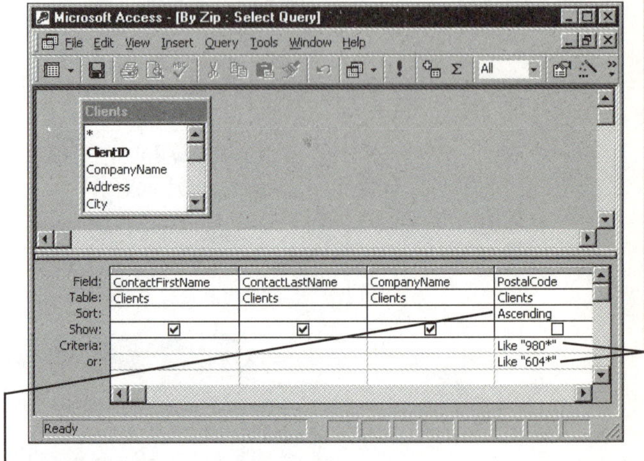

11 To sort the result table by a field, select **Ascending** or **Descending** in the Sort field to determine the sort order.

For example, the above query retrieves clients located in a particular range of zip codes.

12 Click **Save** on the Database toolbar to save the query design.

13 To run the query and view the results, select **View**, **Datasheet View**.

Add or Remove a Table in a Query

Add a related table to an existing query. Or, remove a table from a query.

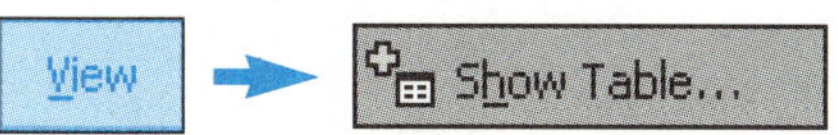

Notes:

- A field list for each data source in the query is displayed above the query grid. Use the field list to add fields to the query. See **Add or Remove a Field in a Query**.

1 Open a query in Design view.

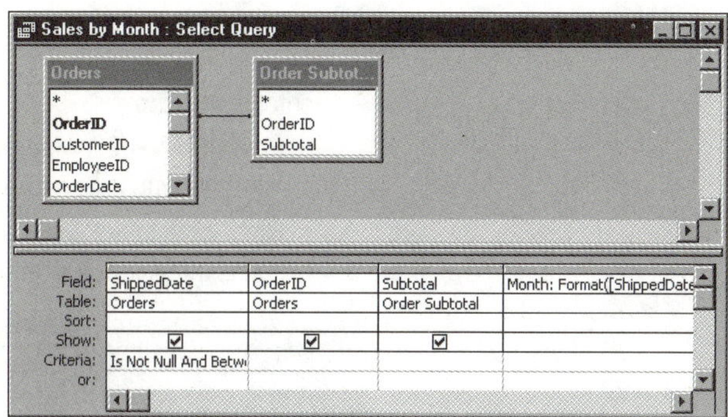

2 Click **Show Table** on the toolbar to open the Show Table dialog box.

3 Click the **Tables** tab to show table data sources, **Queries** to show query data sources, or **Both** to list both tables and queries.

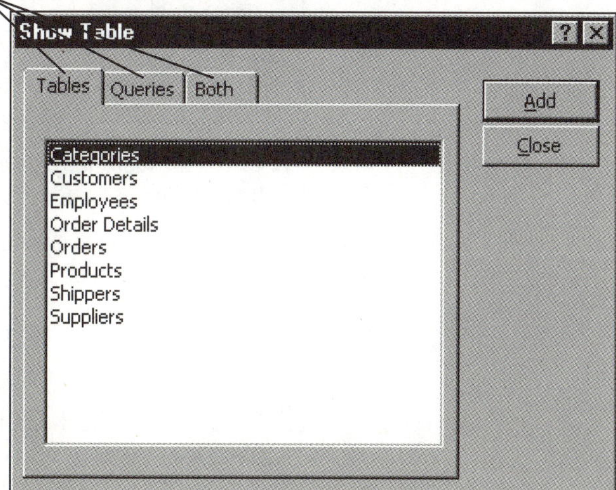

Notes:

- If relationships are defined for the table(s) that you add, they will be inherited in the query. If tables are not related, add a join line between the two common fields (drag the common field from one table to the common field in the second table).

4 Select the table or query to add to the current query.

5 Click **Add**.

6 Repeat steps 4 and 5 to add another data source as necessary.

7 Click **Close** to close the Show Table dialog box. A field list for each data source that you added is displayed above the query grid.

8 Add field(s) from the data source to the query as desired. See **Add or Remove a Field in a Query**.

Notes:

- Removing a table or query from the query does not delete it.

Remove a Table from a Query

1 To remove a table from the query, right-click the table.

2 Select **Remove Table**.

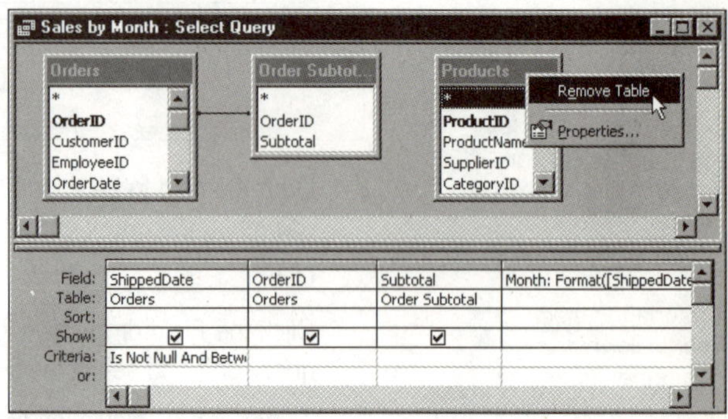

3 Close the Query window.

4 Save the changes when prompted.

Add or Remove a Field in a Query

Add a field from a data source to the query grid in Design view. Or, remove a field from the query.

Notes:

- Before you can add a field, the field list for the table or query containing the field must appear above the query grid. See **Add or Remove a Table in a Query**.
- Use the asterisk (*) in the field list to add all of the fields in the list to the query.
- When you add a field to a query you can specify that the result table be sorted on or grouped by the field. You can also use criteria to select particular records from the underlying data source(s). You can also choose to show or hide the data in the field in the result table.

1 Open a query in Design view.

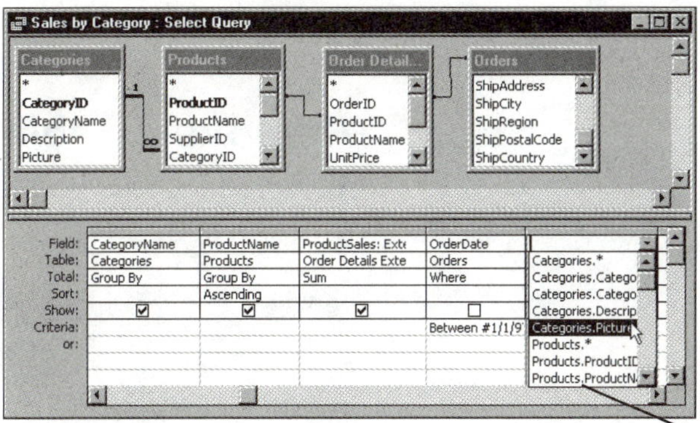

2 Drag the field to be added from the field list to a blank column in the query grid.

OR

Click the Field drop-down list in a blank column in the query grid and select the field to add.

3 To perform a calculation or group the query result data on a field, select a function from the Total field in the grid.

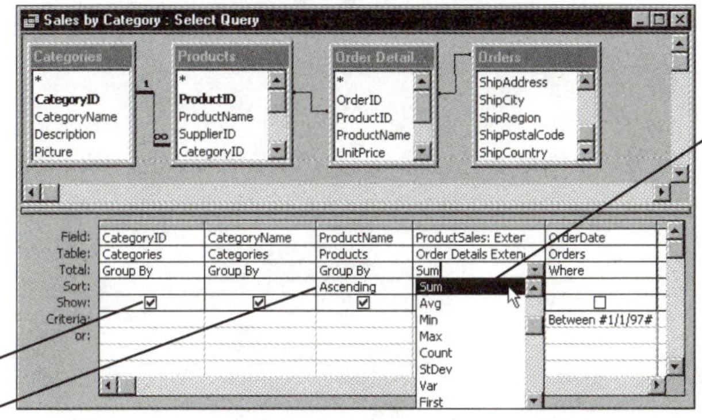

4 To sort the result table by the field, select **Ascending** or **Descending** from the Sort field.

5 To show the field data in the result table, select the **Show** check box; to hide the field, clear the check box.

Notes:

- To create a calculated field in a query, type the expression for the calculation in the Field row.
- The illustration in step 6 of this procedure, from the Northwind sample database, shows two fields with criteria that determine the data to select. The result table for this query will include all records where the subtotal of the order is greater than $2,500 and the order was shipped during 1997.

Note: *Even if you do not show the field data in the result table, you can still use the field for sorting, selection criteria, and other purposes in the query.*

6 Enter a criteria expression in the Criteria field, if desired, to use the field data to determine which records to select in the result table.

Field:	SaleAmount: Subtot	OrderID	CompanyName	ShippedDate
Table:	Order Subtotals	Orders	Customers	Orders
Sort:				
Show:	☑	☑	☑	☑
Criteria:	>2500			Between #1/1/97# And #12/31/97#
or:				

For help on entering criteria you can:

- Press **Shift+F2** to open the zoom box to give you more room to type long expressions, or
- Right-click in the Criteria field and select **Build** to start the Expression Builder.

Notes:

- Removing a field does not delete it in the underlying data source. It is simply not used in the query.

Remove a Field from a Query

1 Click the column header above the field name to select the column containing the field.

2 Press **Delete**.

3 Close the Query window.

4 Save the changes when prompted.

Display All Fields in Query Results

Specify that all fields from the underlying data source(s) will appear in the query results.

Notes:

- Use the OutputAllFields query property to have Access automatically add all fields from all data sources to new queries that you create in Design view.
- When you use the OutputAllFields property, you do not have to add every field to the query grid in order for them to appear in the result table.
- If you do not want to show a particular field in the results, clear the **Show** check box in the query grid in the field to hide. See **Add or Remove a Field in a Query** for an illustration of the check box.

1 Open a query in Design view.

2 Click in the query window background, anywhere outside the query grid and field lists.

Note: This selects the query so that you will open the properties for the entire query, rather than for a table, field, or other individual item in the query.

3 Click **Properties** . The Query Properties dialog box displays.

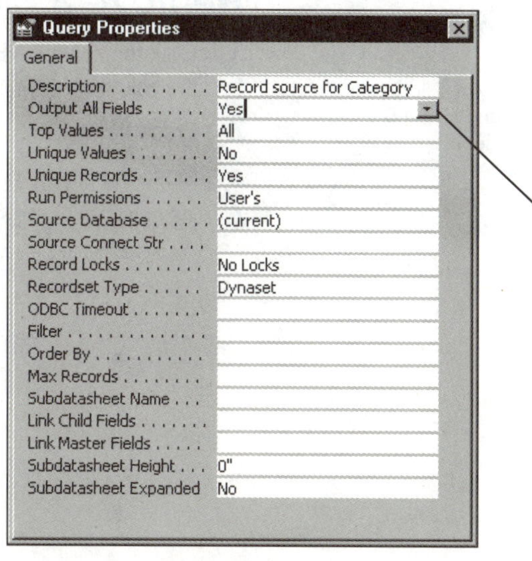

4 Select **Yes** in the **Output All Fields** property.

5 Click to close Query Properties.

Notes:

- Access will assume that you always want to display all fields from data sources in query result tables.
- This setting applies to all future queries that you create. It does not change existing queries.

Display All Fields by Default

1 Select **Tools**, **Options**.

2 Click the **Tables/Queries** tab. The Tables and Queries options display.

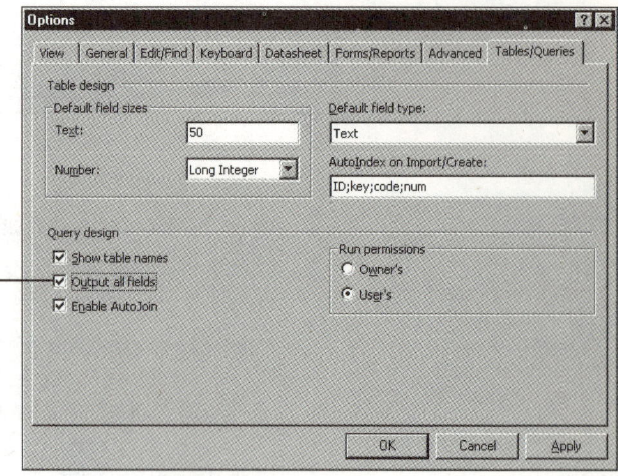

3 Select the **Output all fields** check box.

4 Click OK.

5 Close the Query window.

6 Save the changes when prompted.

Exclude Duplicate Records in a Query

Include only unique records in the query result table.

Notes:

- Use the **UniqueRecords** query property to eliminate duplicate data (entire records) in the query result table.
- The **UniqueRecords** property applies to select queries, append queries, and make-table queries. You can use it only in queries that use multiple tables.

1 Open the query in Design view.

2 Click in the query window background, anywhere outside the query grid and field lists.

Note: *This selects the query so that you will open the properties for the entire query, rather than for a table, field, or other individual item in the query.*

3 Click **Properties** . The Query Properties dialog box displays.

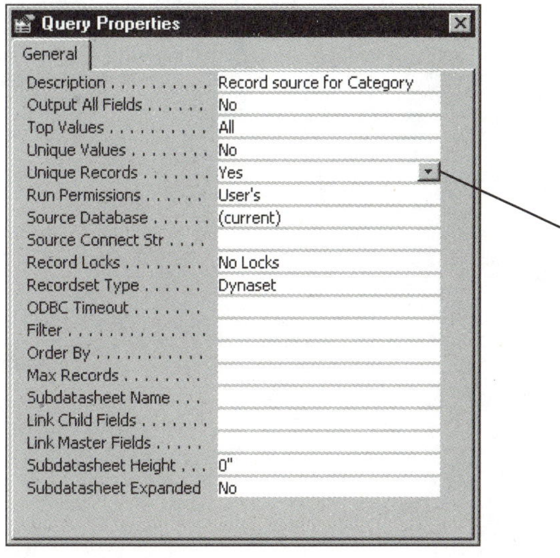

4 To exclude duplicate records in the query results, select **Yes** in the **UniqueRecords** property.

5 Click to close Query Properties.

6 Close the Query window.

7 Save the changes when prompted.

Enter Data

You can use either Datasheet view or create a form to edit the data in a table.

In Datasheet view, records in the table are listed in rows and columns similar to a spreadsheet format. Each row in the datasheet is a record and each column is a field.

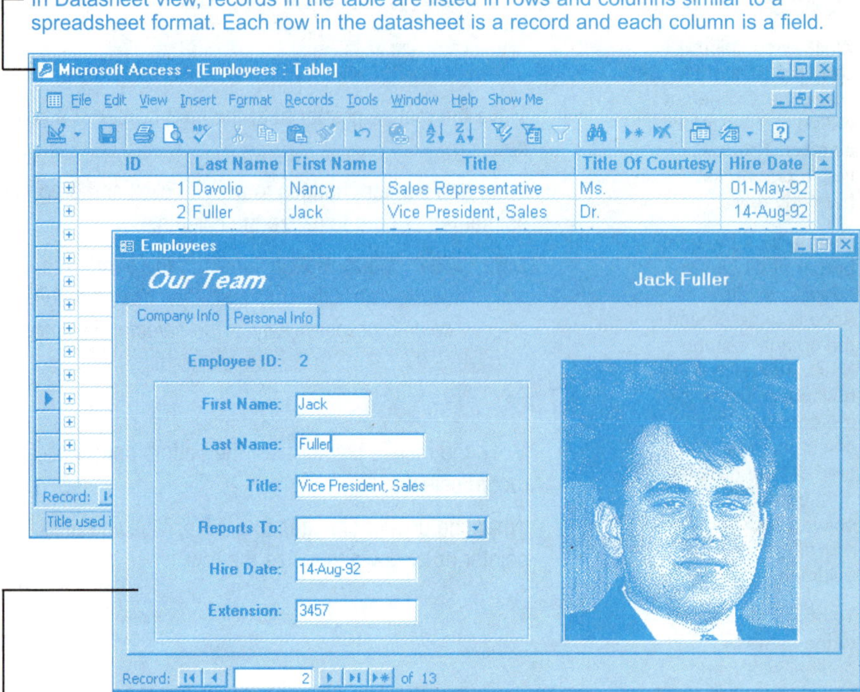

A form displays a single record at a time.

Adjust Datasheet Column Width and Row Height

The column width and row height settings are saved when you save the table.

Notes:

- While each column can be a different width, the row height will be the same for all rows. The row height can be set from any row.
- Double-click the right border of a column heading to allow Access to determine the optimal column width. To resize multiple columns to the optimal width, select them all first, then double-click the right border of the column heading of any of the selected columns.
- To resize all columns to the same or optimal width, first select the entire datasheet.

Open a table, query, or form in Datasheet view.

Column Width

1. Move the mouse pointer near the right border of a column heading.
2. When the pointer changes to a ✛, click and drag the pointer left or right to resize the column.

   Note: *To resize multiple columns to the same or optimal width, select them all first, then drag the right column border of any of the selected columns.*

Row Height

1. Move the mouse pointer near the bottom border of a record selector.
2. When the pointer changes to a ✛, click and drag the pointer up or down to resize the rows.

Notes:

- The new column width applies to all new datasheets that you create, even datasheets in other databases.

Set the Default Column Width

1 Click **Tools**, **Options**.

2 Click the **Datasheet** tab in the Options dialog box.

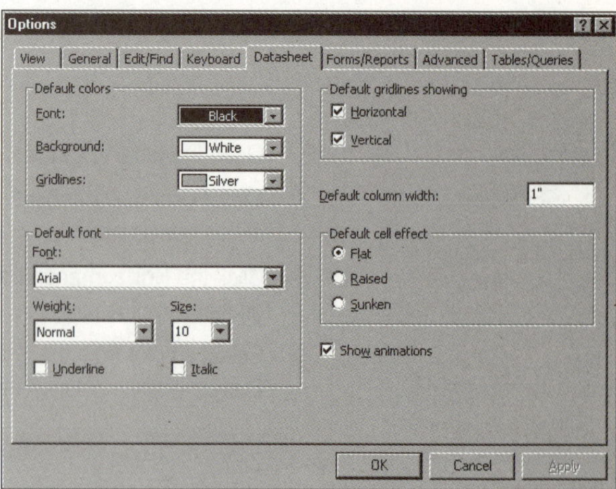

3 Type a measurement in the **Default column width** box.

4 Click OK.

5 Close the table, query, or form.

6 Save the changes when prompted.

Hide or Show Datasheet Gridlines

Hiding the gridlines on a datasheet lets you more clearly see the data. You can hide or show vertical and horizontal gridlines separately.

Notes:

- Show or hide the vertical and/or horizontal gridlines in the datasheet that is currently open on the screen. You can also change gridline colors and line style.
- To show hidden gridlines, repeat the procedure.

1. Open the table in Datasheet view (see **Open a Table**).
2. Click **Format**, **Datasheet**. The Datasheet Formatting dialog box displays.
3. Click the **Horizontal** and/or **Vertical** option(s) to set which gridlines to hide or display.
4. Select a color from the **Gridline color** drop-down list to change gridline colors if desired.

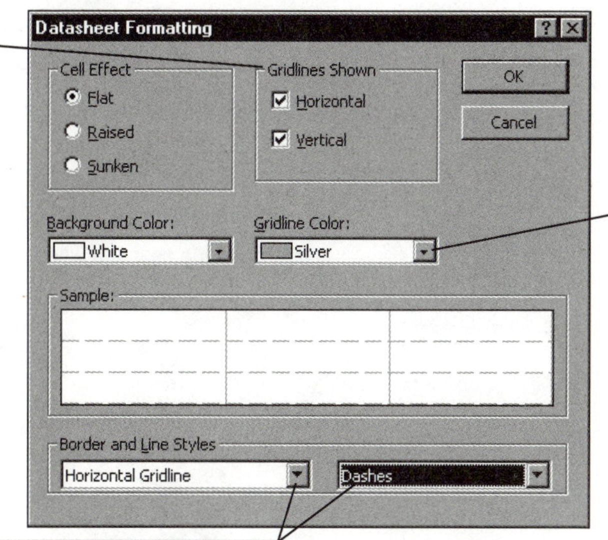

5. To change line styles if desired, select **Horizontal** and **Vertical Gridline** and then select a line style.
6. Click OK.

Notes:

- Hide or show gridlines by default in all datasheets.
- You can also change the default datasheet colors and the appearance of cells.
- These settings apply to all datasheets in all databases. However, changes to gridline defaults do not change formatting that you applied using the Format menu in any individual datasheet. You can override the default gridline settings in individual datasheets as described in this section.

Hide or Show Gridlines for All Datasheets

1 Click **Tools**, **Options**.

2 Click the **Datasheet** tab in the Options dialog box.

3 Click the **Horizontal** and/or **Vertical** options to set which gridlines to hide or display.

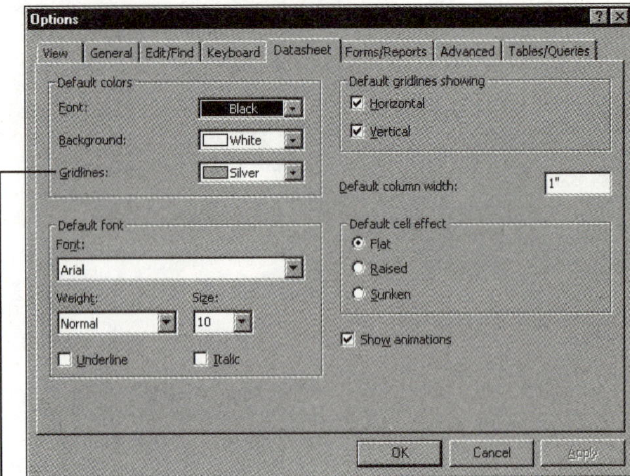

4 Select a color from the **Gridlines** drop-down list to change gridline colors if desired.

5 Click OK.

Hide a Column in a Datasheet

Temporarily hide a column so that you can view more columns in a large datasheet.

Notes:

- You can choose which columns to unhide. For example, if you have hidden two columns, you can unhide one or both.

1 Right-click the column heading in Datasheet view to open the shortcut menu.

2 Click **Hide Columns**.

Unhide a Hidden Column

1 Click **Format**, **Unhide Columns**.

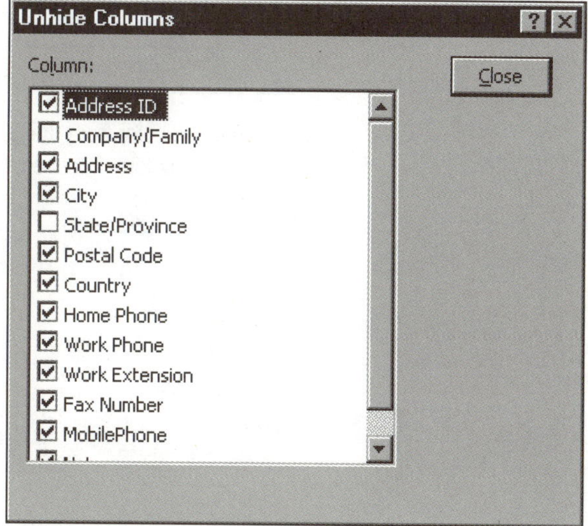

2 Select the check box next to each column that you wish to display.

3 Click Close.

Continue

Enter Data in a Datasheet, Form, or Page

Use Datasheet view or Form view to edit the data in a table. These procedures also apply to data access pages that include data entry capabilities.

Notes:

- If a datasheet has a form created for it, you can switch between Datasheet view and Form view using the View button on the toolbar or the **View** menu.
- A datasheet might be a query result table. To view the datasheet for the query result table, run the query.
- A data access page is posted on a server on the Internet or an intranet. Open the page in Internet Explorer.

Notes:

- Add a new record at the end of existing records.
- Access automatically saves new records after you enter data.

Open a Form or Datasheet for Data Entry

1 To open a datasheet, click **Tables** in the Database window.

OR

Click in the first blank field of the first blank row of the datasheet or form.

OR

To open a form, click **Forms** in the Database window.

2 Double-click on the form or datasheet name to open it.

Add a Record

1 Click **New Record** .

OR

If you enter data in the last record, a new blank record will automatically appear at the end of the table.

2 Type data in the first field.

3 Press **Tab** to move to the next field.

Note: You can also use arrow keys to move from field to field.

4 Repeat steps 2 and 3 to enter data in fields.

5 When finished adding records in the datasheet or form, click to close it.

Zoom to Enter Field Data

1 Position the cursor in the field you want to edit in the Zoom box.

2 Press **Shift+F2**. A Zoom box opens.

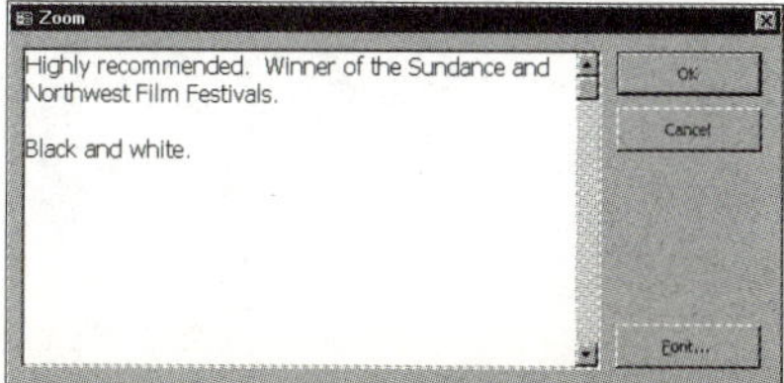

Notes:

- When a field is long, you can open the current field in a zoom box to see all of the data in the field.
- If the font on the datasheet is small, you can relieve your eyes by using the Zoom box to edit fields. You can change the font size in the zoom box to a larger font.

3 To view field contents in a smaller or larger font if desired:

a. Click Font... . The Font dialog box displays.

b. Select font and/or font size.

c. Click OK to return to the Zoom box.

4 Type field data. To start a new paragraph, press **Ctrl+Enter**.

*Note: If you press **Enter** the Zoom box will close.*

5 To close the Zoom box, press **Enter**.

Notes:

- To save data entry time, you can copy the record from the field directly above the current field into the current field.

Copy Data from Previous Field

1 Click in a blank field below a filled-in field.

2 Press **Ctrl+ '** (apostrophe). Access copies the value from the same field in the previous record.

Notes:

- You can only undo changes to the current field or the last record that you edited. Access automatically saves your edits when you start editing another record. After you start editing the next record, you cannot undo changes to the previous record.

Undo Last Edit

Click [Undo button] or press **Ctrl+Z** to undo the last edit in the current field. Repeat if desired to undo previous edits in the current field.

OR

Press **Esc** to undo all edits in the current field.

OR

Press **Edit**, **Undo Saved Record** to undo all edits to an entire record if you have already moved to another record but have not yet started editing it. If this command does not appear on the Edit menu, then you cannot undo changes to the record.

Notes:

- You cannot undo a record deletion.

Delete Record

1 Position the cursor in the record you want to delete.

OR

Select the records you want to delete.

2 Click [Delete Record button]. Access displays a prompt to confirm that you want to delete the record(s).

3 Click Yes to permanently delete the record(s).

4 Close the datasheet or form.

Copy and Move Data in Forms, Datasheets, and Pages

Use the Office Clipboard to store multiple items that you cut or copy.

Notes:

- The Office Clipboard holds up to 12 items that you cut or copy. As you cut or copy items, they are automatically added to the Office Clipboard. The 13th item that you cut or copy causes Access to prompt you for what to do next.
- The Office Clipboard includes a toolbar where you can work with the individual items stored in it.
- The Office Clipboard toolbar can be docked (displays only at the top of the window) or floating (position it anywhere on the screen).

Use the Office Clipboard Toolbar

- Click **View**, **Toolbars**, **Clipboard** to show or hide the toolbar.
- To dock the toolbar at the top of the window if desired, click in its title bar and drag it to the top of the window under any toolbars already displayed.

Note: The toolbar displays automatically when you cut or copy the second item during an editing session.

- To change the docked toolbar to a floating toolbar that you can move anywhere on the screen, drag it by its handle from its docked position to anywhere in the window.
- To view an item stored in the Office Clipboard:

  a. If the toolbar is docked, click Items.

  b. Hover the mouse pointer over an item. The content (up to the first 50 characters) is displayed in a pop-up tip:

Notes:

- The Windows Clipboard stores only one item at a time. If you copy another item to the Clipboard, it replaces any existing data already on the Clipboard. The last item that you cut or paste is stored in the Windows Clipboard. Pasting the contents of the Windows Clipboard pastes the data that you last copied or cut to the Clipboard.
- The contents of both the Windows Clipboard and the Office Clipboard are deleted when you close all Office programs.
- Clearing the Clipboard clears both the Windows Clipboard and the Office Clipboard.
- You can use clipboards to cut and copy data between Access datasheets and forms and other Office documents.

Copy or Cut the Selection to the Office Clipboard

1 Select the data to copy or cut.

2 To copy the data, press **Ctrl+C** or click **Copy** on either the regular toolbar or the Clipboard toolbar.

OR

To move the selected data to the Clipboard, press **Ctrl+X** or click **Cut** .

Note: *The item will be added to the Office Clipboard. It will replace any existing data on the Windows Clipboard.*

Paste Item(s) from a Clipboard

1 Position the cursor where the Clipboard contents will be pasted.

2 To paste the contents of a particular item in the Office Clipboard, click  in the Office Clipboard toolbar.

OR

To paste the item that you last cut or copied, press **Ctrl+V** or click **Paste** on the regular toolbar.

Note: *The item that you last cut or copied is stored in both the Office Clipboard and the Windows Clipboard.*

OR

To paste all items in the Office Clipboard in a data access page, click **Paste All** on the Office Clipboard toolbar.

Note: *The Paste All feature is not available in forms and datasheets. It is available in data access pages.*

Clear Clipboards

Click **Clear Clipboard** in the Office Clipboard toolbar.

Navigate in a Datasheet, Form, or Page

Move around when editing table data.

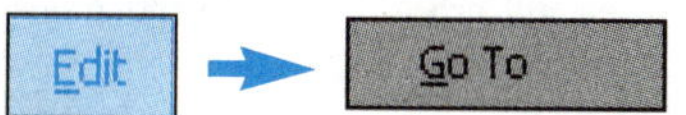

Notes:

- Both forms and datasheets include navigation buttons (unless specifically removed in a form). Data access pages created for data entry purposes also include navigation buttons.
- Navigation buttons are located at the bottom of the window.

Use Navigation Buttons

1 Open a datasheet, form, or page for editing.

2 Click a record navigation button:

- first record
- previous record
- next record
- last record
- new record

Go To a Record Number

1 Press **F5**.

2 Type the number of the record to go to.

3 Press **Enter**.

Notes:

- The Go To Field list shows all the fields in the datasheet. It is located on the Formatting toolbar, which is not displayed by default. If working in a datasheet with many fields, display the Formatting toolbar so that you can access this handy tool for navigating the datasheet.

Go to a Field by Selecting the Field Name (Datasheet View)

1 Select **View, Toolbars, Formatting**.

2 Select the field to go to from the **Go To Field** list at the left of the Formatting toolbar: 

Find Data in a Form or Datasheet

Find particular data in a field in a form or datasheet.

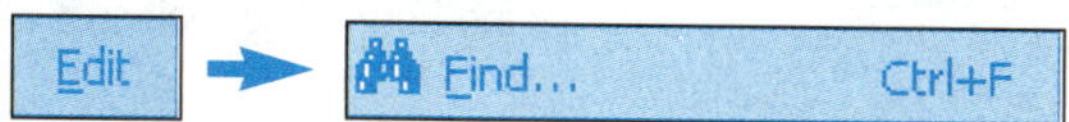

Notes:

You can use the following wildcard characters in both the Find and Replace dialog boxes:

- * Matches any number of characters. Example: "*one" finds "fone" and "phone."
- ? Matches any single character. Example: "r?n?" finds "ran" and "run."
- [] Matches any character in the brackets in the current position in the word. Example: "Hamm[oe]nd" finds "Hammond" or "Hammend"
- [!] Matches any character not found in the brackets (excludes characters in brackets). Example: "Hamm[!oe]nd" will not find "Hammond" or "Hammend" but will find "Hammind"
- [-] Matches a range of characters in ascending order. Example: "b[a-c]d" finds "bad" and "bbd" and "bcd"
- # Matches a single numeric character. Example: "980#0" finds 98010, 98020, etc.

1 Click on the toolbar. The Find and Replace dialog box opens with the Find tab selected.

2 Type the text to find in the **Find What** text box.

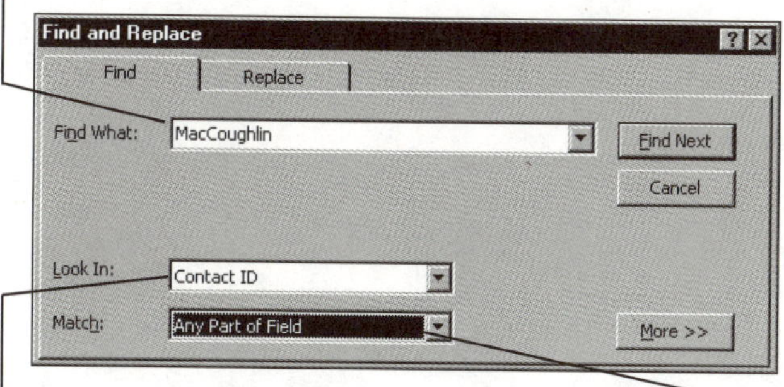

3 Select the field to search for the text.

4 Use the **Match** field to specify where the data can be located in the field in order for Access to find it.

5 To show additional options, click More >>.

Notes:

- You can also use filters to find records meeting criteria. Filters hide any data not meeting your criteria. See **Filter Records in a Datasheet or Form**.
- To find zero-length strings, type "" in the Find What box. Do not enter a space between the quotes. To find a null value, type **Null** or **Is Null** in the Find What box. You cannot use these in the Replace dialog box.

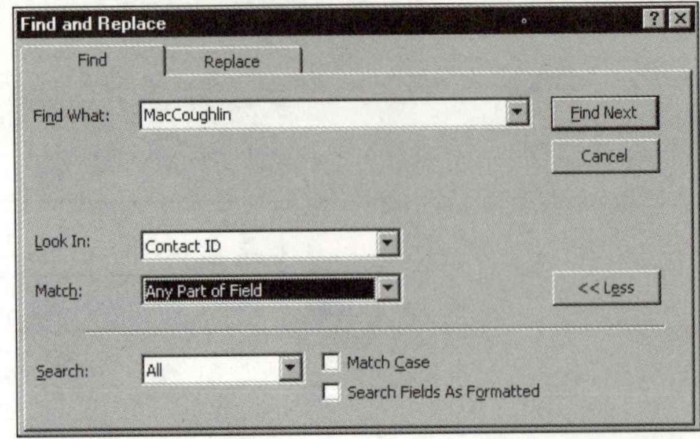

6 To specify which records to search, select a **Search** option:

Up. From the current record to the first record.

Down. From the current record to the final record.

All. From the current record to the end of the database and continuing from the first record.

7 To find field data only when it is in upper/lowercase exactly as typed in the **Find What** box, select **Match Case**.

8 To find data only when it is formatted according to the data type of the text to find, select **Search Fields As Formatted**. For example, if you want to find the date 06-01 only in a formatted date field, select this option.

Note: Selecting this option may slow down search performance.

9 To search for the next instance of the **Find What** text, click Find Next.

10 Repeat step 9 to find data as necessary.

11 Click Cancel or press **Esc** when finished.

Replace Data in a Form or Datasheet

Replace specific data with other data.

Notes:

- For the wildcard characters that you can use to enter find and replace criteria, see the **Notes** sidebar in the **Find Data in a Form or Datasheet** section.

1 Press **Ctrl+H**. The Find and Replace dialog box opens with the Replace tab selected.

2 Type the data to replace in the **Find What** box.

3 Type the replacement data in the **Replace With** box.

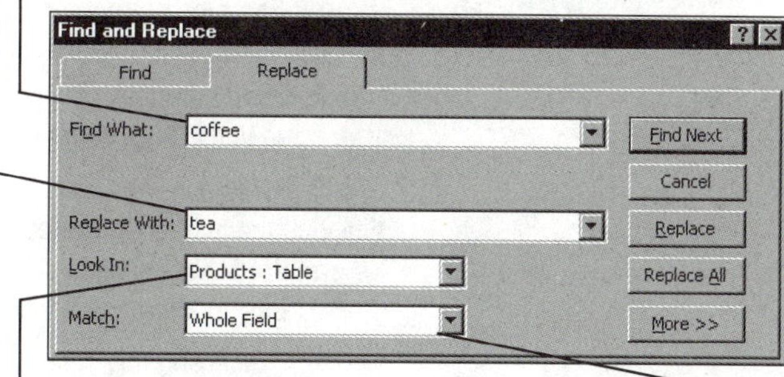

4 Select the field containing the data to replace.

OR

Select the table name to replace in all fields in the entire table.

5 Select where the data can be located in the field in order for Access to replace it.

Note: *If you select Whole Field, then Access will not replace the data if other data is also located in the field.*

6 Click More >> to show more options.

Notes:

- You can also use an Update query to find and replace data in a table. However, you cannot skip replacing individual occurrences of replacement text when you use an Update query. The query will replace all instances.

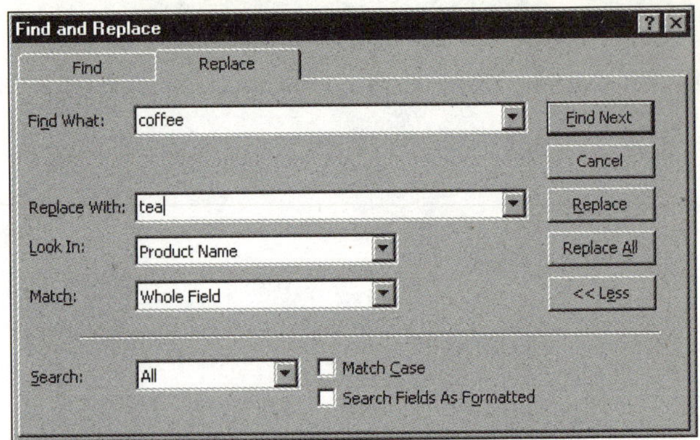

7 To specify which records to replace in, select a **Search** option:

Up. From the current record to the first record.

Down. From the current record to the final record.

All. From the current record to the end of the database and continuing from the first record.

8 To replace field data exactly as typed in the **Find What** box, select **Match Case**.

9 To find data only when it is formatted according to the data type of the text to find, select **Search Fields As Formatted**. For example, if you want to find the date 06-01 only in a formatted date field, select this option.

Note: Selecting this option may slow down search performance.

10 To replace data without prompting you, click Replace All.

OR

Click Find Next to find the next occurrence. To replace the data, click Replace or to skip replacing, click Find Next. Repeat as necessary.

11 Click Cancel or press **Esc** when finished.

Filter Records in a Datasheet or Form

Use filters to display a subset of the data in a table according to the criteria you specify.

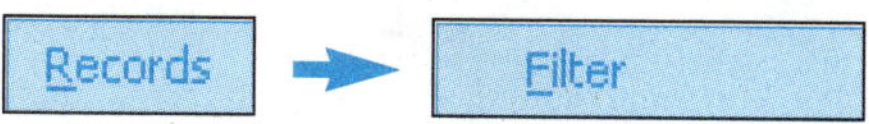

Notes:

- Filters tell Access to hide data that you specify. For example, you can view only records for customers in a particular state or only movies with a certain actor in them.
- You can use Filter by Form in either Datasheet view or Form view. This procedure shows Datasheet view in the illustrations.
- If you enter criteria in an **Or** tab, the resulting filtered recordset will be those records that meet the criteria specified in either the **Look for** tab or the **Or** tab. The **Or** tab effectively broadens the scope of the filter. For example, you could show only records where the state is Washington *or* Missouri.
- To improve the speed of applying a filter, use indexed fields. If you often need to filter on a nonindexed field, consider indexing it. See **Add an Index**.

Use Filter by Form

1 Select **Records, Filter, Filter by Form** in the datasheet or click **Filter by Form** . Access displays a datasheet with one blank row or a blank form. The tab at the bottom of the window is the **Look for** tab.

2 Click in a field to enter criteria.

3 Type the criteria to find.

OR

Click and select the data to find in the field.

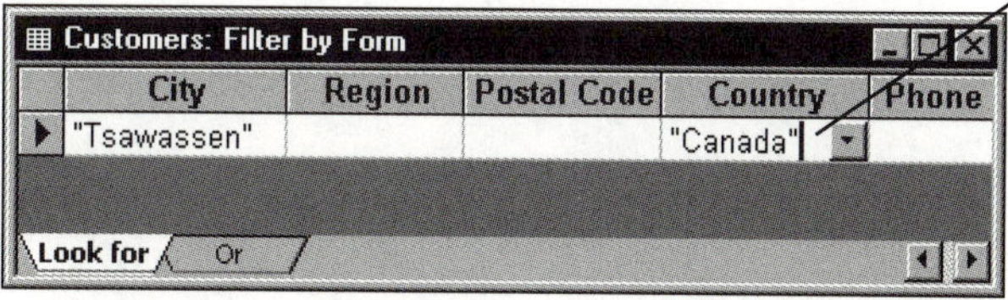

4 To add more criteria if desired, click the **Or** tab at the bottom of the window.

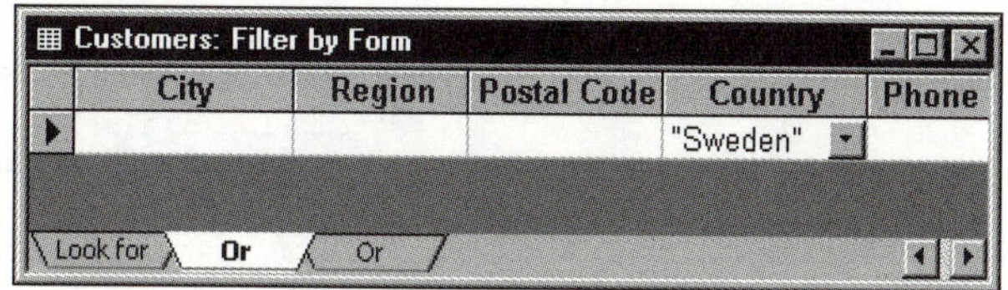

Note: To clear all criteria from the filter if desired, click

*or select **Edit**, **Clear Grid**.*

5 Type or select criteria.

Notes:

- Access places quotation marks around text to find. You do not have to enter the quotation marks.
- In this illustration, only those records where the city is Tsawassen and the country is Canada will be displayed.

6 Repeat steps 4 and 5 to add more criteria if desired.

7 Click **Apply Filter**. Access displays only records matching your criteria. The following illustration shows the records returned using the criteria shown in this procedure.

Customers : Table

City	Region	Postal Code	Country	Phone
Tsawassen	BC	T2F 8M4	Canada	(604) 555-4729
Bräcke		S-844 67	Sweden	0695-34 67 21
Luleå		S-958 22	Sweden	0921-12 34 65

Record: 1 of 3 (Filtered)

Notes:

- The Filter by Selection is a quick way to create a simple filter where you specify the criteria by selecting it directly in the datasheet or form rather than switching to a filter window.
- Filter by Selection allows you to filter records based on the data in a single field. To create more complex filters, use Filter by Form.

Use a Filter by Selection

1 Select the data to include in the filter. The filter will show only those records that have the selected data in them.

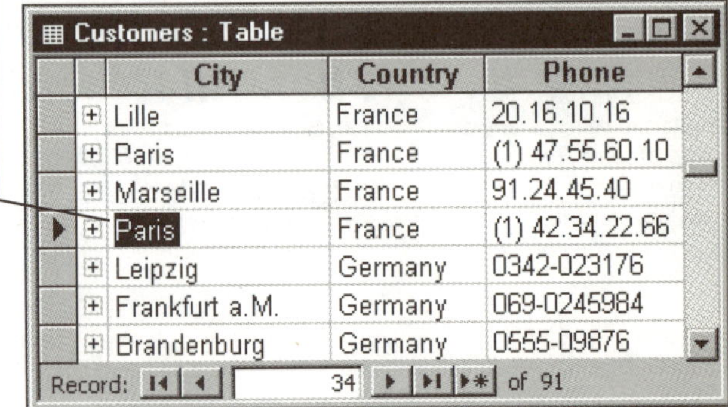

Customers : Table

City	Country	Phone
Lille	France	20.16.10.16
Paris	France	(1) 47.55.60.10
Marseille	France	91.24.45.40
Paris	France	(1) 42.34.22.66
Leipzig	Germany	0342-023176
Frankfurt a.M.	Germany	069-0245984
Brandenburg	Germany	0555-09876

Record: 34 of 91

2 Select **Records, Filter, Filter by Selection** or click .

The filter hides all records that do not have the selected data in the field. The following illustration shows the results of the Filter by Selection set up in this procedure in Datasheet view.

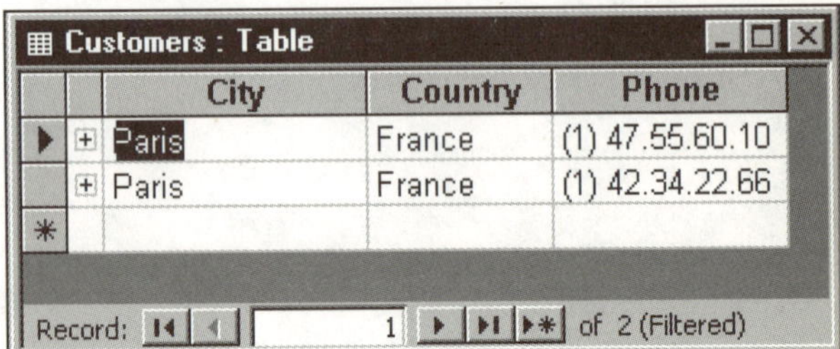

Customers : Table

City	Country	Phone
Paris	France	(1) 47.55.60.10
Paris	France	(1) 42.34.22.66

Record: 1 of 2 (Filtered)

Filter Records in a Datasheet or Form

(continued)

Notes:

- The Filter Excluding Selection shows all records in the datasheet except for records that contain the data that you select. For example, if you select "Paris" in the City field, the filter hides all records except those with "Paris" in the City field.

Use a Filter Excluding Selection

1 Select the data to hide.

2 Select **Records, Filter, Filter Excluding Selection**.

Notes:

- Use this toolbar button to remove any type of filter. Records hidden by the filter are now shown.

Remove Filter and Show All Records

Click **Remove Filter** .

Continue

Sort the Data in a Datasheet or Form

Perform a quick sort in Datasheet view or Form view if you only need to sort on one field. Or, use the Advanced Filter/Sort window to sort on multiple fields.

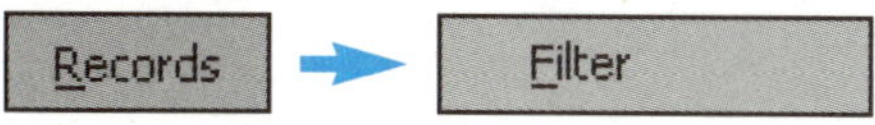

Sort on the Current Field

1 Open the table in Datasheet view or Form view.

2 Position the cursor in the field to sort on.

3 Click [A-Z] to sort in ascending order.

OR

Click [Z-A] to sort in descending order.

Notes:

- Sort in either ascending or descending order by one field only.

Sort on Multiple Fields

1 Open the table in Datasheet view or Form view.

2 Select **Records**, **Filter**, **Advanced Filter/Sort**.

3 Drag a field to sort on from the field list to the grid.

OR

Click [▼] in the Field row and select the field to sort on.

4 Select a Sort order for the field.

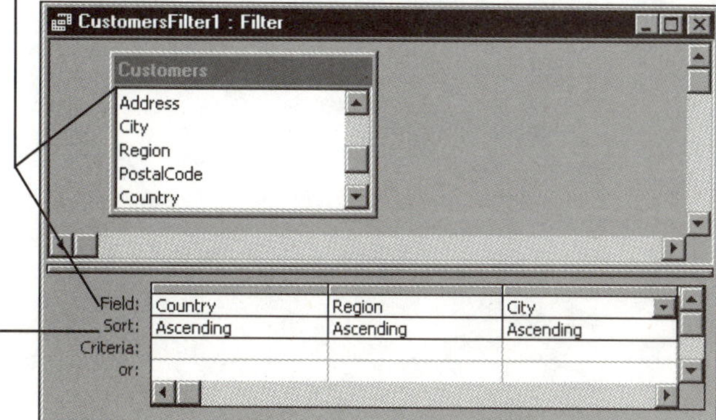

Notes:

- Data will be sorted on fields in the order that they appear in the grid (left to right) in the Advanced Filter/Sort window. For example, to sort by last name and then first name, you would first add the Last Name field to the grid. The sort order set up in the illustration is first by country, then region, then city.

Notes:

- The data remains in the sort order until you either close the database or remove the Advanced Filter/Sort. The filter is saved with the database so that you can reapply it.

5 Repeat steps 3 and 4 for each field you want to sort on. The above illustration shows a sort order with three fields.

6 Set up the sort order as desired:

- To reorder fields, you can move a field by clicking the column selector (above the field name) and then dragging it to a different position in the grid.
- To insert a column after a field in the grid, position the cursor in the field and select **Insert**, **Columns**. The new column is inserted after the field containing the cursor.
- To remove a field from the sort order, click the column selector for the field and press **Delete**.
- To completely clear the design grid so that you can start over, select **Edit**, **Clear Grid**.

7 Select **Filter**, **Apply Filter/Sort**. Access sorts the data and returns to Datasheet view or Form view.

8 Click **Remove Filter** to remove the sort order if desired.

Forms

Use a form to view and edit data in a table.

If there are many fields in a table, you can create a multiple-tab form and place groups of fields on each tab. This allows you to create forms that are not crowded with many fields. Multiple-tab forms are also useful for creating custom dialog boxes.

To show related records from another table, create a subform and add it to the form. For example, in a form that displays customer records, you could show information about a customer's latest order from the Orders table.

Create a Form Using a Wizard

Forms are usually used to provide a user interface for data entry.

Notes:

- A form displays the data in one or more data sources (tables or queries). When you create a form using the Form Wizard, you choose which fields from which tables or queries will appear on the form.

1 Click **Forms** in the Database window.

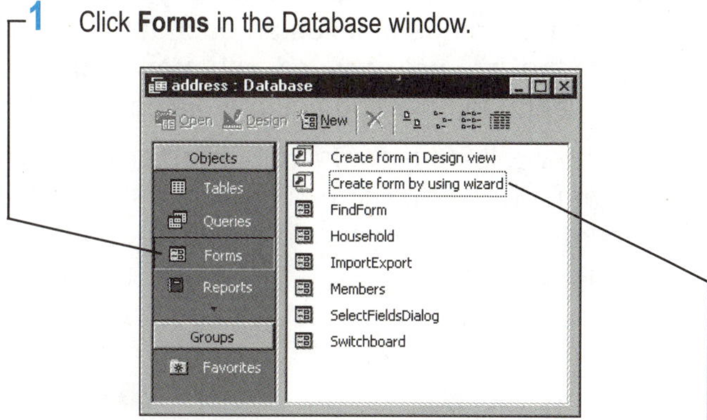

2 Double-click **Create form by using wizard**. The Form Wizard starts.

3 Select the record source for the form.

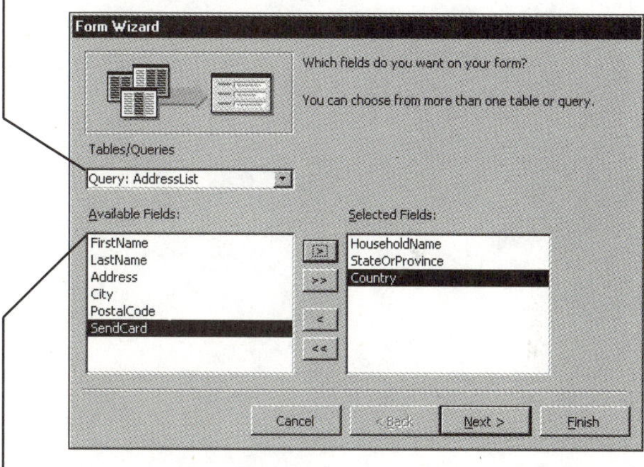

4 Select fields to include in the form in the **Available Fields** list and click [>].

*Note: To select multiple fields, press **Ctrl** and click the next field to select.*

OR

Click [>>] to include all of the available fields in the form.

Notes:

- Display the form in Form view to enter data in the underlying tables or queries.
- In addition to data entry, forms are also used to create custom dialog boxes. However, you would create a dialog box form in Design view rather than using the Form Wizard.

5 Repeat steps 3 and 4 to add fields from other record sources to the form as desired.

6 Click Next >.

7 Select a layout for the form.

Note: Click on a form layout to see a sample of the layout in the preview pane. See also ***Create a Form using AutoForm*** *for examples of the Tabular and Columnar layout.*

8 Click Next >.

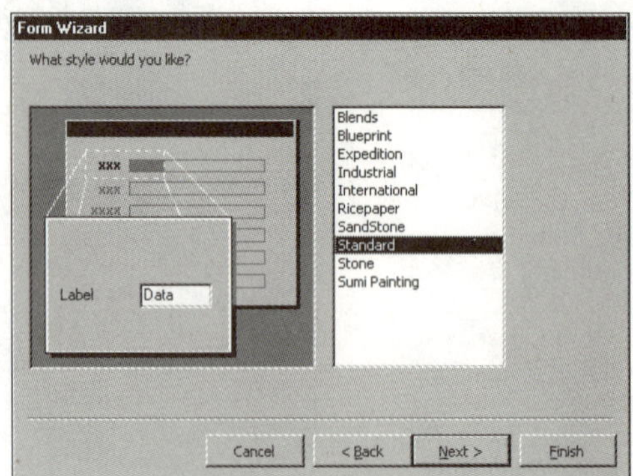

9 Select a style for the form.

10 Click Next >.

11 Type a name for the form.

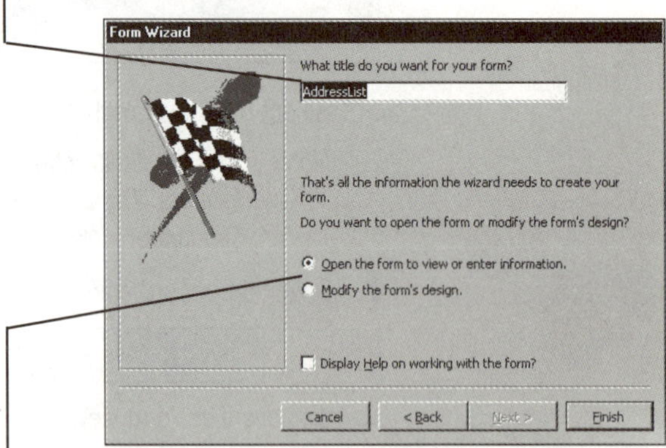

12 Specify what you want to do next: view the form, or open it in Design view for further customizing.

13 Click Finish. The form appears.

Create a Form Using AutoForm

AutoForm creates a form from a single data source (table or query).

Notes:

- You can include only one table or query (record source) in an AutoForm. The AutoForm includes all fields from the data source. If the data source is related to another table (set up in the Relationships window), then all fields in the related table are also included in the form.

1 Click **Forms** in the Database window.

2 Click New. The New Form dialog box displays.

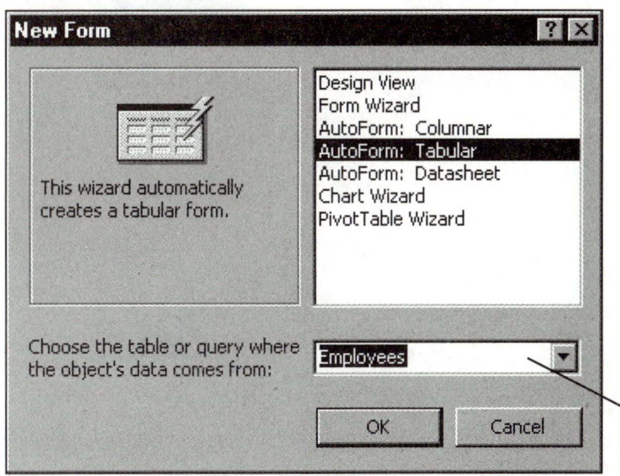

3 Select the layout of the AutoForm that you want to create.

Note: *See the illustrations of the tabular and columnar formats. The Datasheet format is similar to Datasheet view.*

4 Select the record source for the AutoForm.

5 Click OK. Access creates the AutoForm and displays it in Form view.

Notes:

- An AutoForm is the fastest way to create a form. You can open it in Design view and edit the design. For example, you could remove fields from the form in Design view.
- You can also create a form using the **View, AutoForm** command rather than the **New** button as described in this procedure. However, you cannot select a form layout if you use that method.

TABULAR AUTOFORM

In a tabular form, fields appear in a row and field labels appear above each field.

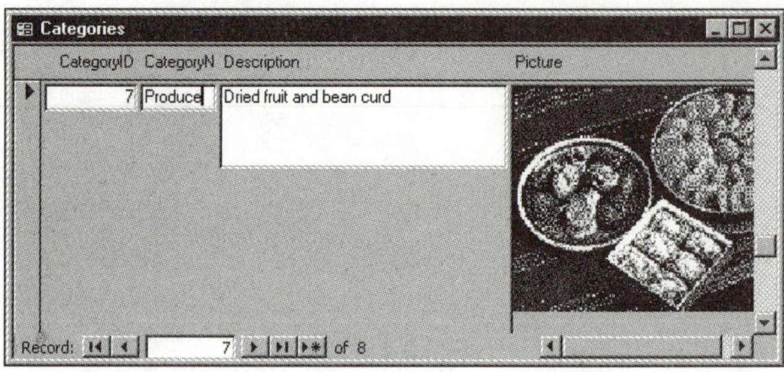

COLUMNAR AUTOFORM

In a columnar form, fields are stacked in a column and field labels appear to the left of each field.

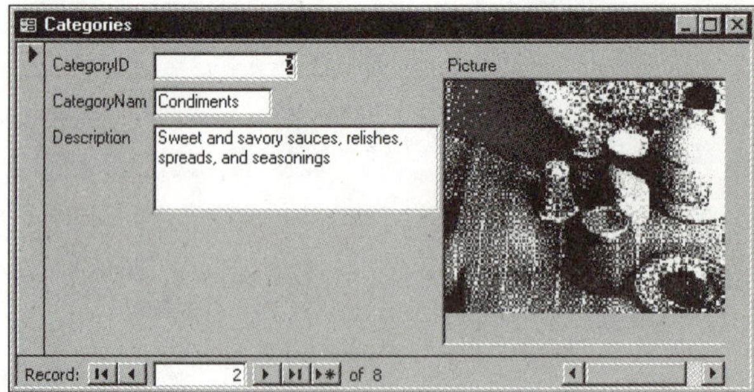

DATASHEET AUTOFORM

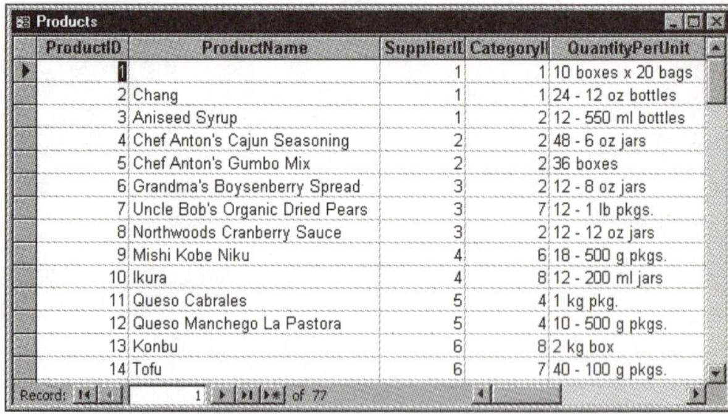

Products

ProductID	ProductName	SupplierII	CategoryI	QuantityPerUnit
1		1	1	10 boxes x 20 bags
2	Chang	1	1	24 - 12 oz bottles
3	Aniseed Syrup	1	2	12 - 550 ml bottles
4	Chef Anton's Cajun Seasoning	2	2	48 - 6 oz jars
5	Chef Anton's Gumbo Mix	2	2	36 boxes
6	Grandma's Boysenberry Spread	3	2	12 - 8 oz jars
7	Uncle Bob's Organic Dried Pears	3	7	12 - 1 lb pkgs.
8	Northwoods Cranberry Sauce	3	2	12 - 12 oz jars
9	Mishi Kobe Niku	4	6	18 - 500 g pkgs.
10	Ikura	4	8	12 - 200 ml jars
11	Queso Cabrales	5	4	1 kg pkg.
12	Queso Manchego La Pastora	5	4	10 - 500 g pkgs.
13	Konbu	6	8	2 kg box
14	Tofu	6	7	40 - 100 g pkgs.

Record: 1 of 77

Create a Multiple-Tab Form

Use tab controls to divide a form into multiple pages. Tab forms have a tab at the top, which you can click to move between them.

Notes:

- Use a multiple-tab form to organize fields into different pages.
- Multiple-tab forms are often used to create dialog boxes. If you use Microsoft software, this type of form is already familiar to you.

1 Select **Insert**, **Form**. The New Form dialog box displays.

2 Select **Design View**.

3 Select the data source (table or query) for the form.

4 Click OK. A blank form design window opens.

5 Click **Tab Control** on the Toolbox. The mouse pointer changes shape as shown in the illustration below.

*Note: If the Toolbox is not displayed, select **View**, **Toolbox**.*

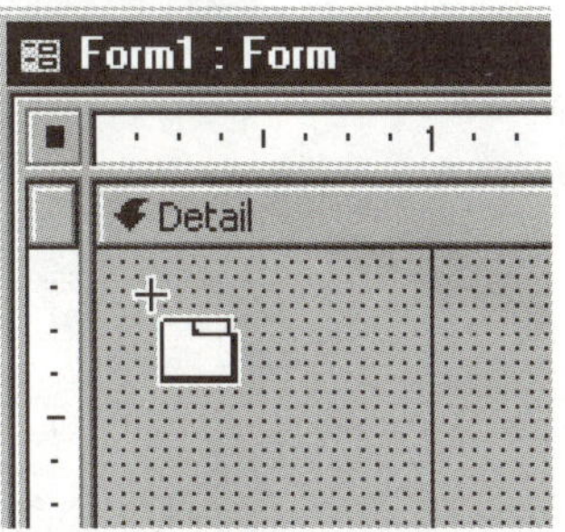

6 Drag across the form grid to create a form of the desired size. When you release the mouse button, a tab control with two tabs is added to the design grid.

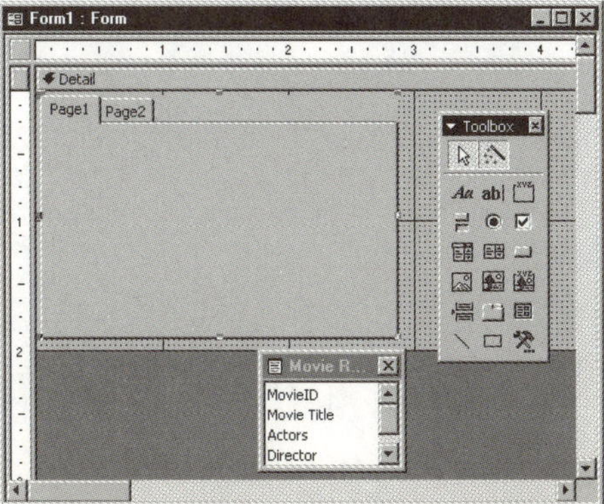

Notes:

- Multiple-tab forms are useful when using forms to create custom dialog boxes that have many options on them. You can use tabs to organize dialog box options into categories.

7 To change the text on the tab:

a. Right-click the tab and select **Properties**. The tab page properties display.

b. Click the **Format** tab.

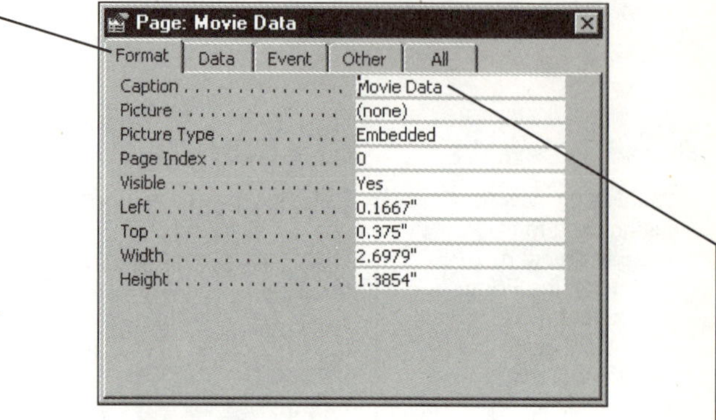

c. Type tab text in the **Caption** property.

d. Press **Enter.**

8 To add another tab if desired, right-click an existing tab and select **Insert Page**. Following is an illustration of a multiple-tab form with three tabs.

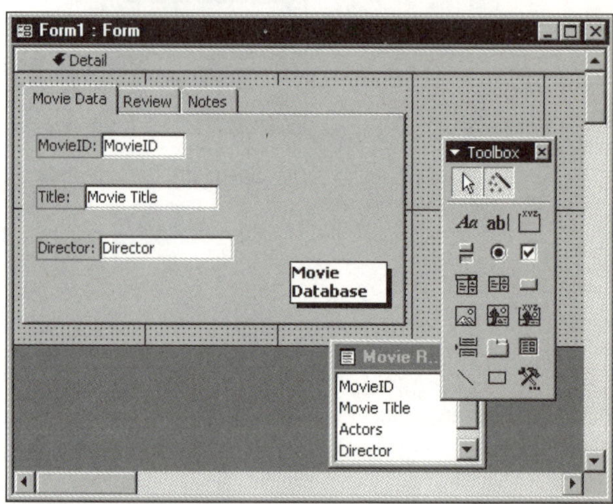

Notes:

- To delete a tab if desired, right-click the tab to delete and select **Delete Page**.
- To move tabs into a different order, right-click a tab and select **Order Pages**.

9 Add fields, controls, and other objects to the form as desired.

10 Press **Ctrl+S** to save the form.

11 Type a name for the form.

12 Click OK or press **Enter**.

13 Click [X] to close the form.

Open a Form

Open a form in Design view to customize the form structure. Open it in Form view to edit data.

Notes:

- Use Design view to customize a form. You can create a form using the Form Wizard and then open it in Design view to add and remove fields, change the style, add controls, and otherwise modify it.

In Design View

1 Click **Forms** in the Database window.

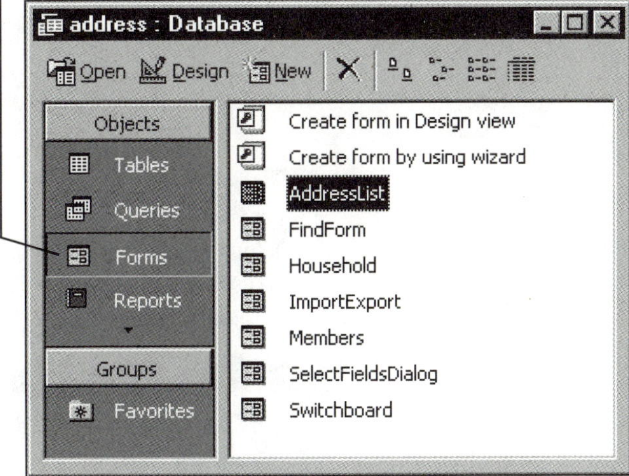

2 Select the form to open.

3 Click Design or press **Ctrl+Enter**.

Notes:

- Use Form view to use the form to enter data.
- For a description of the navigation buttons at the bottom of the form, see **Navigate in a Datasheet, Form, or Page**. For procedures on entering data in a form, see **Enter Data in a Datasheet, Form, or Page**.

In Form View

1 Click **Forms** in the Database window.

2 Double-click the form to open. The form opens in Form view.

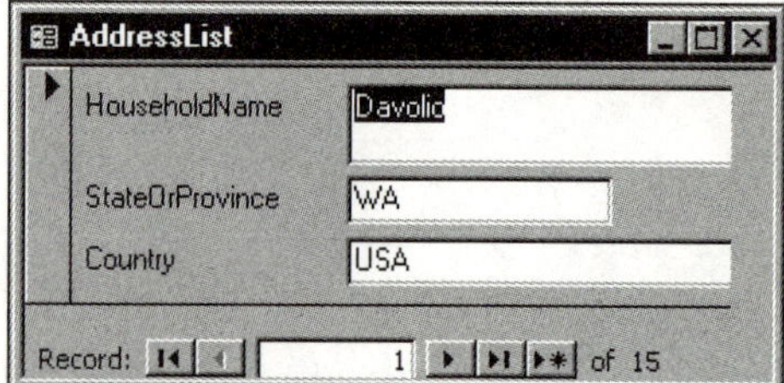

Notes:

- Switch to Datasheet view from Form view.

Switch to Datasheet View

Select View, **Datasheet View**.

Apply an AutoFormat to a Form

AutoFormats are predefined styles that you can apply to a form. They help you apply consistent formatting among the various elements in a form.

Notes:

- If you created the form using the Form Wizard, you chose an AutoFormat to apply when you selected a style for the form. You can use this procedure to apply a different style.
- An AutoFormat contains formatting such as colors, font styles, backgrounds, and borders. You can choose to apply all styles in a particular AutoFormat or only styles that you select (such as formatting text only).

1. Open the form in Design view (see **Open a Form**).
2. Click **AutoFormat** .
3. Click Options >> to display more options at the bottom of the AutoFormat window.
4. Select the format to apply from the **Form AutoFormats** list.

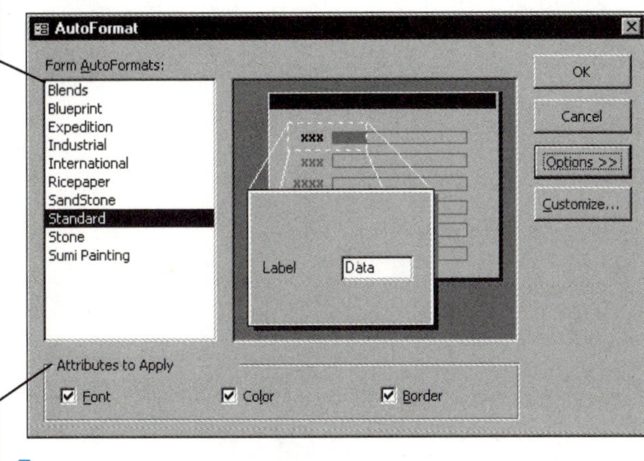

5. Clear any formatting elements that you do not wish to apply.
6. Click OK. The AutoFormat is applied to the form.
7. Switch to Form view.
8. Close the form when finished.

Continue

Create a Subform and Add It to a Form

A subform displays related data from another table or query when you edit records using a form.

Notes:

- The form that contains the subform is called the main form.
- Subforms are often used to display one-to-many relationships. For example, the main form might display a particular customer. The subform displays all open orders for that customer. Or, the main form displays an actor and the subform displays information about all of the movies that actor has been in.
- The tables for the main form and the subform must be related (see **Add or Edit Table Relationships**). For example, if both the Directors table and the Movies table have a DirectorID field, you could show a director in the main form and all movies by that director in the subform.
- Access uses the common field on which the data sources are linked to synchronize the main form and the subform. For example, when you display a record in the main form (such as a customer), the corresponding information (such as all orders the customer has on file) is displayed.

1 Open the main form in Design view (see **Open a Form**).

2 Make sure the **Control Wizards** tool on the Toolbox is active.

3 Click **Subform/Subreport** on the Toolbox.

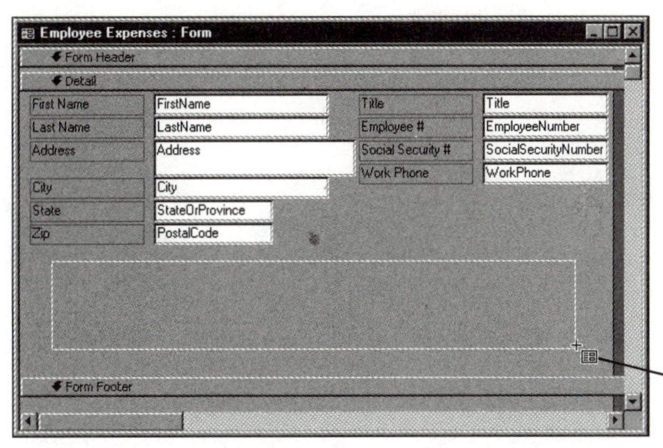

4 Drag on the form to create the Subform control. The Subform Wizard starts.

Note: You can resize the subform later if you need to.

5 Click **Use existing Tables and Queries** in the first Subform Wizard dialog box.

6 Click **Next >**.

Notes:

- There are a number of ways to create a subform. This procedure shows you how to create a subform and add it to an existing form.
- The subform is a separate form and is listed in the Database window. Use a name such as "Orders Subform" or "Members Subform" to identify it as subform.
- See **Edit a Subform** to further customize the subform after you create it.

Notes:

- If the Toolbox is not displayed, select **View**, **Toolbox**.
- The Control Wizards tool has a pressed-in appearance when it is active:

7 Select a record source for the subform.

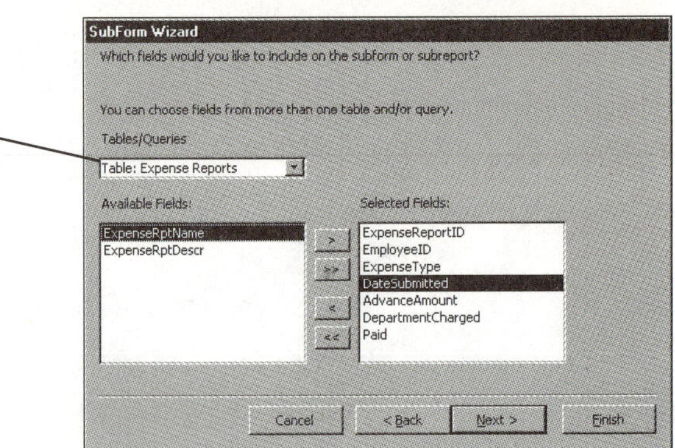

8 Select a field to include in the subform and click >. Repeat to add more fields.

OR

Click >> to include all fields in the record source in the subform.

9 Click Next >.

10 Select the field that relates the form record source and the subform record source.

11 Click Next >.

12 Type a name for the subform.

13 Click Finish.

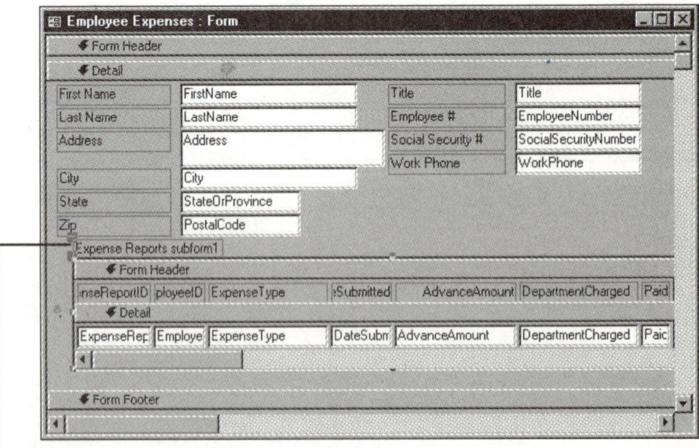

The Subform Wizard adds the subform to the main form. The illustration shows a subform added to a main form.

Note: You will probably need to adjust the subform. See the next section, ***Edit a Subform****.*

Edit a Subform

Work with a subform in Design view to customize it.

Notes:

- Subforms are listed with main forms in the Database window.
- Some of the work that you do to modify a subform must be done by working with the main form. For example, to resize the subform on the main form, you open the main form in Design view. Other modifications require that you work with the subform. For example, in order to remove a field from a subform, you must open the subform in Design view.
- Switch to Form view (**View**, **Form View**) to see how your changes to a subform will look. Switch back to Design view (**View**, **Design View**) to continue editing.

Resize a Subform

1 Open the main form in Design view.

2 Click on the outside border of the subform control to select it.

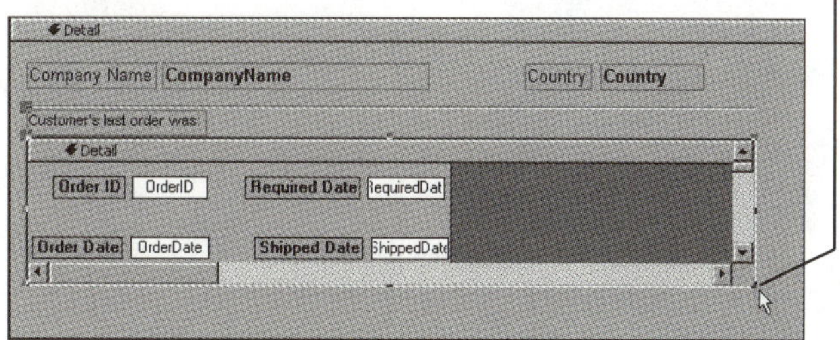

3 Place the pointer on a sizing handle on the border of the subform until it changes to a two-headed arrow: ↕

4 Drag to resize.

Move a Subform

1 Open the main form in Design view.

2 Click on the outside border of the subform control to select it.

3 Place the pointer on the subform border until it turns into a hand:

4 Drag to move the control.

Notes:

- Removing a field from a subform does not remove it from the underlying table or query.
- Field labels appear to the left of or above field controls, depending on the design of your form.

Remove a Field from a Subform

1 Open the subform in Design view.

2 Click on the field you want to remove.

3 Press **Delete**.

4 Repeat to remove the field label if necessary.

Set the Tab Order in a Form

Set the order in which fields are activated when you press the **Tab** key in a form displayed in Form view.

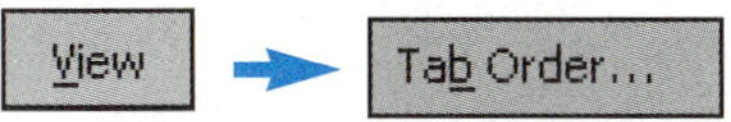

Notes:

- The tab order is the order in which fields are activated when you press **Tab** to move to the next field in a form. This is called moving the focus. By default, the tab order is from left-to-right across the form and then to the next row.
- Changing the tab order changes the order in which fields appear in Datasheet view. Fields will appear in the tab order set using this procedure.
- The new tab order does not rearrange fields in Form view. It only changes the order in which fields are activated.

1 Open the form in Design view (see **Open a Form**).

2 Select **View**, **Tab Order**. The Tab Order dialog box displays.

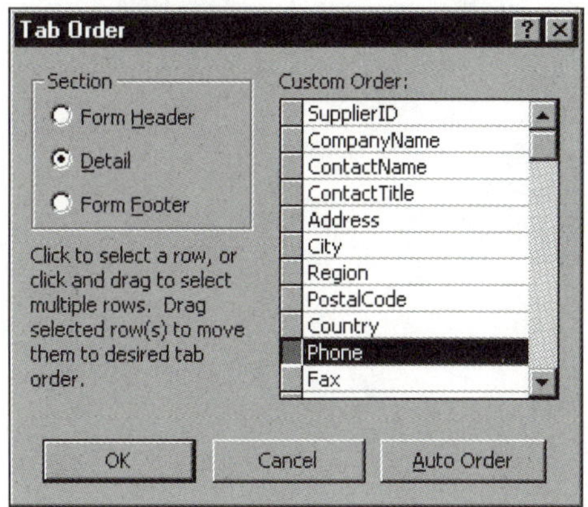

3 To move a field in the tab order, click the field selector (box to the left of the field name).

4 Drag the field to the new position in the field list.

5 To reset the tab order to the default order, click

Note: The default tab order is left-to-right across the form and then to the next row of fields.

6 Click OK.

7 Click **Save** to save the design changes.

Set Tab Behavior for the Last Field

1 Open the form in Design view.

2 Press **Ctrl+R** to select the form.

3 Click to open the form properties.

4 Click the **Other** tab.

Notes:

- This procedure determines which field receives the focus (is activated) when you press **Tab** from the last field in Form view.

5 Click the Cycle property.

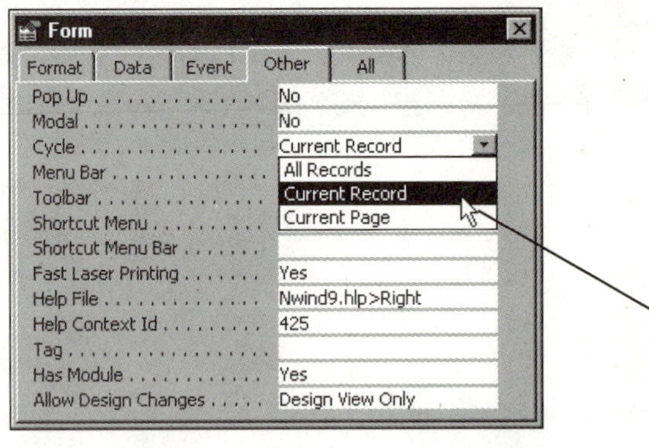

6 Click the drop-down button and select an option that determines what happens when you press **Tab** at the last field in the form:

All Records. Focus moves to the first field in the next record.

Current Record. Focus moves to the first field in the current record.

Current Page. Focus moves to the first field in the current page.

7 Click **Save** to save the design changes.

8 Close the Properties dialog box.

Notes:

- This deactivates a control so that it is not activated when **Tab** is pressed in Form view. When you press **Tab**, the focus skips the control and moves to the next control set in the tab order.
- To activate the control in Form view, click it or use the hot key if one is provided.

Remove a Field or Other Control from the Tab Order

1 Right-click the control and select **Properties**.

2 Click the **Other** tab.

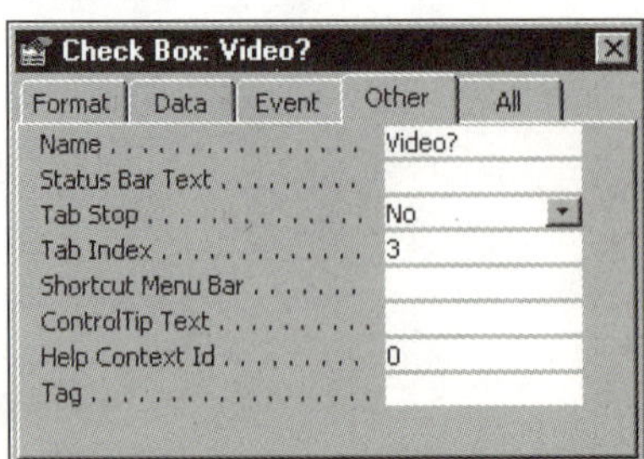

3 Click the Tab Stop property and select **No**.

4 Click the close button to close the Properties dialog box.

5 Click **Save** to save the design changes.

Add a Form Header and Footer

Use a header or footer to display a title, instructions for filling out the form, command buttons, and other information that always appears on the form no matter which record is displayed.

Notes:

- A form header appears at the top of the form and a form footer appears at the bottom.
- The information in form headers and footers does not change from record to record. It does not matter which record is displayed in the form—the header and footer information is always displayed.
- You must add both the header and footer. If you do not wish to use one of them, set its **Visible** property to **No** so that it does not appear.

1 Open the form in Design view (see **Open a Form**).

2 Click **View**, **Form Header/Footer**. Access adds both a form header and form footer.

3 Add title text, borders, and/or other controls to the header and footer areas as desired.

4 To resize the header or footer area, drag the section bar below it up or down. To resize a header, drag the Detail bar. To resize a footer, drag the Form Footer bar.

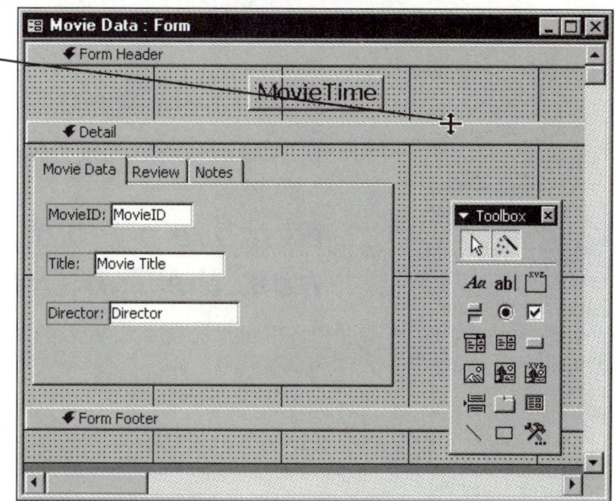

5 To hide an unused form header or footer:

a. Right-click the section to hide (Form Header or Form Footer).

b. Click **Properties**. Section properties are displayed.

Notes:

- Form headers and footers are not the same as page headers and footers. Page headers and footers appear on forms only when you print them. Form headers appear on both printed forms and forms displayed on the screen.

c. Click the **Format** tab.

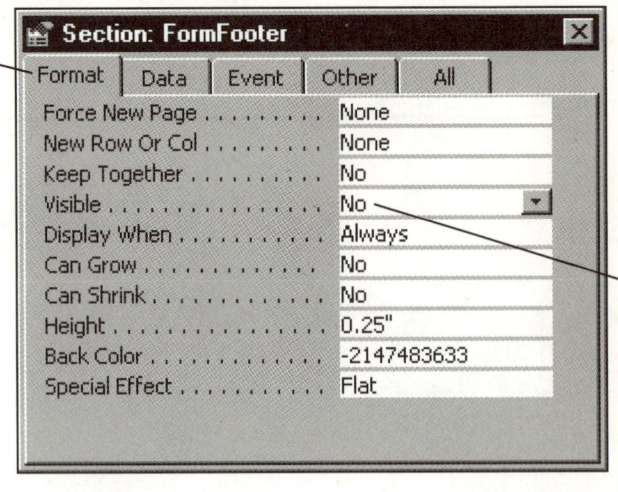

d. Click in the Visible property.

e. Click ▾ and select **No**.

f. Click ☒ to close section properties.

Note: The hidden section will be visible in Design view but not in Form view.

6 Press **Ctrl+S** to save changes.

7 Click ☒ to close the form.

Change the Form Window Title

Set the text that will display in the title bar of the window when the form is opened in Form view.

Notes:

- By default, Access displays the name of the form in the form window. Use this procedure to customize the form window by entering your own text in the form window title bar.
- You can also specify that the window not display any text at all in the title bar.

1 Open the Form in Design view (see **Open a Form**).

2 Press **Ctrl+R** to select the form.

3 Click . Form properties display.

4 Click the **Format** tab.

5 Type the text to appear in the Form window title bar in the Caption property.

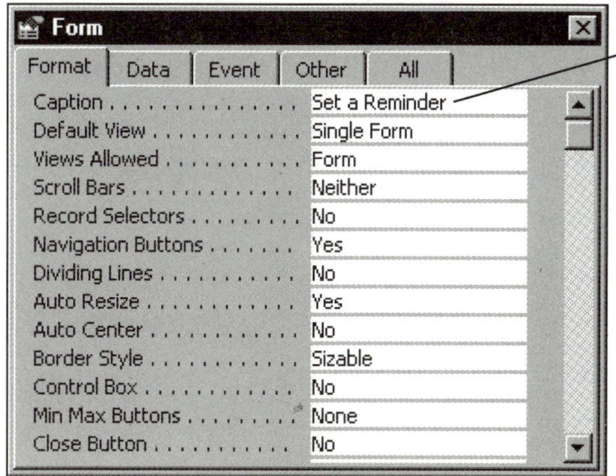

Note: *To leave the window title blank, type a space in the Caption property.*

6 Click to close form properties.

7 Click to save changes.

8 If the form has a subform, Access displays a prompt asking if you want to apply the change to the subform also. Select **Yes** or **No**.

9 Click to close the form design when you have finished modifying it.

Show the Result of a Calculation on a Form

Calculations that you might want to display on a form could be, for example, the amount of state tax for an order or the commission percentage of a sale.

Notes:

- Use a text box with an expression to show a calculation for each record on a form. For example, you could calculate the amount of tax for an order and display it in the form.
- If the form is based on a query, create a calculated field in the query and then add the field to the form.
- Surround fields that you use in the expression in square brackets. Example: [Quantity]*[Price]

1. Open the form in Design view (see **Open a Form**).
2. Click **Text Box** in the Toolbox.

   Note: If the Toolbox is not displayed, select ***View, Toolbox****.*
3. Drag across the form to create the text box. Release the mouse button when the text box is the size you want.
4. Click **Properties** on the toolbar. The text box properties display.
5. Click the **Data** tab.

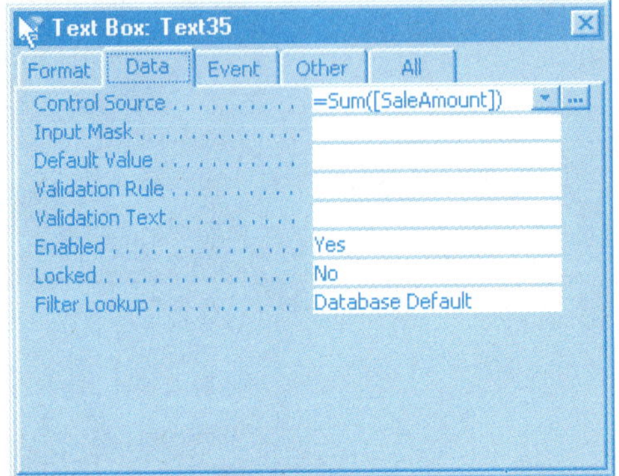

6. Type = in the Control Source property.

   Type the expression in the Control Source property.

   Note: Press ***Shift+F2*** *to open a zoom window to type long expressions if desired.*

   OR

   Click to open the Expression Builder to create the expression, if desired. When you have finished, click OK to close the Expression Builder. The expression is placed in the Control Source property.
7. Click to close text box properties.

Apply an Input Mask to a Field on a Form

An input mask ensures that field data (for example, telephone numbers, dates, zip codes) is entered correctly.

Notes:

- An input mask is a property setting for a data entry field that determines the format of data that is entered in the field. For example, an input mask for a telephone number might be (xxx) xxx-xxxx.
- You can apply an input mask to a text or date field only.

1. Open the form in Design view (see **Open a Form**).
2. Right-click the field text box control.
3. Click **Properties**.
4. Click the **Data** tab.
5. Click **Input Mask** property and then click [...]. The Input Mask Wizard starts.

   Note: *If this is the first time you have used the Input Mask Wizard, Access might display a prompt asking you if you want to install the wizard. Click the **Yes** button. Access will install and start the wizard.*

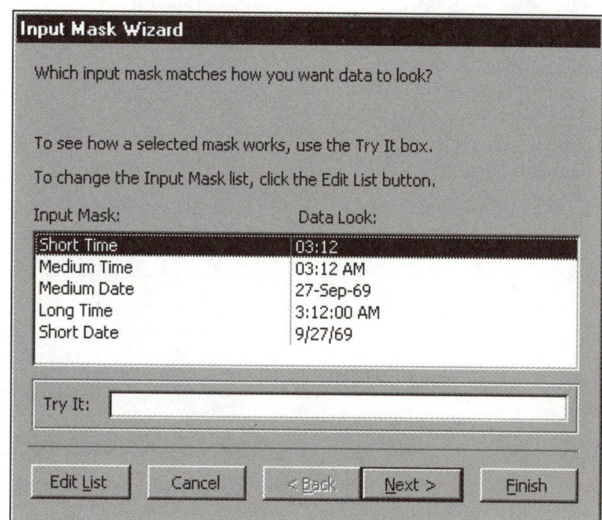

6. Select the format to apply to the field.

   Note: *The formats shown in the dialog box depend on the format of the field you are editing.*

7. To see what the format will look like and how it will work, click the **Try It:** text box and type data.

Notes:

- You can have Access show a template of the format in the field with characters such as asterisks. The template appears in the field in Form view. It shows the format of how data should be entered in that field. For example, a telephone template using asterisk characters might look like: (***) ***-****.

8 Click Next >.

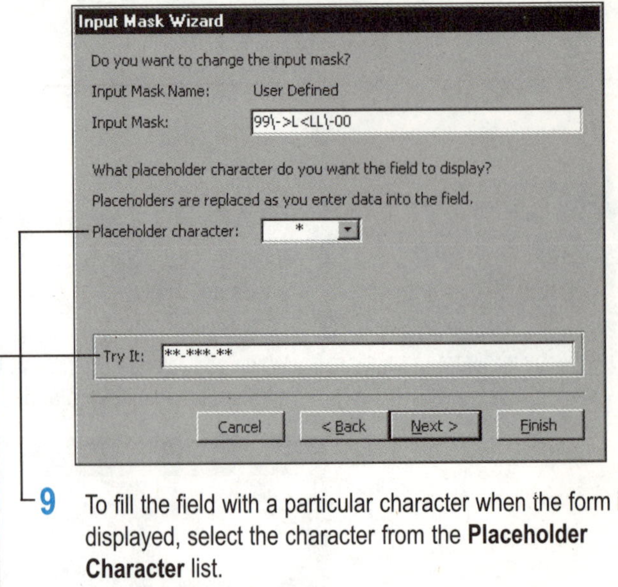

9 To fill the field with a particular character when the form is displayed, select the character from the **Placeholder Character** list.

10 Click the **Try It:** text box to see how the placeholder characters will appear in the form.

11 Click Next >.

12 The dialog boxes that the Input Mask Wizard displays depend on the field data type (text or date) and the input mask that you are creating. Follow the prompts on the screen.

13 Click Finish at the last Input Mask Wizard dialog box. The Input Mask property shows the input mask that you selected.

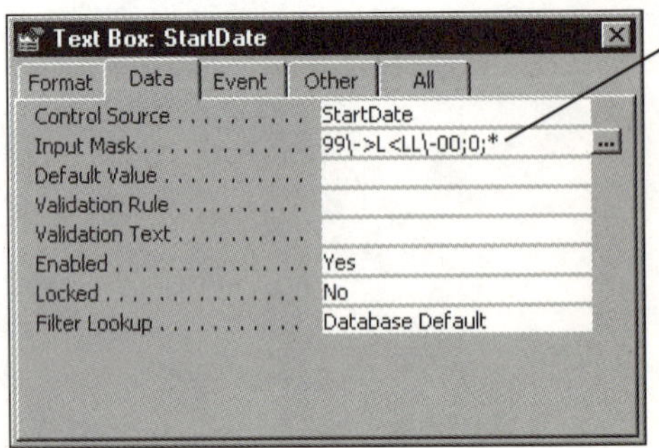

14 Click [X] to close the field properties.

Add a Field to a Form or Report

Add a field from one of the tables on which the form or report is based.

Notes:

- You might need to add a field from a table to a form or report if you modified a table by adding a field.

1. Open the form or report in Design view (see **Open a Form**).
2. If the field list of the table or query that contains the field to add is not displayed, click **View**, **Field List**.
3. Drag the field name from the field list to the design grid. When you release the mouse button, a field control and corresponding label are added to the form or report.

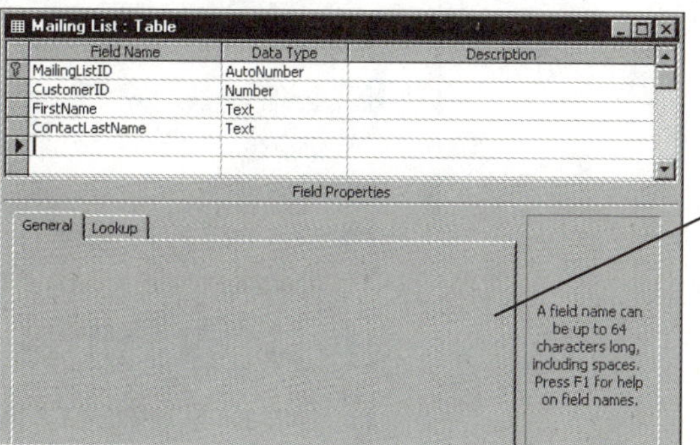

Note: *The field name appears in the field control in Design view only. It is not visible in the form or report.*

Notes:

- This procedure does not show you how to create a new field, such as a calculated field, that does not exist in a table. It is only for adding an existing field from a table to the form or report.
- Adding a field creates a text box control for the field data and an attached label for the field name.

4 To type different text in the field label (caption) if desired:

a. Double-click the label. The Label properties box displays.

b. Click the **Format** tab.

c. Type new text in the Caption property.

d. To format the text if desired, use the Font properties.

e. Click to close the Properties dialog box.

5 To apply a special effect to the field, such as a raised appearance or a shadow, if desired:

a. Right-click the field.

b. Select **Special Effect**.

c. Select from one of the special effects. Access applies the effect.

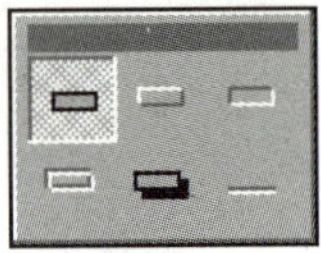

6 Press **Ctrl+S** to save changes.

7 Switch to Form or Report view to see your changes.

8 Close the form or report.

Reports

Reports display data in one or more tables. You can group data from tables in a report. For example, the following report from the Northwind sample database is grouped by product type.

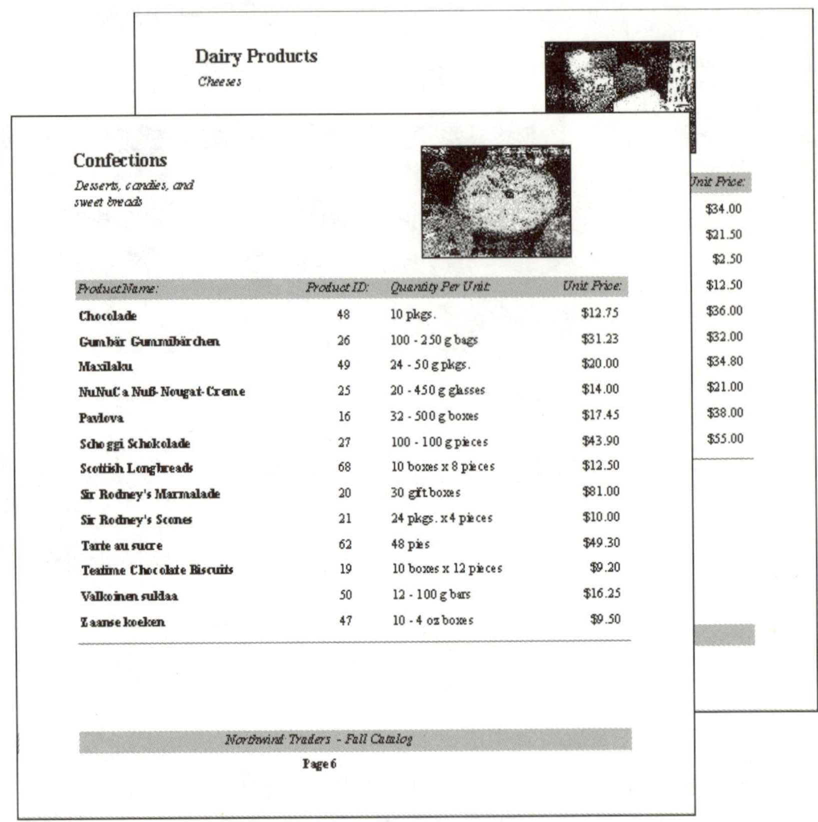

Dairy Products

Cheeses

Unit Price:
$34.00
$21.50
$2.50
$12.50
$36.00
$32.00
$34.80
$21.00
$38.00
$55.00

Confections

Desserts, candies, and sweet breads

Product Name:	Product ID:	Quantity Per Unit:	Unit Price:
Chocolade	48	10 pkgs.	$12.75
Gumbär Gummibärchen	26	100 - 250 g bags	$31.23
Maxilaku	49	24 - 50 g pkgs.	$20.00
NuNuCa Nuß-Nougat-Creme	25	20 - 450 g glasses	$14.00
Pavlova	16	32 - 500 g boxes	$17.45
Schoggi Schokolade	27	100 - 100 g pieces	$43.90
Scottish Longbreads	68	10 boxes x 8 pieces	$12.50
Sir Rodney's Marmalade	20	30 gift boxes	$81.00
Sir Rodney's Scones	21	24 pkgs. x 4 pieces	$10.00
Tarte au sucre	62	48 pies	$49.30
Teatime Chocolate Biscuits	19	10 boxes x 12 pieces	$9.20
Valkoinen suklaa	50	12 - 100 g bars	$16.25
Zaanse koeken	47	10 - 4 oz boxes	$9.50

Northwind Traders - Fall Catalog

Page 6

Create a Report Using a Wizard

The Report Wizard prompts you for the information it needs to create a report.

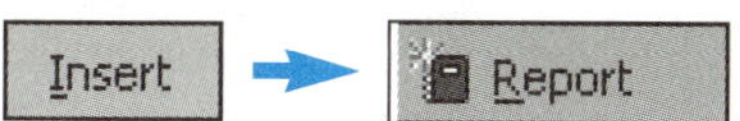

Notes:

- The Report Wizard helps you through creating a report. After you create the report, you can customize it in Design view.

1. Click **Reports** in the Database window.
2. Double-click **Create report by using wizard**. The Report Wizard starts.
3. Select a data source (table or query) for the report.

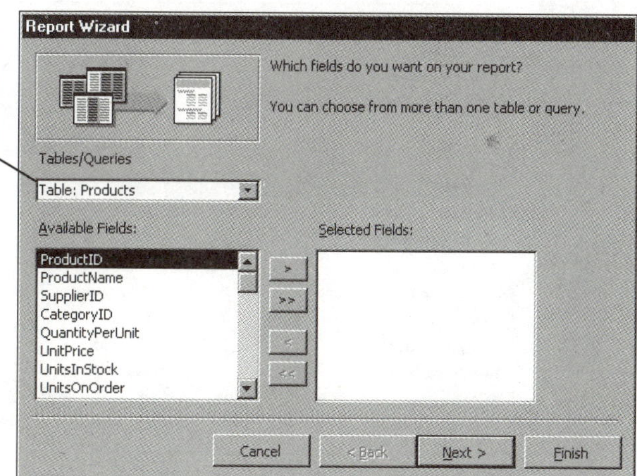

4. Select one or more field(s) to include in the report and click .

   OR

   To add all fields to the report, click >>.
5. Repeat steps 3 and 4 to add another data source if desired.
6. Click Next >.
7. Choose **Layout** and **Orientation** options as desired.

Notes:

- You can use the Report Wizard to create a report from one or more data sources. A data source (also called a record source) is a query or table that supplies data to the report.

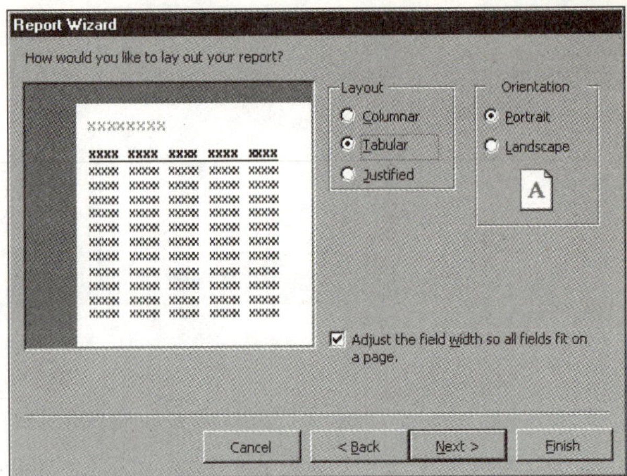

8 At this stage, the Report Wizard screens vary depending on the data source(s) that you selected. Make your choices and click Next > to continue.

The steps in the Report Wizard converge again at the style screen.

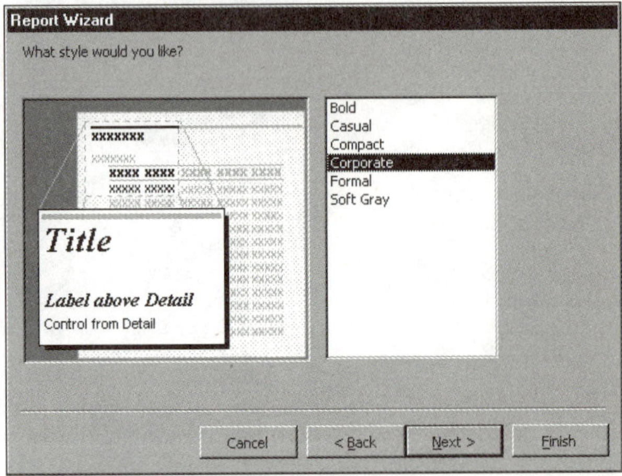

9 Select a style for the report.

10 Click Next >.

11 Type a title for the report.

12 Choose what you want to do next. You can **Preview the report** or **Modify the report's design** by opening it in Design view.

13 Click Finish.

14 Close the report.

Create an AutoReport

Use the AutoReport feature to quickly create a simple report in a single step.

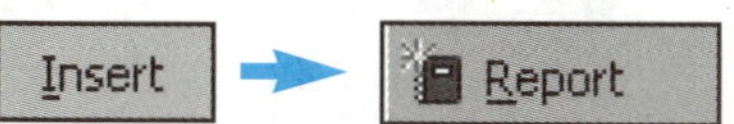

Notes:

- You can select from two different report layouts when you create an AutoReport. A columnar layout lists field names in a column down the left side of the report. Field data appears in a column to the right of labels. A tabular layout lists field names across the top of the report and field data appears below.
- You can specify only one data source for an AutoReport. To create a report that includes multiple data sources, use the Report Wizard.
- You can open an AutoReport in Design view and customize it.

1 Select **Insert**, **Report**. The New Report dialog box displays.

2 Select **AutoReport: Columnar**.

OR

Select **AutoReport: Tabular**.

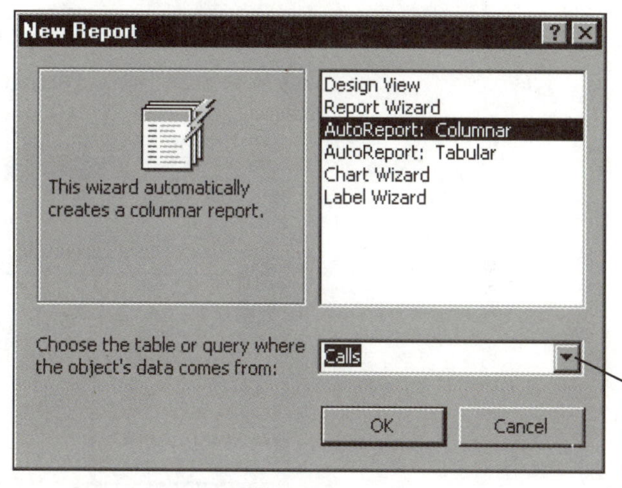

3 Select a record source for the report.

4 Click OK. Access creates the report and displays it in Print Preview.

5 Close the report.

Apply an AutoFormat to a Report

AutoFormats are predefined styles that are used to apply a consistent look among the different elements of a report. They do much of the formatting work for you.

Notes:

- An AutoFormat contains formatting such as colors, font styles, backgrounds, and borders. You can choose to apply all formatting in the AutoFormat or only particular styles (such as text formatting only).
- If you created your report using the Report Wizard, you applied an AutoFormat when you created it. You can apply a different AutoFormat using this procedure.

1 Open a report in Design view (see **Open a Report**).

2 Click **AutoFormat** .

3 Click Options >> to display more options at the bottom of the AutoFormat window.

4 Select the format to apply from the **Report AutoFormats** list.

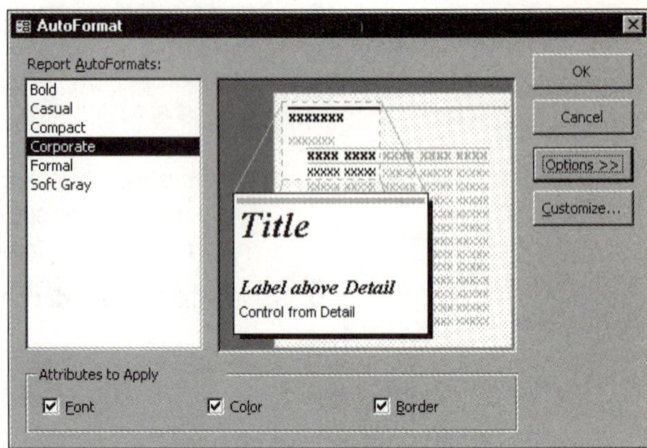

5 Clear any formatting elements that you do not wish to apply.

6 Click OK. The AutoFormat is applied to the report.

7 Switch to Print Preview to view your changes.

8 Close the report.

9 Save the changes when prompted.

Create Mailing Labels Using a Wizard

Create labels for names and addresses stored in an Access database.

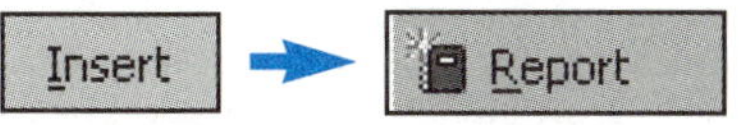

Notes:

- Print labels from a database that stores names and addresses.

1 Select **Insert**, **Report**. The New Report dialog box opens.

2 Select **Label Wizard**.

3 Select the record source for the labels.

4 Click OK. The Label Wizard starts.

5 Select the label manufacturer.

Note: *If the manufacturer of the labels you will be using is not listed, click Customize... and enter measurements and other specifications to create custom labels. You need to enter label specifications such as the size of each label and the number of labels on a page.*

6 Select the label **Product number**.

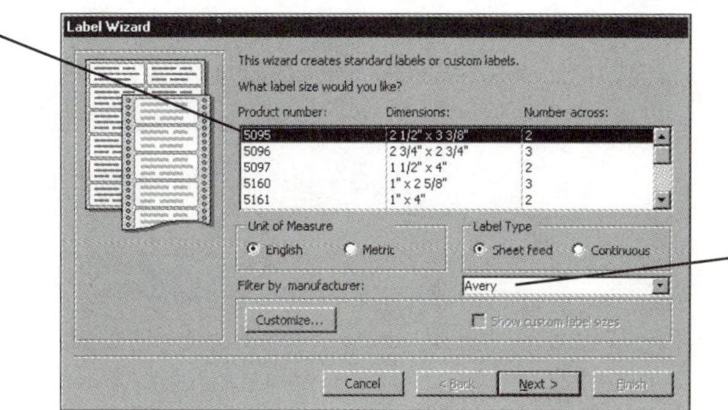

7 Click Next >.

8 Select the font, font size, and other text formatting for the labels.

9 Click Next >.

10 Select a field from the record source to add to the label.

Note: *Add fields in the order that they will appear on the label.*

Notes:

- Access organizes labels by the manufacturer. For example, if you are printing on Avery labels, all you have to do is select the product number of the labels you are using and Access will use the label specifications, such as the measurements of each label and the number of labels on a page.

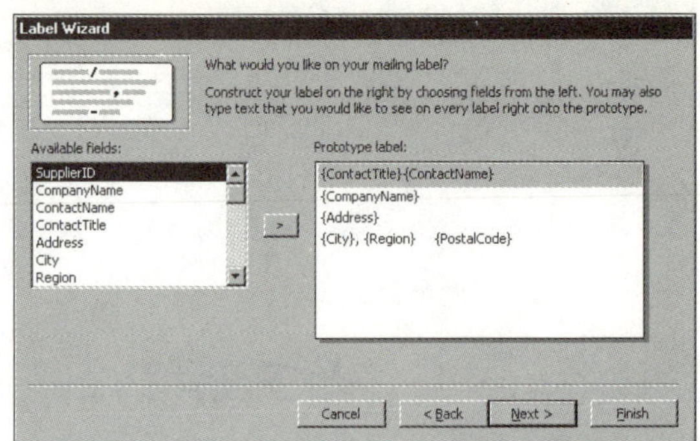

11 Click >. The selected field is placed in the label prototype in the right pane.

12 Type any text or spaces if necessary.

Note: For example, in the illustration, there is a comma and a space after the City field. A space will need to be added between the ContactTitle and the ContactName fields.

13 Press **Ctrl+Enter** to start a new line if necessary.

14 Repeat steps 10–13 until all fields that you wish to place on the label are added.

15 Click Next >.

16 Select a field to sort on and click > if you want to print labels in a certain order.

17 Repeat step 16 to sort by multiple fields if desired. For example, you could sort by zip code and then by state.

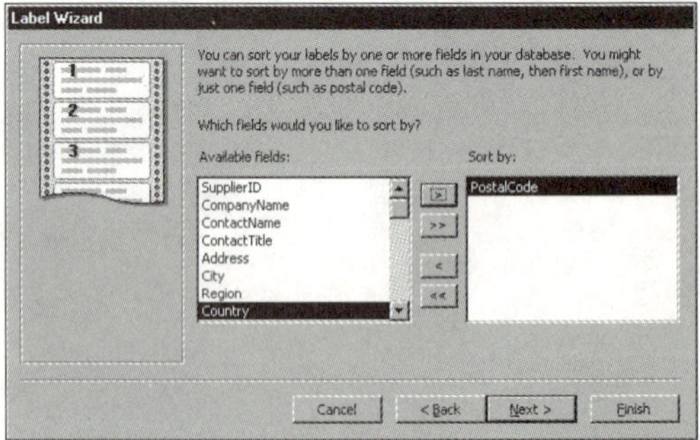

18 Click Next >.

19 Type a name for the label report.

20 Specify whether you want to **See the labels as they will look printed** (shows you a sample label with data) or **Modify the label design** (opens the report in Design view).

21 Click Finish.

Open a Report

Reports have two views—Print Preview and Design view.

Notes:

- Print Preview shows your report with all the data the report will have when it prints. Use it to make sure your report is well-designed before you print it.
- For information on working in Print Preview, see **Preview a Report**.

In Print Preview

1 In the Database window, click **Reports**.

2 Double-click the report that you want to open. The report opens in Print Preview.

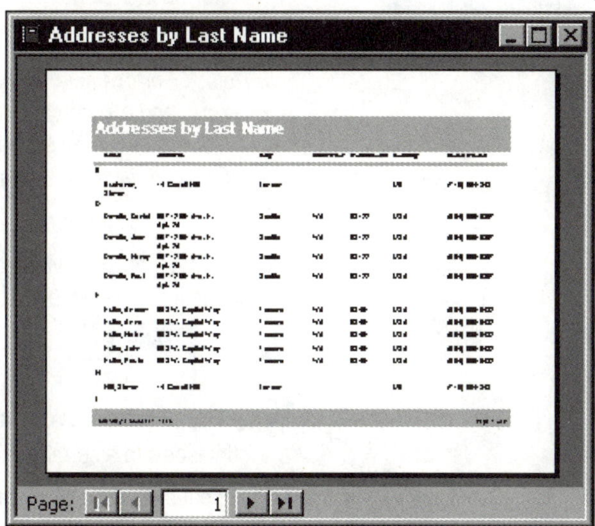

3 Close the report.

Notes:

- Use Design view to customize a report. For example, you can apply AutoFormats, add or remove fields, add headers and footers, and otherwise create the report exactly as you want it.
- In Design view, the report displays in an area of the screen called the design grid. You add and format report elements against the background of the grid. To adjust the design grid, see **Use the Grid in Design View**.

In Design View

1 In the Database window, click **Reports**.

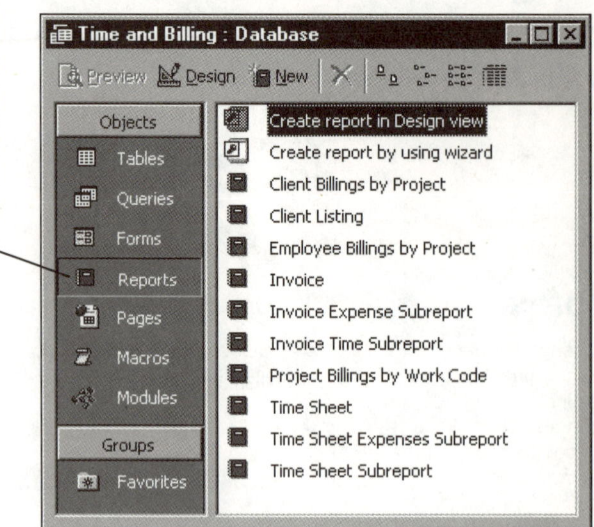

2 Click the report to open.

3 Click Design.

Switch Between Print Preview and Design View

- In Design view, click **View** on the toolbar to switch to Print Preview.
- In Print Preview, click **View** on the toolbar to switch to Design view.

Set Report Page Margins and Orientation

By default, margins are one inch all the way around the page.

Notes:

- Change the margins and/or orientation for a single report. You can also change the page margins for the current report just before you print it. See **Print a Report**.

1 Open the report in any view.

2 Select **File**, **Page Setup**. The Page Setup dialog box displays.

3 Click the **Margins** tab.

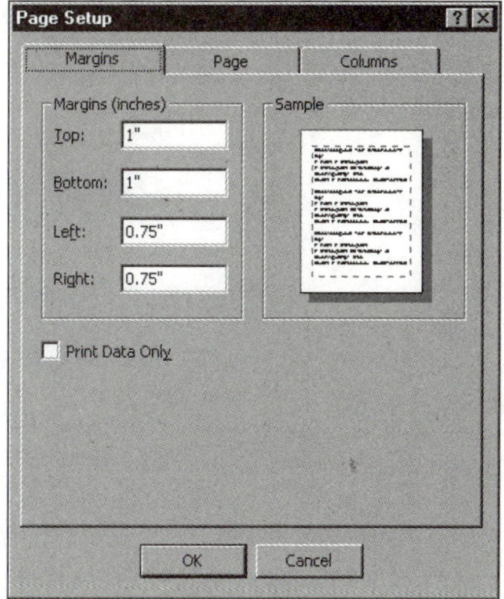

4 Type the desired margin measurements.

Notes:

- Use Landscape orientation to print pages sideways.

5 To change the report orientation, click the **Page** tab.

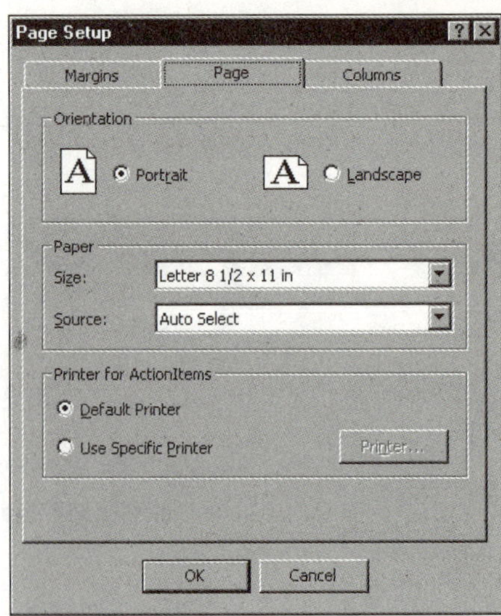

6 Select **Portrait** or **Landscape** orientation.

7 Click OK.

Notes:

- This setting also applies to forms that you print.

Set Default Margins for All Reports

1 Select **Tools**, **Options**.

2 Click the **General** tab.

3 Type margin measurements.

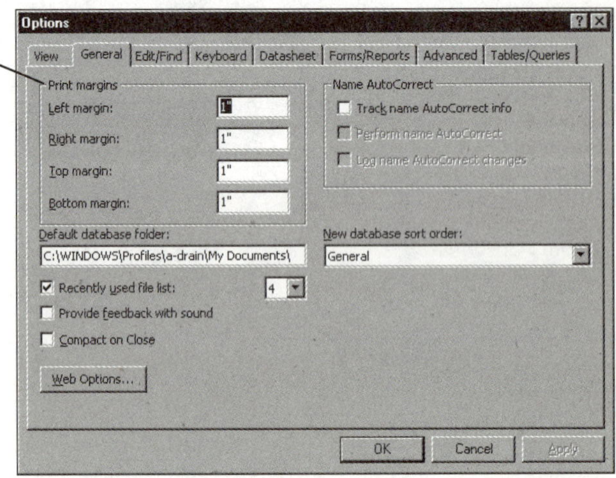

4 Click OK.

Add a Header and Footer to a Report

Page headers and footers contain information such as a date or report title that will print on every page. Report headers and footers print once at the beginning and once at the end of a report.

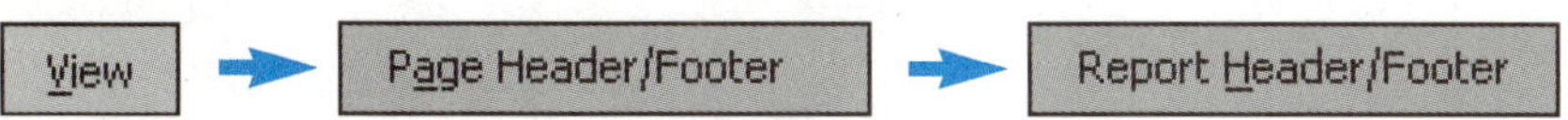

Notes:

- These procedures tell you how to add page and report headers and footers. Page headers and footers and report headers and footers are not the same thing.
- Page headers and footers print on each page of the report. The header prints at the top of each page and the footer prints at the bottom. The date and/or page number often appears in the page header or footer.
- The report header prints once on the first page of the report and the footer prints once on the last page of the report. Use report footers to place totals, subtotals, and summary information at the end of a report.
- You can insert an updating date in a page header or footer. See **Insert the Date/Time in a Report**.

1 Open the report in Design view (see **Open a Report**).

2 Open the **View** menu.

3 Select **Page Header/Footer** if it is not already selected.

OR

Select **Report Header/Footer** if it is not already selected. The illustration below shows a report with both page and report header and footer sections.

4 To resize a section, if desired, drag the section bar below it up or down. For example, dragging the Page Header bar resizes the Report Header section. Dragging the Detail section bar resizes the Page Header section.

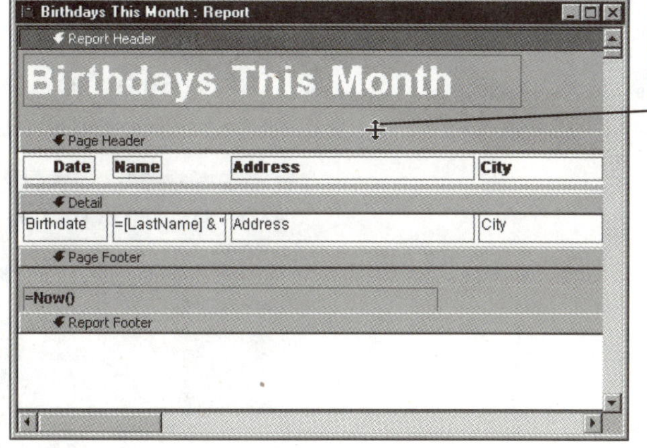

Notes:

- To add page numbers to the page header or footer see **Add Page Numbers to a Report**.
- Adding headers and footers adds two sections to the form—one section for the header and another for the footer. The section bar shows the section name. You must add headers and footers in pairs—you cannot add just a header or just a footer. However, you do not have to use both sections. You could enter information in the footer but leave the header blank, for example.

5 Add page numbers, text, fields, the date, controls, or other information as desired to headers and footers.

6 Click **Save** to save the report design.

7 Click to close the report when you have finished modifying it.

Add Page Numbers to a Report

Add a page number field to automatically number report pages.

Notes:

- If you add page numbers to a report using this procedure, Access automatically adds a page header or footer. Page headers and footers print on each page and Access assumes that you want to number every page. If you have already added page headers and footers (see **Add a Header and Footer to a Report**), it places the page number field in the header or footer as you specify.
- You can add just the page number (example: Page 2) or you can include the number of pages in the document (example: Page 2 of 5).

1 Open the report in Design view (see **Open a Report**).

2 Select **Insert**, **Page Numbers**. The Page Numbers dialog box displays.

3 Select a page number **Format**.

4 Select a **Position**. You can place numbers in the page header or footer.

Note: *You can move page numbers in Design view after you add them.*

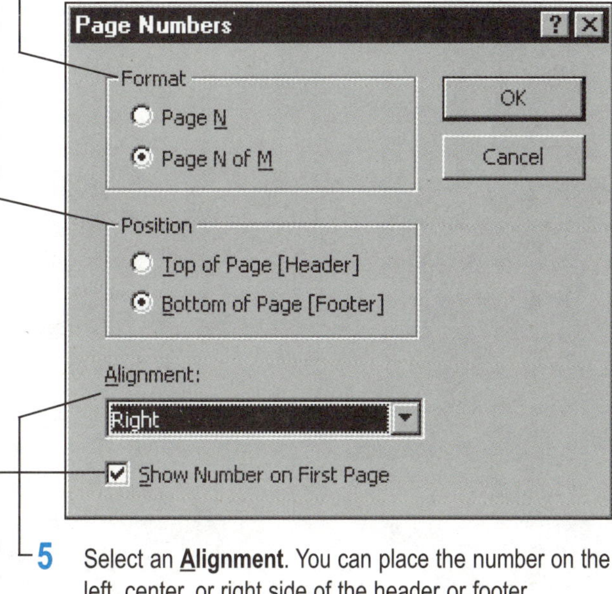

5 Select an **Alignment**. You can place the number on the left, center, or right side of the header or footer.

6 Specify whether or not to **Show Number on First Page**.

7 Click OK.

Notes:

- You can specify whether or not to print the page number on the first page. If the page number might detract from the report title, which appears only on the first page, you can skip printing the page number.

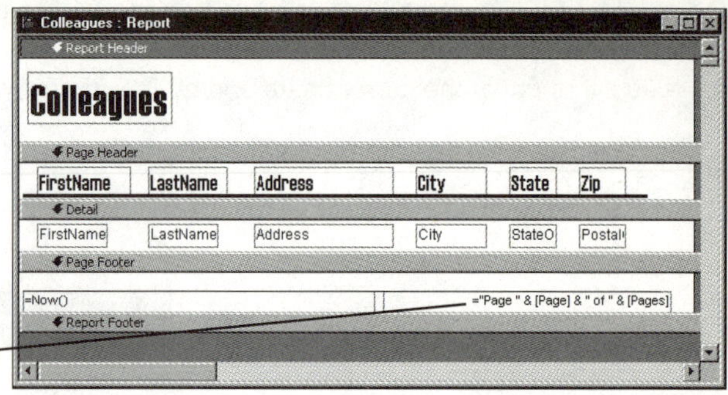

Access inserts a text box that contains a function to add the page number in the format that you selected. In this report, the page number has been added to the Page Footer section.

8 To move the page number, if desired, drag the field.

9 Switch to Print Preview to view your changes.

10 Press [save icon] to save the report design.

11 Click [close icon] to close the report when you have finished modifying it.

Insert the Date/Time in a Report

Place a field that prints the current date and/or time in a report footer.

Notes:

- The date and time update automatically so they are current each time you print the report. If you want to add a date that does not update, create a label and type the date as text.

1 Open the report in Design view (see **Open a Report**).

2 Click **Insert**, **Date and Time**. The Date and Time dialog box displays.

3 Select a date format.

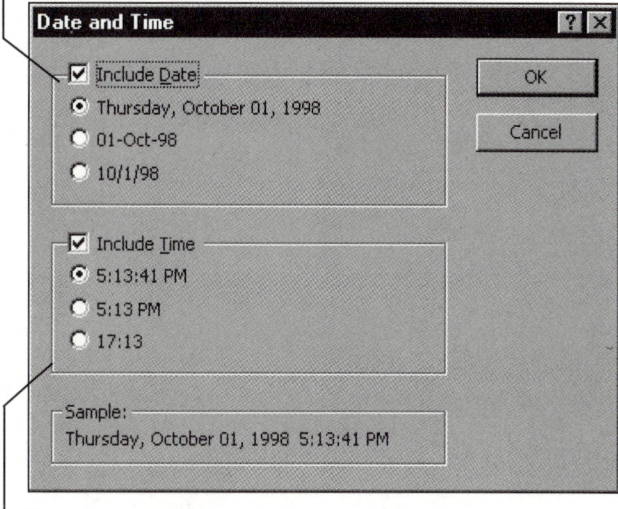

4 Select a time format.

*Note: To include only the date in the report and not the time, clear **Include Time**.*

5 Click OK. Access inserts a text box with a date function to add the date/time in the format that you selected.

Notes:

- If you have not created a page header or footer for the report, Access automatically adds them when you add the date and time. Page headers and footers print on every page and Access assumes that you want to include the date/time on every page. See **Add a Header and Footer to a Report**.

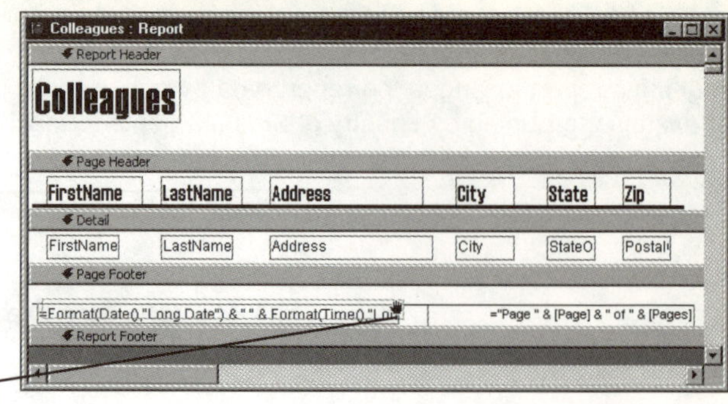

6 Drag the date to position it in the report as desired.

7 Switch to Print Preview to view your changes.

8 Press [save icon] to save the report design.

9 Click [close icon] to close the report when you have finished modifying it.

Group a Report

Grouping a report arranges the report data by one or more fields that you specify. For example, grouping by country groups all clients for each country together.

Notes:

- Report data is more readable when data is sorted and grouped. For instance, you can sort a list of companies by the country in which they are located. Each country would have its own group header above the group to identify it. Customers in the same country could be grouped and sorted by region, then by company name.
- You can group up to ten fields or expressions in a report.
- You sort records in ascending or descending order within each group.

1 Open the report in Design view (see **Open a Report**).

2 Click **Sorting and Grouping** on the toolbar. The Sorting and Grouping dialog box displays.

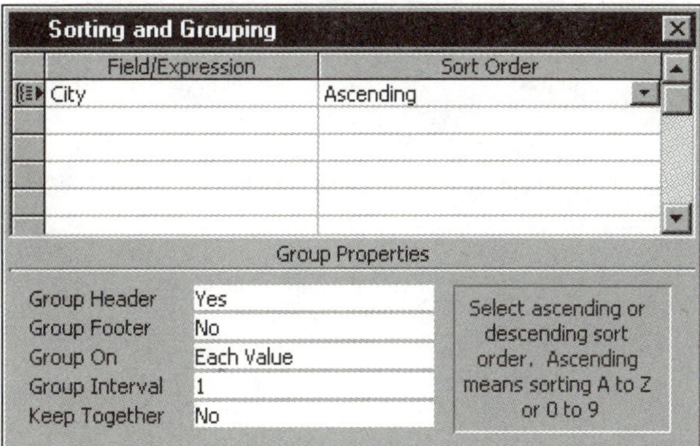

3 Select the field or type the expression to group the report on in the Field/Expression column.

4 Select a **Sort Order**.

5 Repeat steps 3 and 4 to add more groups if desired.

6 Add a group header or footer, if desired, in the Group Properties section.

7 Click ☒ to close the Sorting and Grouping box.

Notes:

- If you want text to appear before and/or after each group when the report is printed, add a group header/footer. For example, if grouping customers by country you could include the country name in the group header. Or, you can use group footers to calculate totals for the records in the group.

8 If you added a group header or footer, enter the data that you want to appear in the section. For example, the following illustration shows a report grouped by city. The City field has been added to the group header section so that the city name will print before each group.

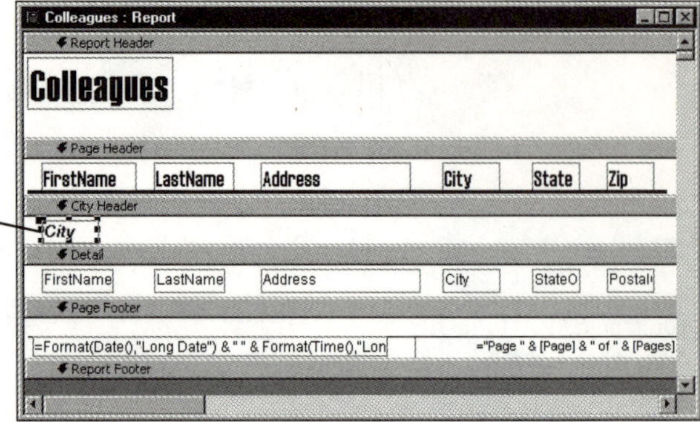

9 Switch to Print Preview to view the results of your changes.

10 When you have finished, click **Save** to save the report design.

11 Click to close the report design when you have finished modifying it.

The following illustration shows how the report appears after it has been grouped. This is a simple report design listing names and addresses grouped by city. The group header shows the City name.

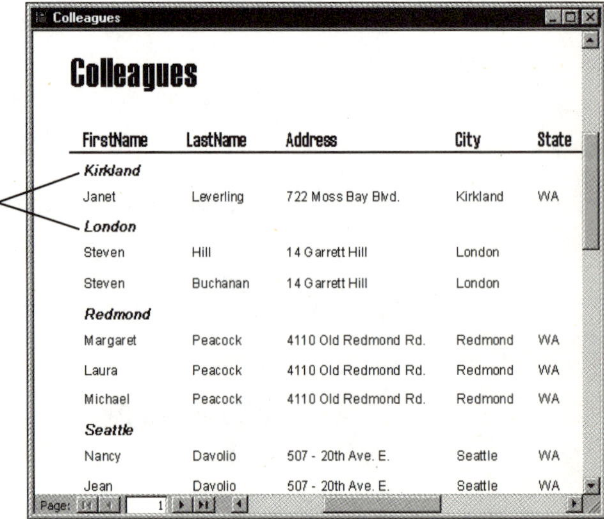

Preview a Report

Preview a report to view it with the report data.

Notes:

- Preview reports after you create them to make sure that the report will print the way you expect it to.

1 Double-click the report to preview in the Database window.

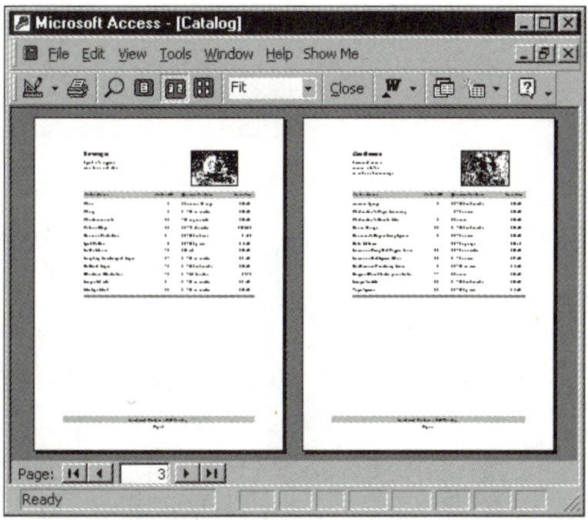

2 Use the following toolbar buttons in the Preview window:

Print	Opens the Print dialog box.
Zoom	Click this tool, then click the page to zoom in. Repeat to zoom out.
One Page	Shows one page at a time in the preview window.
Two Pages	Shows two pages at a time in the preview window.
Multiple Pages	Sets the number of pages to show in the window. Click the button and select the number of pages. You can also use the **View**, **Pages** menu.

Notes:

- You cannot edit a report in Preview. Do all your editing in Design view.

Zoom Sets the magnification level. You can also use the **View**, **Zoom** menu. When you select **Fit** , the report fits in the window even when you resize the window.

Close Exit Print Preview.

Move Between Pages

Click a navigation button at the bottom of the window to move between pages in the report:

- first page
- previous page
- next page
- last page

Go to a Specific Page Using a Page Number

1 Press **F5**.

2 Type the number of the page to display.

3 Press **Enter**.

Preview a Report Layout

1 To switch to Design view, select **View**, **Design View**.

2 Select **View**, **Layout Preview**.

3 Close the report.

Notes:

- In Layout view, only enough data for you to see the report layout is included.
- Use Layout view instead of Print Preview when it takes a long time to display the report because there is a lot of report data.

Print a Report

Print all or part of a report.

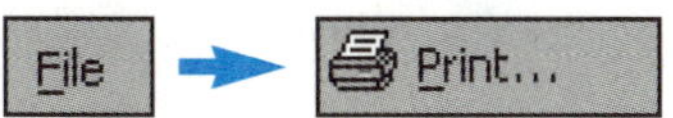

Notes:

- Always check the report in Print Preview before you print it. Print Preview will reveal any problems with the report such as truncated data. You can adjust the report to solve problems before printing.

1 Select the report in the Database window.

2 Select **File**, **Print**. The Print dialog box displays.

3 Change the printer if necessary to print to a different installed printer.

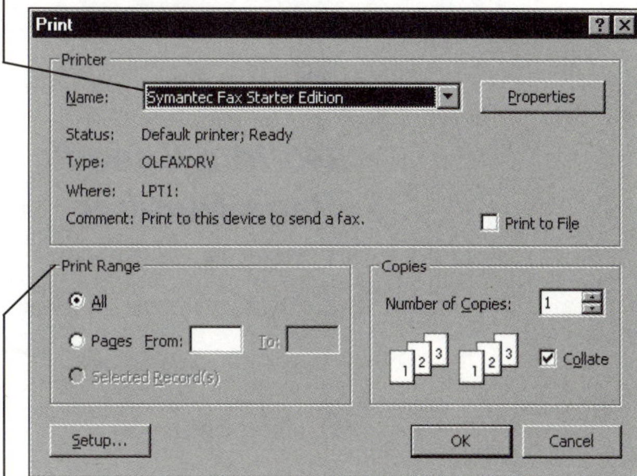

4 By default, Access assumes that you want to print **All** pages in the report. To print particular pages, click **Pages** and then type the number of the first page to print in the **From** text box and the last page to print in the **To** text box.

Notes:

- You can print all pages in the report or a range of pages.
- This procedure includes instructions on setting the margins for this report only. To set the default margins for all reports, see **Set Report Page Margins and Orientation**.

5 To change page margins if desired:

a. Click [Setup...]. The Page Setup dialog box displays.

b. Click the **Margins** tab.

c. Type margin measurements.

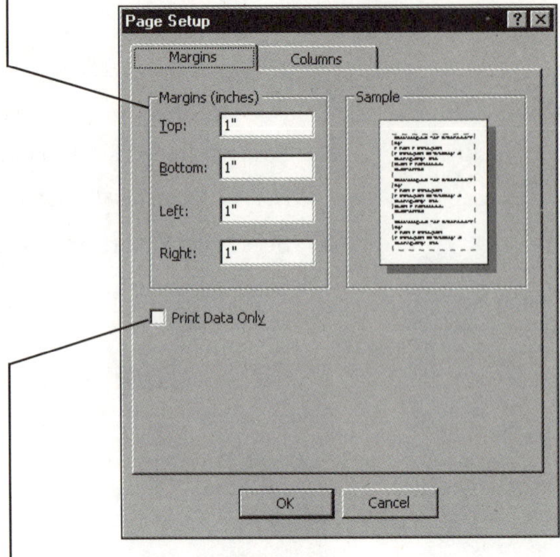

d. To print only the report data, excluding all headers, footers, titles, field headings, and other information added to the report, select **Print Data Only**.

e. Click [OK] to return to the Print dialog box.

6 Click [OK] in the Print dialog box to print the report.

Create a Report Snapshot

A report snapshot is a picture of a report. You can print, e-mail, or fax the snapshot and you can embed it in a data access page.

Notes:

- Use report snapshots when all you need to show is a completed report with static data.
- Use the Snapshot Viewer to view, print, or mail a snapshot that you created in Access. Access installs the Snapshot Viewer the first time you create a report snapshot.

1 In the Database window, click **Reports**.

2 Select the report that you want to create into a snapshot.

Note: The original report will not be modified.

3 Select **File**, **Export**. The Export Report dialog box opens.

4 Select the folder in which to save the file from the **Save in** list if necessary.

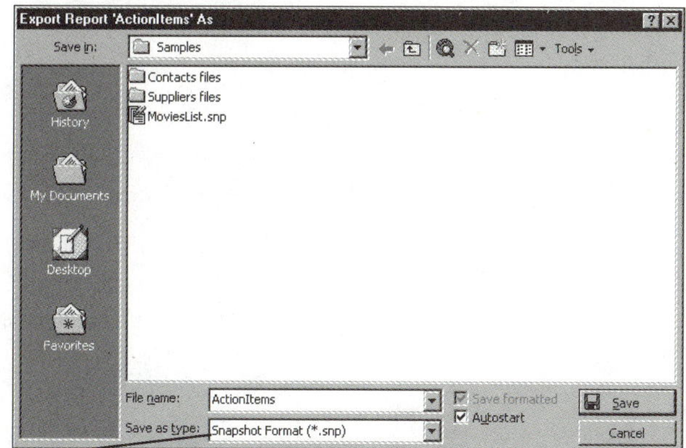

5 Select **Snapshot Format (*.snp)** from the **Save as type** list.

6 Type a **File name** for the snapshot file.

7 Click [Save]. Answer [Yes] to the prompt if asked if you want to install the Snapshot Viewer. Access creates the snapshot file, installs the Snapshot Viewer if necessary, and opens the report snapshot in the Snapshot Viewer.

Notes:

- In order to e-mail a report snapshot, both the sender and the recipient must use a mail program that supports ActiveX controls. In addition, the recipient must have the Snapshot Viewer to view the snapshot.

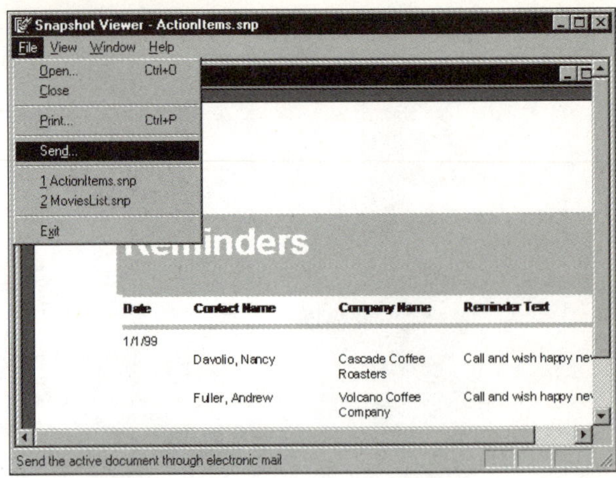

8 In the Snapshot Viewer select an action:

- Select **File**, **Print** to print the report snapshot.
- Select **File**, **Send** to open the default e-mail program on your computer and create a message for mailing the snapshot.
- Select **File**, **Close** to close the report snapshot.
- Select **File**, **Exit** to close the Snapshot Viewer.

Data Access Pages

Data access pages (also called simply pages) are designed to be placed on an intranet or Web site. You can create data access pages that accept data, which is useful for gathering information by having people enter data in the page. Data access pages can also display data in report formats. You can add command buttons and other controls to data access pages in Design view to create Web applications using back-end SQL Server databases. This guide shows you how to create simple data access pages. Creating and publishing an intranet or Web application is beyond the scope of this book.

Create a Data Access Page Using a Wizard

A data access page is a Web page based on database data. The page can be placed on an Internet site or on an intranet.

Notes:

- You can create three types of data access pages: 1) data entry pages (similar to forms) that accept data, 2) read-only reports where you can filter and otherwise work with the data in Page view but you cannot modify the data, and 3) data analysis pages that include analysis tools such as PivotTables and charts.
- A data access page can be similar to a form–you can use it to collect data from people who visit your Web site. It can also work like a report–users can sort, filter, and otherwise work with the data source for the page.

1 Click **Insert**, **Page**. The New Data Access Page dialog box opens.

2 Double-click **Page Wizard**. The first Page Wizard screen displays.

3 Select the data source (tables or queries) for the page.

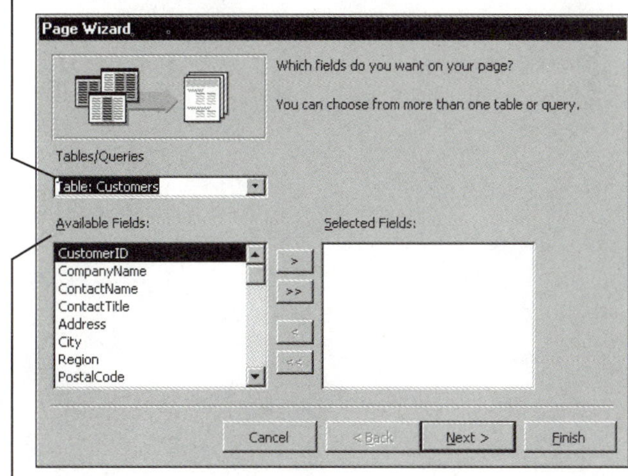

4 Select the fields to add to the page in the **Available Fields** list and click [>].

*Note: To select multiple fields, press **Ctrl** and click the next field.*

OR

Click [>>] to include all of the fields in the record source.

5 Repeat steps 3-4 to add record sources as desired.

6 Click [Next >].

Notes:

- Access comes with a number of themes that you can apply to a page when you create it using the Page Wizard. A theme consists of predesigned formatting styles. For example, a theme includes a background picture, font styles, colors, and other formatting options. To apply a different theme to a page after you create it, see **Apply a Theme to a Data Access Page**.

* Data access pages are saved outside the database in the current folder. A shortcut to the page is added to the Database window so that you can open it from within the database.

- Data access pages are stored in HTML files with an .htm extension.

- You must have Internet Explorer version 5.0 or later installed on your computer in order to create or open a data access page.

- You can use the Page Wizard to create a data access page and then modify it in Design view.

7 To set up the page as a read-only report (users cannot edit the database data from the page), group the data. Use the **Grouping Options** button to further define the layout.

OR

To create a data entry page, skip this step. Do not add a grouping level.

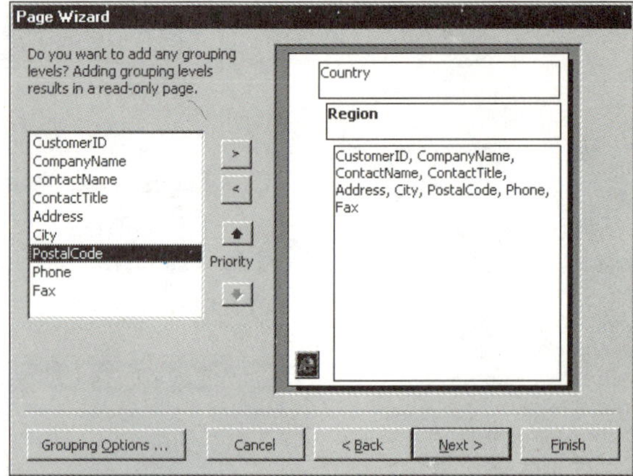

8 Click Next >.

9 Select a sort order for data if desired.

10 Click Next >.

11 Enter a title for the data access page.

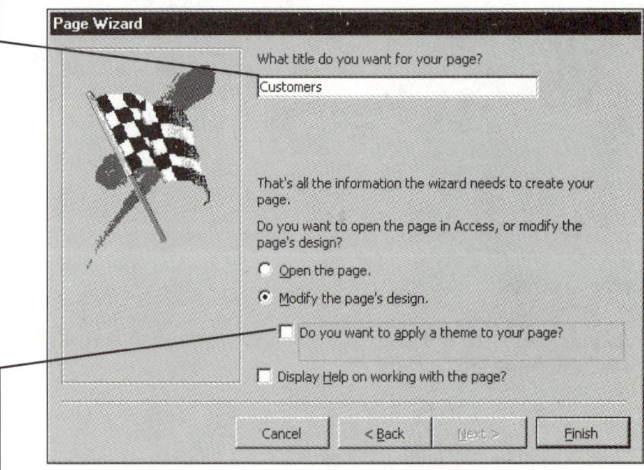

12 Specify what you wish to do next. You can open the page in Page view (select **Open the page**) or Design view (select **Modify the page's design**).

13 To apply the default theme to the page if desired, select the theme option.

14 Click Finish.

Create a Data Access Page Using AutoPage

Using AutoPage is the quickest way to create a simple data entry page using a single data source.

Notes:

* AutoPage creates a data access page that includes all of the fields in a data source (table or query) that you specify. It does not include fields that contain pictures.

- You can use only one data source in a data access page created using AutoPage.

- AutoPage creates a data access page used for data entry. To create other types of data access pages, see **Create a Data Access Page Using a Wizard**. Or, create the page in Design view.

- AutoPage applies the default theme to the page. To change the default theme, see **Apply a Theme to a Data Access Page**.

1 Click **Pages** in the Database window.

2 Click New. The New Data Access Page dialog box opens.

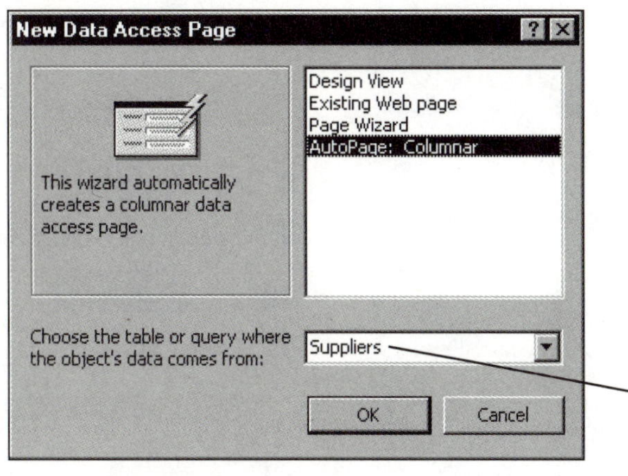

3 Select a record source for the data access page.

Notes:

- You must have Internet Explorer version 5.0 or later installed on your computer in order to create or open a data access page.
- You can open the page in Design view to customize it after creating it.

4 Double-click **AutoPage: Columnar**.

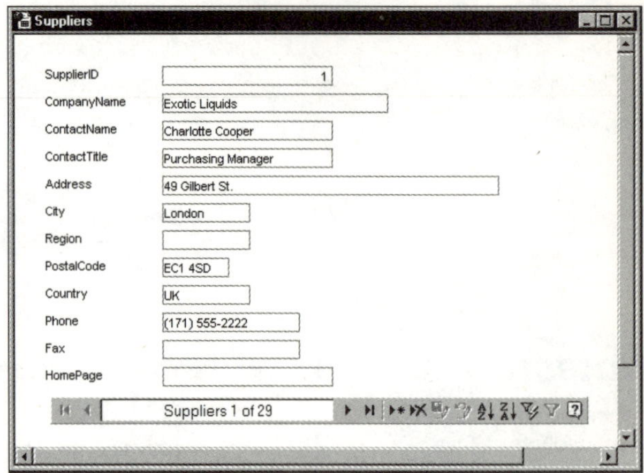

Access creates the page and displays it in Page view as shown above. Note the toolbar at the bottom of the page. This toolbar contains navigation buttons and buttons for working with data.

Apply a Theme to a Data Access Page

Applying a theme does the work of formatting page elements using consistent design styles.

Notes:

- A theme is similar to an AutoFormat for a form or report. It formats your data access page with graphics, background pictures, borders, animated graphics, fonts, colors, and other elements.
- You cannot preview animated graphics in Design view. Open the page in Internet Explorer 5.0 to see animations.
- When you install Access, the default theme is the Straight Edge theme. You can use this procedure to set the default for new data access pages that you create using the AutoPage feature.

1 Open the data access page in Design view (see **Open a Data Access Page**).

2 Click **Format**, **Theme**. The Theme dialog box opens.

3 Click the theme in the **Choose a Theme** list.

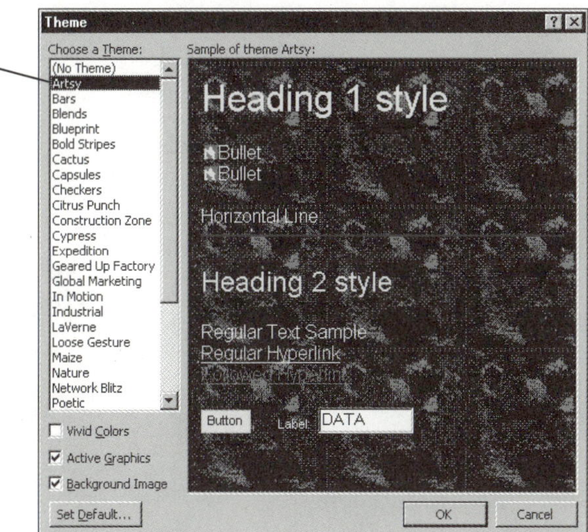

4 Select attributes to apply as desired:

Vivid Colors. Apply brighter colors.

Active Graphics. Uses animations in themes that have animated graphics. You cannot preview the animation in Access. It is visible when you open the page in Internet Explorer.

Background Image. Include or remove the background picture with the theme.

Notes:

- If you have FrontPage 98 installed, you can use FrontPage themes in data access pages.
- Not all available themes are installed using Typical installation. The Theme dialog box displays all themes, even those not installed. If the theme is not installed, the preview pane will display a message rather than a sample of the theme. Run Setup to add uninstalled themes.
- You can download more themes from the Microsoft Web site (select **Help**, **Office on the Web** to connect).

5 To set the selected options as your default data access page theme, click Set Default...

Note: To set the default theme without applying it to the current page, click Cancel *rather than* OK *at step 6.*

6 To apply the theme to the current page, click OK

7 Click **Save** to save the page design changes.

8 Click to close the page design when you have finished modifying it.

Create a Hotspot Control That Opens a Web Page

A hotspot control is a picture on a data access page that is a hyperlink to another Web page. When you click the control in Page view, it opens the Web page.

Notes:

- A hotspot control is a hyperlink. When you click on it, it jumps to a Web page. The control looks like a picture on the data access page. In Page view, when you hover the mouse pointer over the control, it changes to a hand pointer just as with any other hyperlink.
- You can include a pop-up tip that displays when you hover the mouse over the control in a Web browser. This feature is generally used for a brief control description, just as with other hyperlinks on Web pages. The tip will display if the page is viewed using Internet Explorer version 4.0 or higher.

1 Open the data access page in Design view.

2 Click **Hotspot** on the Toolbox. When the Hotspot tool is active, the pointer changes shape: 

*Note: If the Toolbox is not on the screen, click **View**, **Toolbox**.*

3 Click on the data access page where you want to add the tool. The Insert Picture dialog box displays.

4 Double-click the file containing the image to display in the data access page. The Insert Hyperlink dialog box displays.

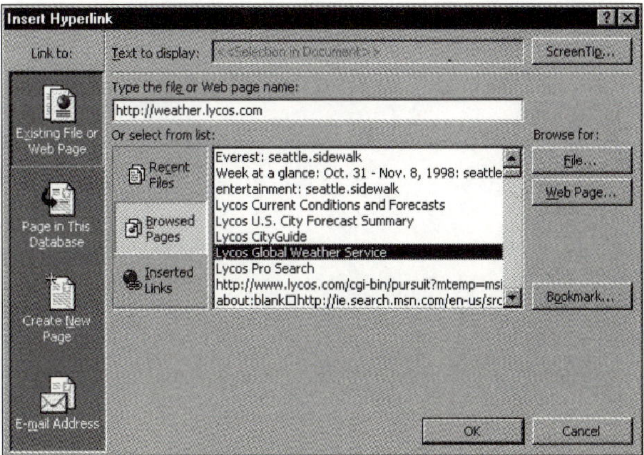

Notes:

- Before you create the control, you should have a file containing the image that you want to use for the control. If you do not know the destination Web page address for the hyperlink, you can connect to the Internet to get it.

5 Enter the hyperlink destination (the address of the Web page that will display when the hotspot is clicked):

- Type the address in the text box.

OR

- Click 

to select an address from Web pages that you have recently browsed.

OR

- Click 

to select from pages in the current database.

OR

To start your Web browser and connect to the Web to find the address of the page you want to link to, click 

.

6 To show a pop-up tip when you hover the mouse pointer over the button:

a. Click ScreenTip....

b. Type the text to display in the pop-up tip.

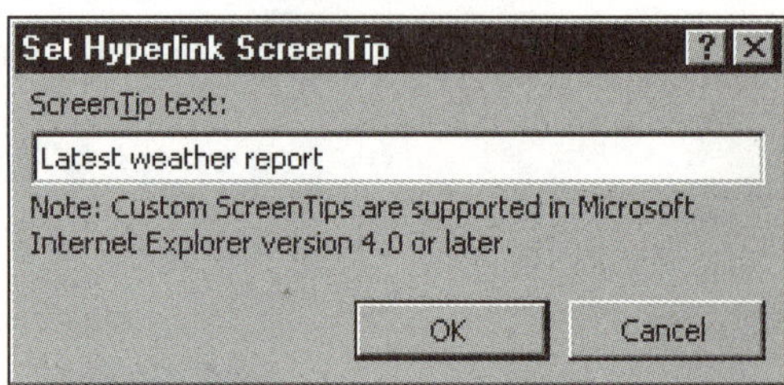

c. Click OK.

7 Click OK in the Insert Hyperlink dialog box. Access creates the hotspot on the page.

8 To view the button as it will appear in the Web browser, select **View**, **Page View**. Hover the mouse pointer over the control to see if the screen tip text appears as you entered it. You can also test the hyperlink—click the control to start your Web browser and display the Web page.

9 Close the data access page.

Open a Data Access Page

Data access pages have two Microsoft Access views: Page view and Design view. You can also open the page in Internet Explorer 5.0.

Notes:

- Page view shows how the page will look when placed on the Internet or intranet.

In Page View

1 Click **Pages** in the Database window.

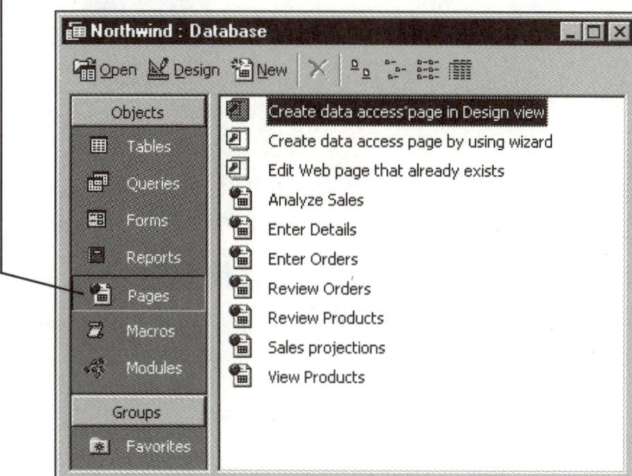

2 Double-click the page to open it.

Notes:

- Use Design view to customize the data access page. Working with data access pages in Design view is similar to working with forms and reports. Work with controls that you create using the Toolbox and use the design grid to position objects.
- You can view the page in HTML source code if you have the HTML Source Editor installed. Select **View**, **HTML Source**.

In Design View

1 Click **Pages** in the Database window.

2 Select the page to open.

3 Click Design.

Notes:

- Opening the page in Internet Explorer shows you what it will look like when you publish it on the Web or intranet.
- You must have Internet Explorer version 5.0 or later installed on your computer in order to open a data access page.
- You can also open the page in Internet Explorer from outside of Access. Double-click the icon for the data access page file in Windows Explorer and it will open in Internet Explorer. Or, start Internet Explorer and enter the page location (pathname) in the Address bar.

In Internet Explorer

1. Open the page in Design view or Page view.
2. Select **File**, **Web Page Preview**. Access starts Internet Explorer and displays the page.

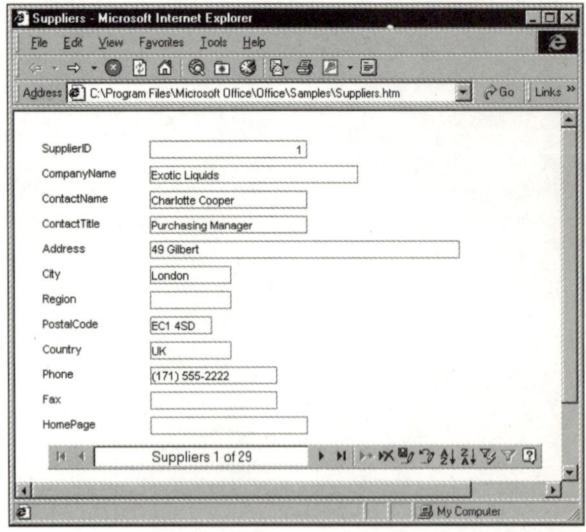

3. Close the page.

Design View

Switch to Design view to create and edit the structure of tables, forms, reports, queries, and data access pages. This section details how to work with the structure of forms, reports, and data access pages in Design view.

Use the Toolbox to create controls in Design view. Set properties for a control to format and otherwise specify its attributes.

Design view includes a grid to help you size and position controls precisely.

Control Basics

Use the Toolbox in Design view to create controls on forms, reports, and data access pages.

Notes:

- This illustration shows the Toolbox for forms. The Toolbox for data access pages has more tools.

Display the Toolbox

1 Open a form, report, or data access page in Design view.

2 Click **Toolbox** on the toolbar if the Toolbox is not already displayed.

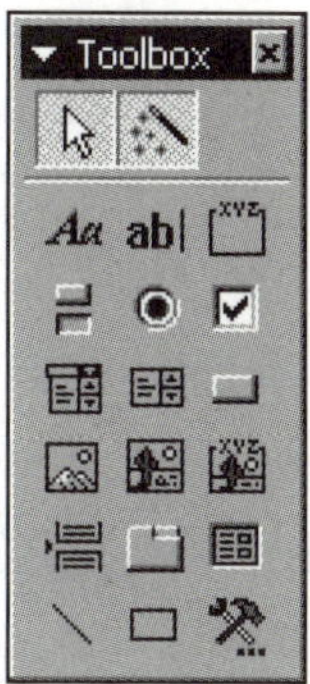

Notes:

- When Control Wizards are enabled, creating a control causes a wizard to start. The wizard guides you through the process of creating the control.
- By default, Control Wizards are enabled.

Enable/Disable Control Wizards

1 Display the Toolbox (see above).

2 Click **Control Wizards** on the Toolbox if it is not already enabled.

Note: *When Control Wizards are enabled, the button has a pressed-in appearance: . When disabled, the button appears as any other button:*

Notes:

- To keep a particular toolbox tool active so that you can create multiple controls of a particular type, lock the tool on the Toolbox. That way you can create controls without pausing to click the control tool again.
- To speed things up even more, you may want to disable Control Wizards (see above) when locking a control tool.

Lock a Tool

1 Double-click the desired control tool in the Toolbox.

Note: The mouse pointer changes to reflect the current control.

2 Create controls.

3 Press **Esc** to unlock the control.

OR

Click the **Select Objects** button  on the Toolbox to unlock the control.

Resize a Control

1 Click anywhere in the control to select it. A border with handles appears around a control when it is selected.

Note: If you select a control that has an attached label, both the control and the label are selected.

2 Place the mouse pointer on a selection handle until the pointer changes to an arrow.

3 Drag to resize the control.

Move a Control

1 Click anywhere in the control to select it. A border with handles appears around a control when it is selected.

Note: If you select a control that has an attached label, both the control and the label are selected.

2 Place the mouse pointer anywhere on the selection border until it changes to a hand pointer.

3 Drag the control on the design grid.

Delete a Control

1 Click the control or label.

2 Press **Delete**.

Notes:

- Selecting the control selects both the control and its attached label (for example, a field and the field label). When you press **Delete**, both will be deleted. Selecting just the label allows you to delete only the label.

Properties

Many of the objects, elements, and controls of Access have Properties settings that you can customize. Properties control additional aspects of objects that are not set using menus or toolbars.

Form or Report Control Properties

1 In Design view, click the object and, on the toolbar, click the Properties button to display the Properties Sheet.

OR

Double-click the object.

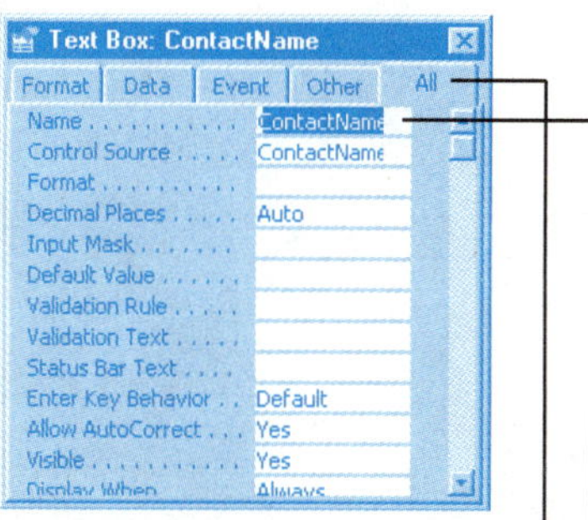

2 Click the desired tab to bring it to the front.

3 Change properties as desired (see below).

Property	Use
Caption	Contains text for column, form or report labels. Otherwise, the field name is used.
Decimal places	Determines the number of decimal places displayed for number fields.
Default value	Specifies a value automatically assigned to the field.
Format	Determines the display of data, such as the associated symbols with number fields, the translation of yes/no data, and the wording of date/time data.
Required	Determines whether it is required to input or enter data into the field.
Can Grow	For printouts, allows field to enlarge to show all data.
Can shrink	For printouts, allows field to shrink around data to close up empty space.

4 Close the Properties sheet.

Notes:

- You can also view an item's properties by right-clicking the item and selecting **Properties** from the pop-up menu.

Form and Report Properties

1 In Design view, click an area in the Form or Report window outside the form or report layout.

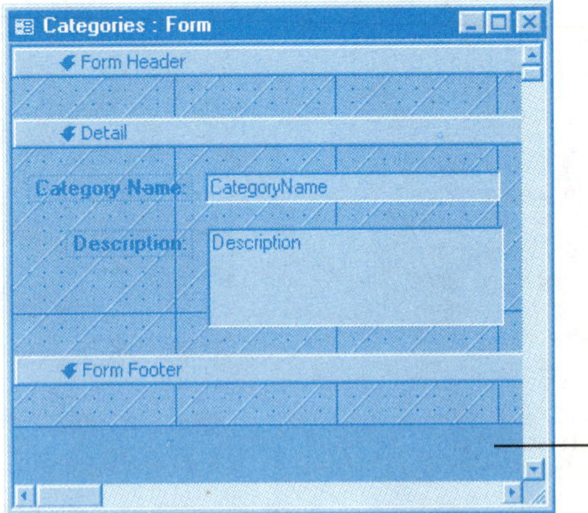

2 On the toolbar, click the **Properties** button to display the Properties Sheet.

3 Change properties as desired.

Property	Use
Record Source	Specifies the table or query from which displayed records are drawn.
Default View	Specifies whether Form or Datasheet view will be displayed on opening.
Views Allowed	Limits view to Form or Datasheet.
Allow Edits/Deletions/Additions	Controls data entry.

4 Close the Properties sheet.

Copy Control Formatting

Copy formatting such as colors, fonts, borders, special effects, text alignment, and other formatting from one control to another.

Notes:

- Format one control the way you want it and then copy the formatting to other controls to perform high-speed formatting.
- You can lock the Format Painter button so that you can apply the copied formatting to more than one control.
- To apply a consistent formatting scheme to all elements in the form, report, or page, use an AutoFormat.
- To change an individual formatting property for a single control, use the Format tab in the control properties. The formatting properties that are available depend on the type of control you are working with. However, formatting for all controls is handled by setting properties.

1 In Design view, click the formatted control.

2 Click to copy the formatting to a single control.

OR

Double-click to copy to multiple controls. When locked, the Format Painter button appears pressed-in: 

3 Click the control you want to apply the formatting to.

4 If you double-clicked the button in step 2:

a. Repeat step 3 as desired to apply more formatting.

b. When you have finished formatting, click to unlock it.

Set Default Properties for Controls

Default control properties determine how new controls will look when you create them using a Toolbox tool. For example, if you want all new titles to use a certain font and color, set the default font and color properties for labels.

Notes:

- Default settings are saved with each form, report, and data access page. You can save different defaults in each database object.
- Control default settings are referred to as the default control style.
- Each type of control has its own default control style. For example, the default control style for text boxes is not applied to labels.
- To set default properties for fields, set text box properties. To set default properties for field names, set label properties.

1. Open a form, report, or data access page in Design view.
2. If the Toolbox is not visible, select **View**, **Toolbox** to display it.
3. Press **Ctrl+R** to make sure the entire form, report, or data access page is selected.
4. Select **View**, **Properties**.
5. Click the Toolbox tool you want to modify. The property title bar changes to the word "Default" followed by the name of the control type that you selected (such as "Default Text Box").

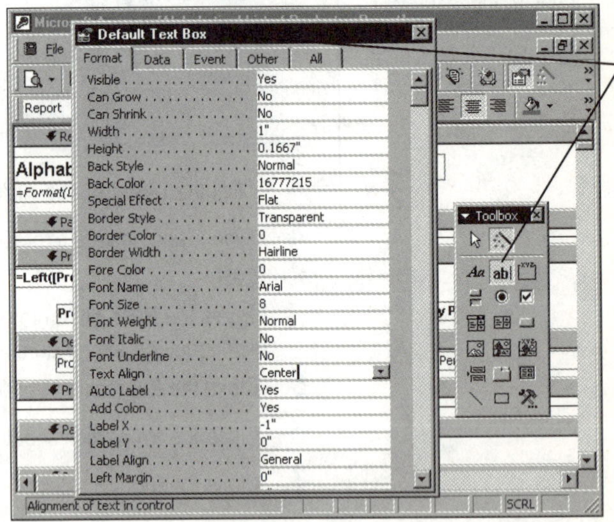

6. Set options as desired. When you click in a property, the status bar displays a brief description of the property.
7. Click to close the Properties sheet.

Expressions

Expressions are used in queries, forms and reports to provide values calculated based on your formulas.

Notes:

- Expressions can be used to display the current date or page number, or to string field values.
- Expressions in Control Source tell Access where to get the data that will be displayed in the text box.
- In a form or report, you will have to create your own label for the text box containing the expression.

Enter the Expression in a Control on a Form or Report

1 Click the text box that you want to contain the expression (see **Edit a Form**).

2 Click the Properties button (see **Properties**).

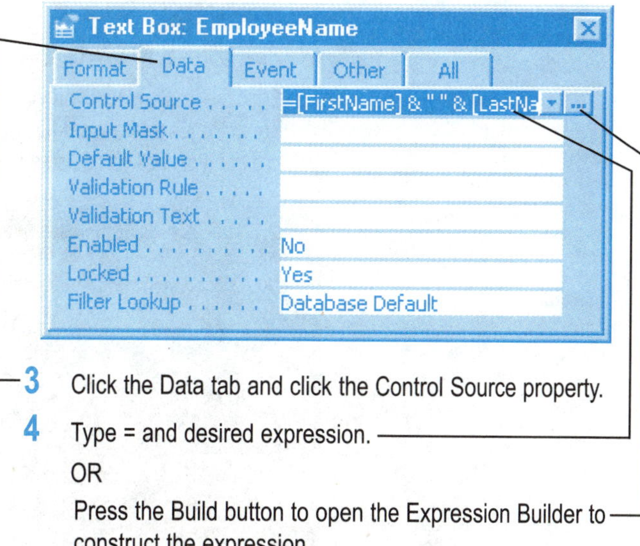

3 Click the Data tab and click the Control Source property.

4 Type = and desired expression.

OR

Press the Build button to open the Expression Builder to construct the expression.

5 Close the Expression Builder if you opened it.

6 Close the Properties sheet.

7 Close the form or report.

Enter the Expression in a Query

1 In the Database window, click **Queries**.

2 Click the query you want to view and click Design.

Notes:

- The name you type before the colon becomes the field label.
- Equal signs do **not** precede expressions in queries.

3 Click an empty field cell to use for the expression.

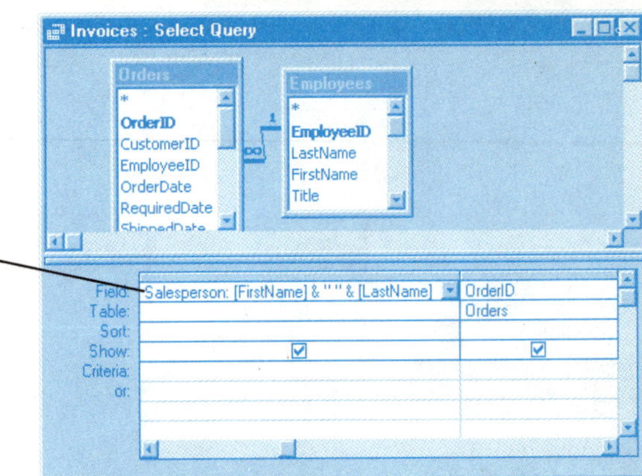

4 Type a name for the expression followed by a colon.

5 Type the desired expression.

OR

On the toolbar, click the **Build** button to open the Expression Builder.

Expressions and Examples

When using a field name in an expression, surround it with square brackets. When using text, surround it with quotation marks. (In the first example below, the space is enclosed in quotation marks so that the fields don't run together.)

Operator	Use	Example	Sample Result
&	Combines text	[first name] & " " & [last name]	Jun Smit
Chr$10 & Chr$13	Inserts a line return	[first name] & " " & [last name] & Chr$10 & Chr$13 & [company name]	Jun Smit Ajax Company
Date()	Current date	=Date	January 24, 1998
Page()	Current page	="page " & page()	page 53
*	Multiplies	=[rate]*[hours]	(20 * 5=) 100
-	Subtracts	=[rate]-5	(20-5=) 15
+	Adds	=[rate]+5	(20+5=) 25
/	Divides	=[rate]/5	(20/5=) 4

Use the Grid in Design View

In Design view, a grid of dotted lines appears on the screen. Use the grid to line up and size objects that you add to a form, report, or data access page.

Notes:

- Using the grid to size or align controls helps you line them up accurately and keeps them a uniform size and distance from each other. You can use the grid to help you visually size and position controls, or you can use the Snap to Grid option.
- Snap to Grid causes objects to jump to the nearest dot in the grid when you move or size them. Creating, sizing, moving, and aligning controls with Snap to Grid enabled forces the control to "snap" to the closest grid points.
- The Snap to Grid option can be enabled even if the grid is hidden.
- To temporarily disable Snap to Grid, hold down **Ctrl** while you move or size a control.
- Changing the granularity of the grid changes the number of dots per square inch.

Show or Hide the Grid

Click **View**, **Grid**.

Enable or Disable Snap to Grid

Select **Format**, **Snap to Grid**.

Set Grid Granularity

1. Press **Ctrl+R** to select the form, report, or page.
2. Select **View**, **Properties** to open the form, report, or page Properties sheet.
3. Click the **Format** tab. Scroll down to the Grid properties.
4. Type a value in the **GridX** property to change the granularity of the horizontal lines in the grid.

   Note: *A higher number results in more dots that are closer together. When you type a new granularity value, you can see the new placement of dots in the grid. If you type too high a value, dots will be placed too close together to be useful.*
5. Type a value in the **GridY** property to change the granularity of the vertical lines in the grid.
6. Click ☒ to close the Properties sheet if desired.

Notes:

- In addition to the grid, you can use the ruler to help you line up objects in Design view.

Show or Hide the Ruler

Click **View**, **Ruler**.

Notes:

- Aligns a group of existing controls to the design grid.

Align Controls to the Grid

1. Select the controls to align.
2. Select **Format**, **Align**, **To Grid**. The selected controls automatically line up with the grid.

Notes:

- Resizes a group of existing controls.
- To size a control to the grid when you create it, enable the Snap to Grid feature. As you drag across the design grid to create the control, it will automatically snap to the next gridline.

Resize Controls to the Grid

1. Select the controls to resize.
2. Select **Format**, **Size**, **To Grid**. The selected controls are resized to the nearest points on the grid.

Draw a Line on a Form, Report, or Page

Enhance the appearance of forms, reports, and data access pages by drawing lines to add borders.

Notes:

- Lines and borders make screens and reports more professional in appearance. They also separate the different elements of a form or report to make them easier to read.
- The Toolbox includes the Line tool which you can use to draw lines in Design view. The Line tool creates a Line control. You can set properties for the Line control just as any other control.

1 Open a form, report, or data access page in Design view.

2 Click **Line** on the Toolbox.

*Note: If the Toolbox is not displayed, select **View**, **Toolbox**.*

3 Drag across the design grid to draw the line.

4 To change line weight if desired:

a. Click the line to select it.

b. Click **Properties** in the toolbar. The properties for the line display.

c. Click the **Format** tab.

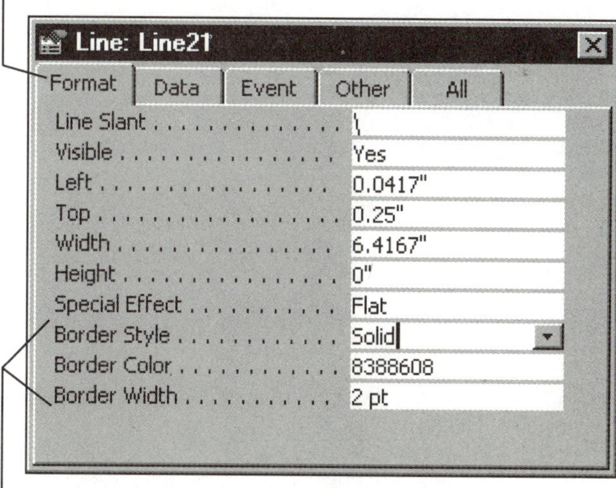

d. Set border line style, color, and width as desired.

e. Click to close Line Properties.

5 Repeat steps 1–3 to draw more borders as desired.

6 Press **Ctrl+S** to save changes.

7 Close the Properties sheet.

Notes:

- You can also add rectangular borders. See **Add Borders to a Form, Report, or Page**.
- Use the design grid to have lines snap to the background grid lines as you draw them. See **Use the Grid in Design View**.

8 Click to close the design when you have finished modifying it.

The following illustration shows a report with two borders. The top line separates the column headings from the data. The bottom line separates the body of the report from the page footer.

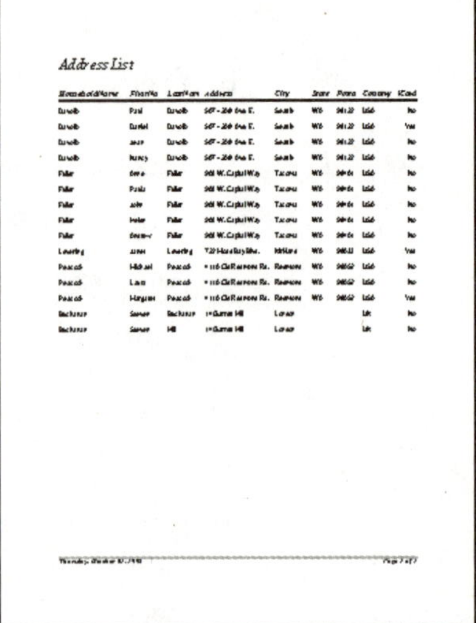

Add Borders to a Form, Report, or Page

Improve the appearance and enhance the organization of input screens and reports, including those displayed in a data access page, with rectangular borders.

Notes:

- This procedure tells you how to draw borders using the Rectangle tool in the Toolbox.

Notes:

- If the Toolbox is not displayed, select **View**, **Toolbox**.
- The illustration shows the Toolbox in form Design view. The data access page Toolbox has more tools.

1 Open a form, report, or data access page in Design view.

2 Click **Rectangle** in the Toolbox.

3 Drag on the design grid to draw the border.

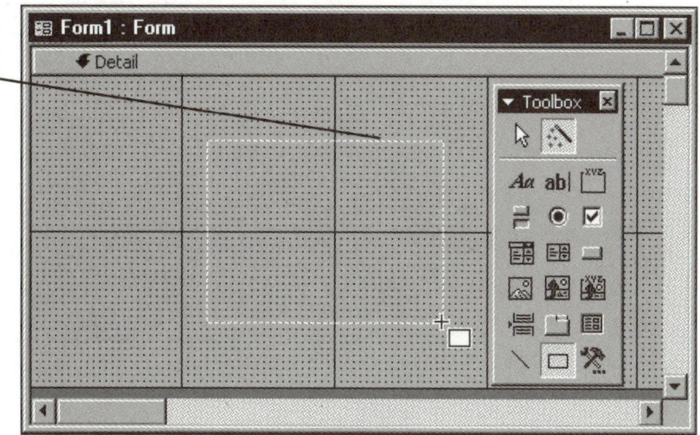

As you drag, the cursor changes shape as shown in the illustration. When you release the mouse button, Access draws the border.

Notes:

- Use the design grid to have borders snap to the background grid lines as you create them. See **Use the Grid in Design View**.
- This procedure draws a rectangular border. To create borders by drawing single lines, see **Draw a Line on a Form, Report, or Page**.

4 To format the border:

a. Right-click the border and select **Properties**. The Rectangle properties display.

b. Click the **Format** tab.

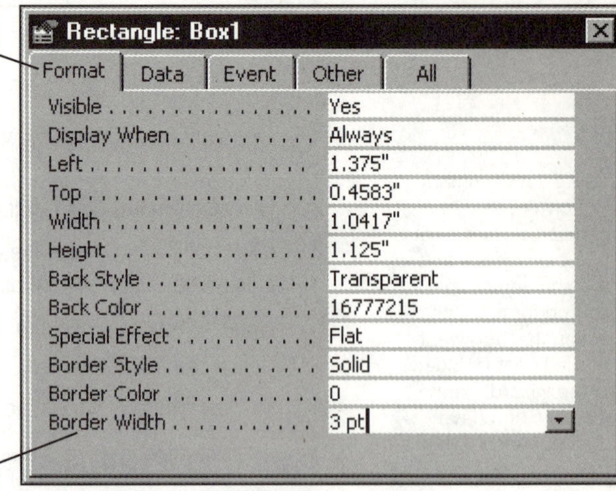

c. Use the Special Effect and Border properties to specify formatting.

d. Click [X] to close the Properties sheet.

5 Click **Save** to save the design.

6 Click [X] to close the design when you have finished modifying it.

The following illustration shows a thin etched border added to one of the sample forms in the Northwind database.

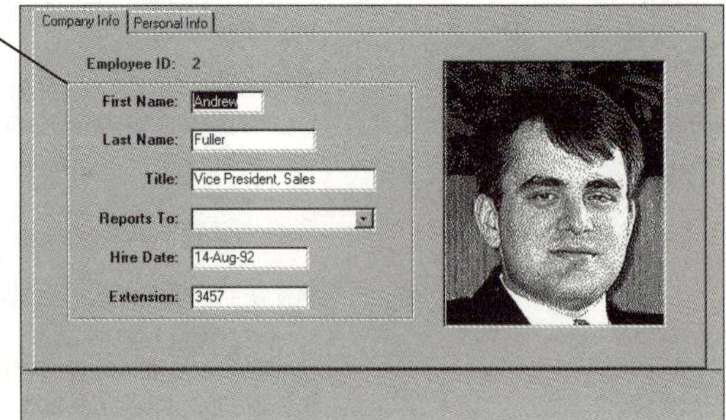

Add a Command Button to a Form

When you click on a command button in Form view, it performs an action such as printing a report, filtering data, or running a macro.

Notes:

- Using the Command Button Wizard, you can select from a list of many actions that a command button can perform. If the action that you want to run is not included in the wizard, create a macro and have the command button run the macro.
- To see the event procedure that runs when the button is clicked in Form view, open the properties for the control. The event procedure is in the On Click property on the **Event** tab.
- This procedure assumes that you have Control Wizards enabled so that the Command Button Wizard will start automatically when you select the Command button. See **Control Basics**.

1 Open a form in Design view.

2 Click **Command** in the Toolbox.

3 Click the form to create the command button. The Command Button Wizard dialog box displays.

Note: You can move and resize the command button after you create it.

4 To view different actions, select a different category.

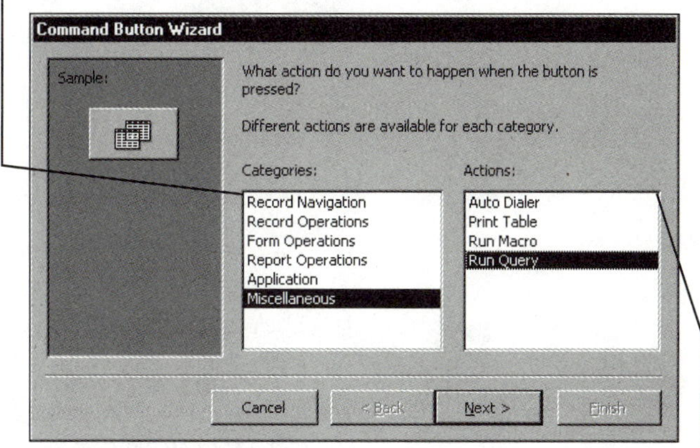

5 Select the action that you want the button to perform from the list of actions.

Note: A preview of the default picture that will be added to the button shows in the Sample pane. The image changes depending on the selected action.

6 Click Next >.

7 Follow Command Button Wizard prompts and click Next > to set up the command button. The prompts that are displayed depend on the action that you selected.

Notes:

- The size of the command button that you create will adjust to accommodate the picture or text that you place on the button face. You can resize the button after you create it. Use control properties to change the typeface and font size of text on a button.

8 The processes for creating a command button converge at the following screen. Select whether to display text or a picture on the button:

- If you select **Text**, type the text to display on the button.

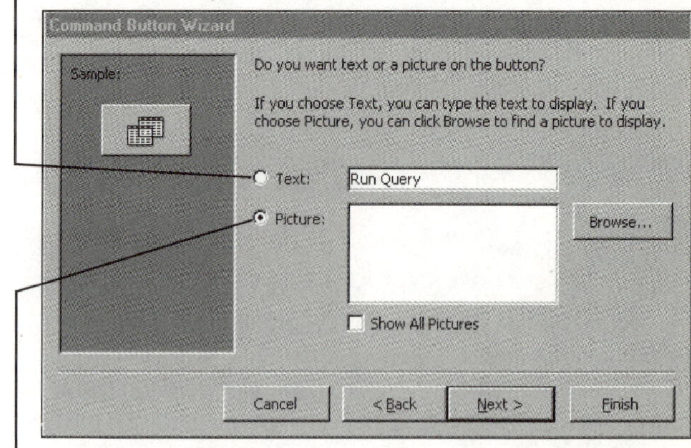

- If you select **Picture**, you can use the picture shown in the Sample pane. Or, select **Show All Pictures** to choose from button pictures included with Access. You can also click the **Browse** button and select a picture file.

9 Click Next >.

10 Type a name for the button.

11 Click Finish.

12 Close the form.

Add a Label to a Form, Report, or Page

Labels display text that does not change from record to record or page to page. For example, you would display a report title or a field name in a label.

Notes:

- There are two kinds of labels: attached labels and stand-alone labels.
- Access automatically creates attached labels when you add certain types of controls to a form, report, or page. For example, when you add a field to a form, Access creates a text box for the field data and a corresponding label for the field name. The label is attached to the text box. The label stays with the text box when you move, select, and otherwise work with it.
- Use stand-alone labels for descriptive text such as titles, subtitles, and instructions on how to use a form. Use this procedure to create stand-alone labels.

1. Open the form, report, or data access page in Design view.
2. Click **Label** in the Toolbox.

   Note: If the Toolbox is hidden, select ***View****,* ***Toolbox****.*
3. Drag in the design grid to create the label. Release the mouse button when the label is the size you want.

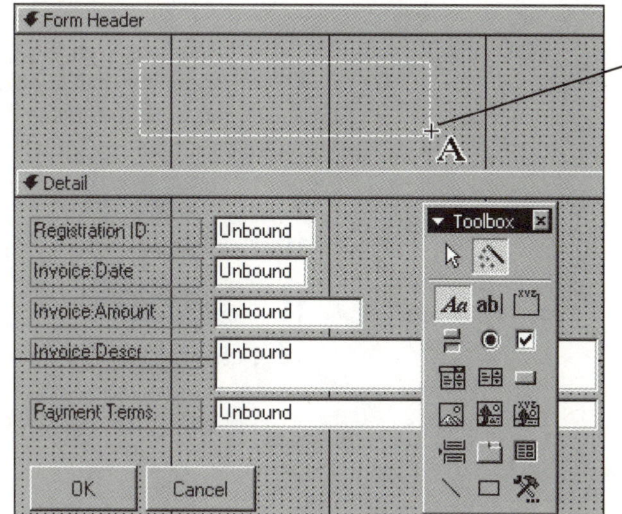

4. Type the text that you want to appear in the label.

5. To start a new line in a label, press **Ctrl+Enter**.
6. Press **Enter** when you are finished entering text.
7. Close the form, report, or page.

Change the Font of Text in a Label

Change the font, attributes (such as boldface or italics), and/or the size of text in a label.

Notes:

- You can format both stand-alone labels that display descriptive text and attached labels that display field names, or other captions for other controls.

1. Open the form, report, or data access page in Design view.
2. Right-click a label.
3. Select **Properties**. The Label properties sheet displays.
4. Click the **Format** tab.
5. Scroll down to the Font property settings.

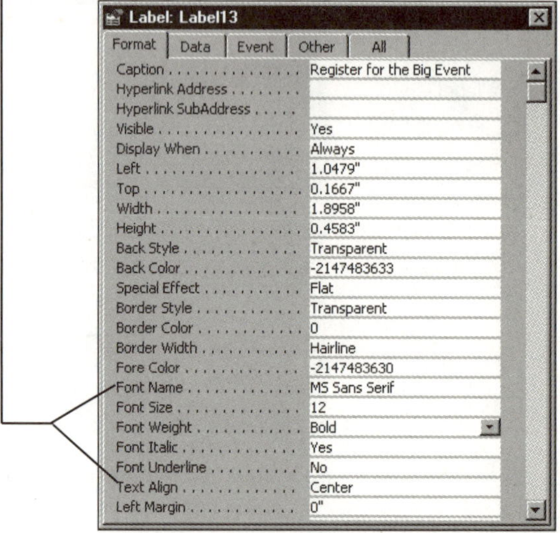

6. Click in a Font property and click ▾ to select a property from the list. For example, change the font name and the font size.
7. Click ☒ to close the Properties sheet. The following illustration shows the above properties applied to the descriptive text in a label.

8. Close the form, report, or page.

Add a Graphic to a Form or Report

Add a picture as a decorative element to a form.

Notes:

- To add a picture to a form or report, place it in an image control. An image control stores a picture that stays the same from record to record. For example, you might display a company logo at the bottom of a form. A picture in an image control is similar to a title or other descriptive text displayed in a label.

1 Open the form or report in Design view.

2 Click **Image** on the Toolbox.

3 Drag in the grid to create the control. Release the mouse button when the image control is the size you want.

Note: *You can automatically size the control to fit the picture after you import it.*

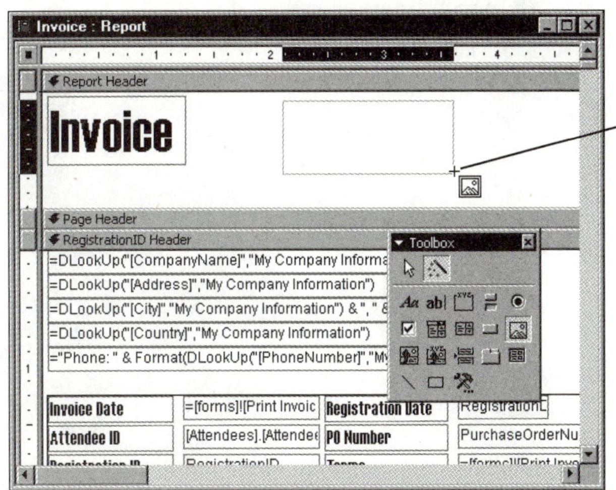

When you release the mouse button, the Insert Picture dialog box displays.

4 Select the picture file in the Insert Picture dialog box.

5 Click OK. Access places the picture in the image control.

6 To resize the image control to fit the picture if desired, right-click the control and select **Size**, **To Fit**.

Note: *To size the picture to the fit the image control, set the **Size Mode** property in the control properties to **Stretch**. When you resize the control, the picture will automatically resize to fit.*

Notes:

- Like titles, pictures in image controls are often added to a header or footer in the form or report.

7 To apply special formatting such as a raised effect, right-click the image control and select **Special Effect**. Select the effect to apply. For example, the following illustration shows an image control with a shadow effect.

Notes:

- By default, Access applies a border around an image control. Use this procedure to remove the border or to change the line style.

Format or Remove the Border

1 Right-click the image control.

2 Select **Properties**. The Image properties display.

3 Click the **Format** tab.

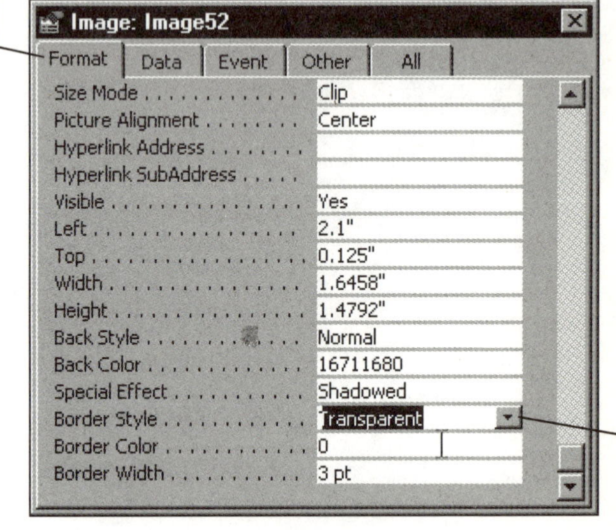

4 Click the **Border Style** property.

5 Select a different line style to apply.

OR

Select **Transparent** to remove the border.

6 Click [X] to close the Image properties sheet.

7 Switch to Form view to view your changes.

Create a Tip for a Control

Add pop-up tips and status bar text to provide assistance on using particular types of controls. You can display text in a tip that displays when the mouse pointer is placed on the control or you can display text in the status bar when a control is selected.

Notes:

- Pop-up tips are usually a brief description of the control. When the mouse pointer is placed over the control, a yellow box pops up with text that you specify.
- You have seen pop-up tips in Office applications. For example, when you place the mouse pointer over a dialog box option, a tip on using the option displays.

Create a Pop-Up Tip for a Control

1. Open the form or data access page in Design view.
2. Right-click the control.
3. Select **Properties**.
4. Click the **Other** tab.
5. Display the ControlTip Text property if you are working in a form (as shown).

   OR

   Display the Title property if you are working in a data access page.
6. Type the text that will appear in the pop- up tip when the mouse pointer is placed over the control. You can use up to 255 characters.

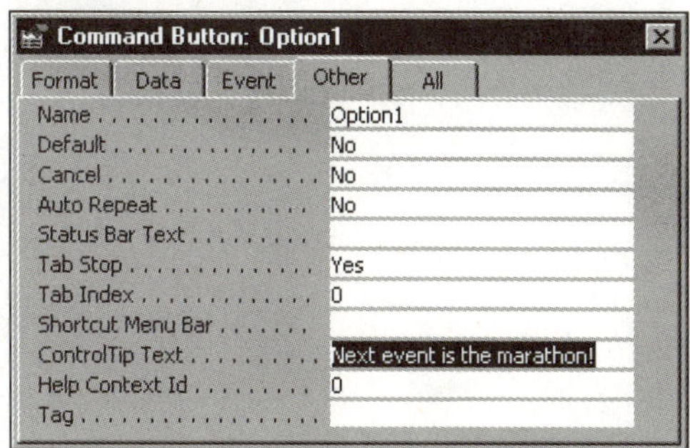

7. Click ☒ to close the Properties sheet.

Notes:

- You can create pop-up tips for text boxes, command buttons, option buttons, and other controls on forms and data access pages.

8 To see the pop-up tip, select **View**, **Form View** (for a form) or **View**, **Page View** (for a data access page) and position the mouse pointer over the control as shown in the following illustration.

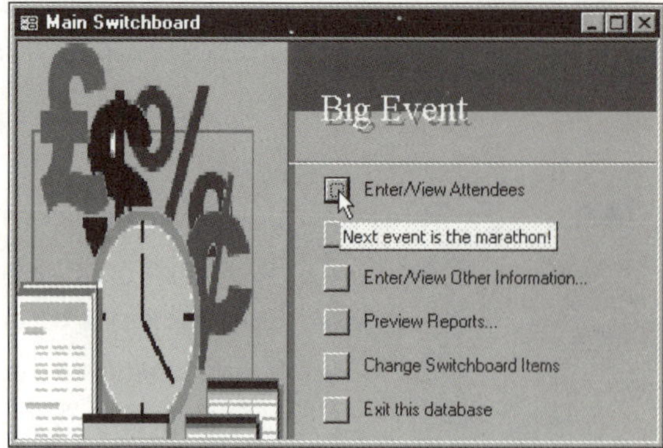

Notes:

- When a control is selected, the text that you specify appears in the status bar of the form. For example, when the cursor is placed in a field, the text will display in the status bar.
- Status bar tips often provide help on how to use a particular control. For example, status bar text for a field might explain the kind of information that should be entered in the field.
- You can create status bar text for text boxes, fields, and other controls on forms.

Display Status Bar Text for a Control

1 Open the form in Design view.

2 Right-click the control.

Note: *The control selected cannot be a label or unbound control.*

3 Select **Properties**.

4 Click the **Other** tab.

5 Type the text to display in the status when the control is selected in the Status Bar Text property.

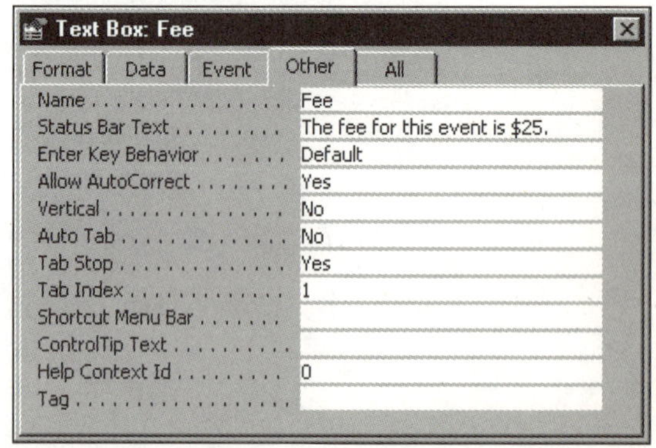

6 Click ☒ to close the Properties sheet.

7 To see the pop-up tip in a form, select **View**, **Form View** and select the control. The text displays in the status bar at the bottom of the application window.

Change the Record Source for a Form or Report

The record source is the table, query, or SQL statement on which a form or report is based.

Notes:

- The Record Source property determines where the data in a report or the data to edit in a form comes from.

1. Open the form or report in Design view.
2. Press **Ctrl+R** to select the entire form or report.
3. Right-click the title bar of the Design window.
4. Select **Properties**. Form properties display.
5. Click the **Data** tab.

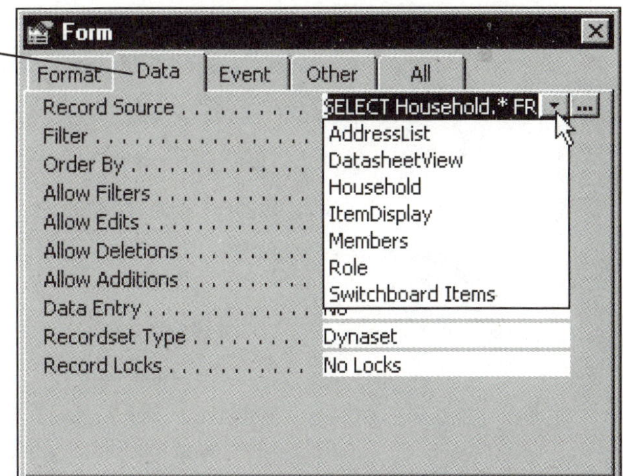

6. Select a record source for the form or report from the drop-down list.

   Note: You can also click [...] to create an expression to specify the data source.

7. Click [X] to close the Properties dialog box.
8. Close the form or report.

Import/Export Data

You can copy Access data into other applications. You can also copy data created in other applications into Access. For example, you can export client names and addresses stored in an Access table to Microsoft Word, where you can use the Access data to create letters and labels for a client mailing.

You can also copy data and other objects, such as toolbars, between Access databases.

Import from Another Access Database

Copy the data or the structure of database objects from another Access database into the current database. You can also import custom menus and toolbars.

Notes:

- You can import the data from a table or query into the current database. Or, you can import the structure of a database object. For example, you can import a report design or a query design.

1. Open the database into which you will import the data.
2. Select **File**, **Get External Data**, **Import**. The Import dialog box displays.
3. Select the database containing the table.
4. Click Import. The Import Objects dialog box displays.

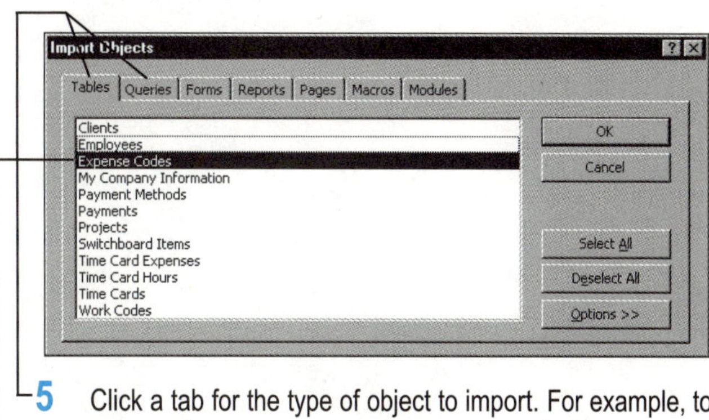

5. Click a tab for the type of object to import. For example, to import queries, click the **Queries** tab.

   Note: To import menus and toolbars, see step 9.

6. Select the database object to import.

   OR

   Click Select All to select all objects in the current tab.

7. Repeat steps 5 and 6 to specify other objects to import if desired.
8. Click Options >> to show additional options in the lower part of the Import Objects window.

Notes:

- To work with data in another database without copying it into the current database, see **Link to a Table in Another Access Database**.

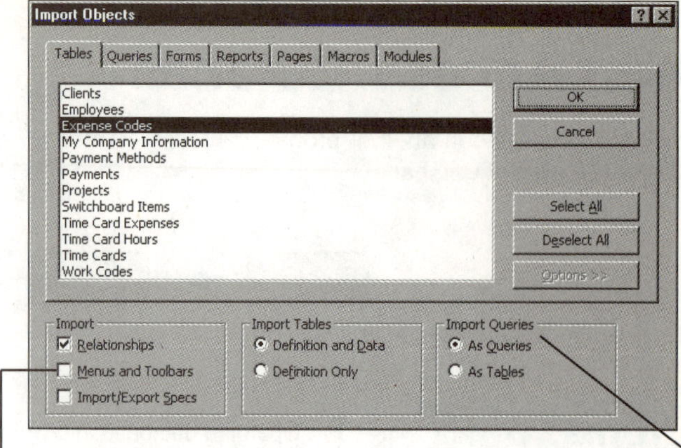

9 Select to import **Menus and Toolbars** if desired.

10 If you are importing queries, specify whether to import the query design (**As Queries**) or the query data (**As Tables**).

11 If you are importing tables:

a. Under **Import Tables**, specify whether to import both the **Definition and Data** (imports the table structure and all data in the table) or the **Definition Only** (imports the table structure without data).

b. To preserve the relationships between tables in the original database, select **Relationships**.

12 Click OK.

Import Data from a Non-Access Database

Import data created in another program. Access creates a new table for the imported data in the current database.

Notes:

- Access starts a wizard based on the type of file that you are importing. For example, if you import an Excel workbook, the Import Spreadsheet Wizard starts.

1 Open the database into which you will import the data.

2 In the Database window, click **Tables**.

3 Click New. The New Table dialog box displays.

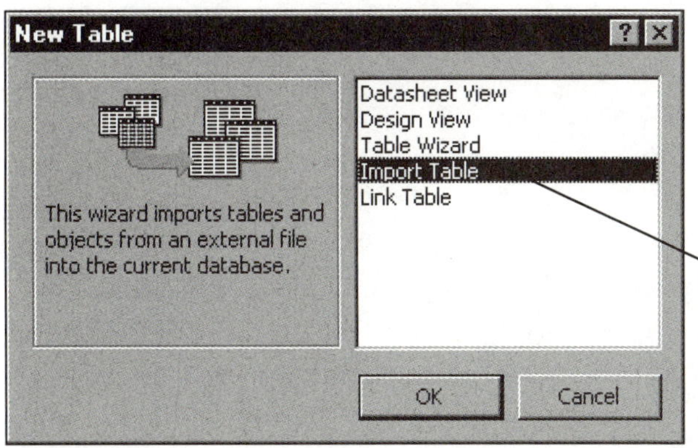

4 Double-click **Import Table**. The Import dialog box displays.

5 Select the type of file you are importing from the **Files of type** list.

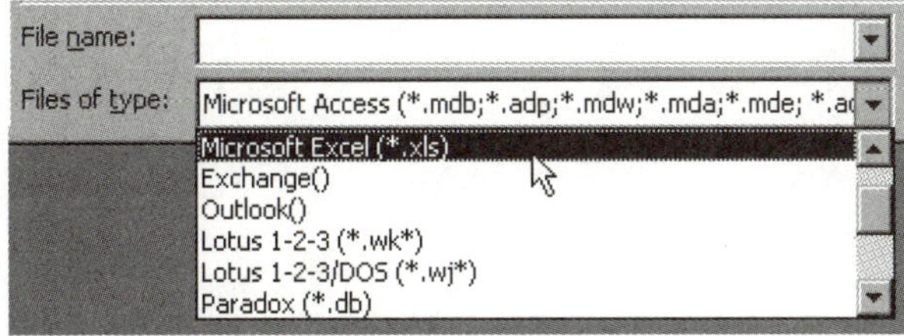

Notes:

- If you are importing a spreadsheet, you can import the entire file or a named range.
- Access creates a new table for the imported data and adds it to the Database window.

6 Select the file containing the data to import.

*Note: To shows files in a different drive or folder, select from the **Look in** list.*

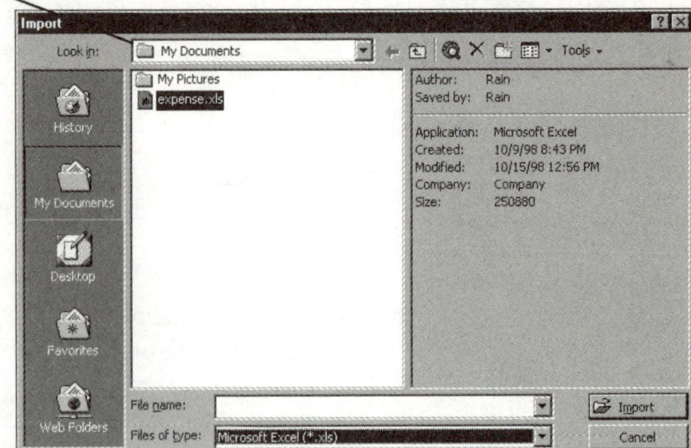

7 Click Import. The wizard for the file type that you selected starts. For example, if you selected an Excel or Lotus spreadsheet, the Import Spreadsheet Wizard starts.

8 Follow the wizard prompts on the screen and click Next >.

9 At the last screen, click Finish. Access imports the data and creates a new table in the current database for it.

Export to a Word Mail Merge Data Source

Create a Microsoft Word mail merge data source file from names and addresses in an Access table.

Notes:

- Use the exported data source file to create form letters in Word.
- The data that you export can be stored in a table or the result of a query. For example, you could create a query that selects name and address information from the Employees table to create a list of employee names and addresses. You would select the query as the data source to export to Word. Access exports the query data, not the query database object.
- Access field names are retained in the mail merge data source. When you add fields to the main document in Word, use the original field names.
- After exporting the table or query, open Word and start the Mail Merge Wizard to create form letters.
- You can start Microsoft Word and the Mail Merge Wizard from within Access. Select the table or query to use as the data source and then select **Tools**, **OfficeLinks**, **Merge It with MS Word**.

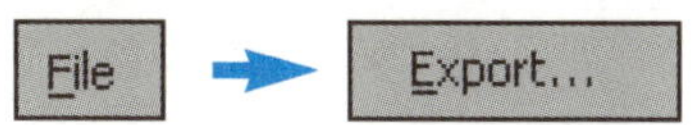

1 Right-click the table or query containing the merge data and select **Export**. The Export dialog box displays.

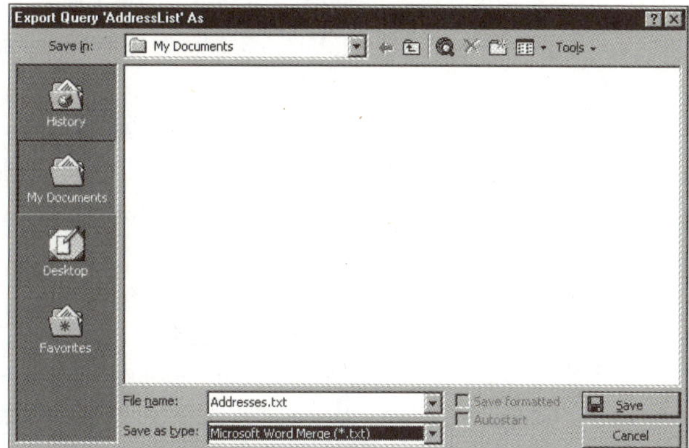

2 Select a location and type a name for the mail merge data source file if desired.

Note: The .txt file extension will be added for you.

3 Select **Microsoft Word Merge** (*.txt) in the **Save as type** list.

4 Click **Save**.

5 Open Microsoft Word and start the Mail Merge Wizard. Specify the exported file as your data source file.

Output Report Data to Microsoft Excel

Use OfficeLinks to output the data in an Access report to a new Microsoft Excel workbook.

Tools
Office Links

Notes:

- This procedure exports report data, not the report database object.
- Microsoft Excel must be installed on your computer in order for this procedure to work.
- If the report is grouped, Excel outlines the report data. Records in report groups become second- and third-level rows in the workbook.

1 Select the report containing the data to export.

2 Select **Tools**, **Office Links**, **Analyze It with MS Excel**. Access exports the data and displays a prompt reporting on the progress of the export.

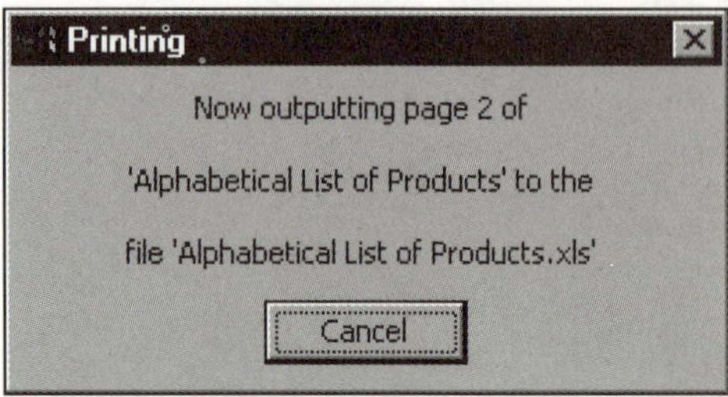
Printing
Now outputting page 2 of
'Alphabetical List of Products' to the
file 'Alphabetical List of Products.xls'
Cancel

When Access is finished, Excel is open with the new workbook containing the exported data on the screen.

Get Help

Access offers two types of Help: Help on the Web and Help that is installed with Access.

To locate Help topics, you can use the Office Assistant, the Answer Wizard, and the Table of Contents.

If you cannot find the information you are looking for in Help, go to the Office of the Web page to search for Help topics in the Microsoft Office Web site.

Get Help Using the Answer Wizard

The Answer Wizard is a tab located in the Help dialog box. Use it to ask questions and browse through topics found.

Notes:

- This procedure assumes that you have disabled the Office Assistant so that it does not pop up when you start Help. If the Office Assistant appears instead of the Help dialog box, see **Disable the Office Assistant** or **Customize the Office Assistant**.

1 Select **Help**, **Microsoft Access Help**. The Microsoft Access Help dialog box opens.

Note: If the Office Assistant is enabled, it appears rather than the Help dialog box. To disable the Office Assistant, see ***Customize the Office Assistant****.*

2 Click the **Answer Wizard** tab.

3 Type your question. You can enter English-language queries such as "create appointment" or "exit Access."

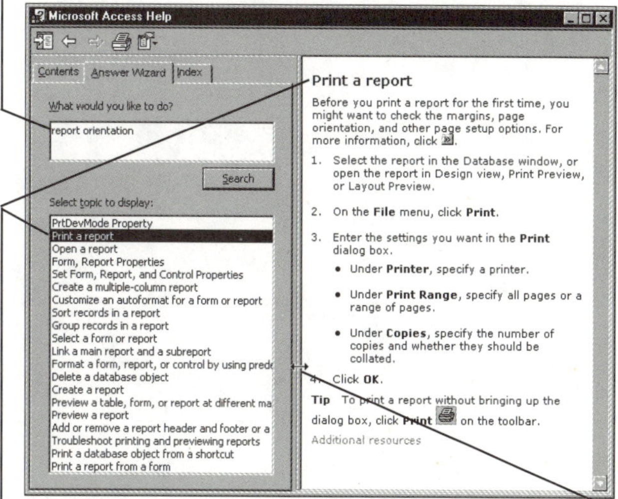

4 Press **Enter**. Topics that might be related to your question appear in the **Select topic to display** list.

5 To resize panes so that you can see more of the topic titles, place the mouse pointer between the two panes until the pointer changes to a double-headed arrow. Drag to resize.

6 Click the topic to read. The topic is displayed in the right pane.

Notes:

- You can ask questions of the Answer Wizard in much the same way as you do the Office Assistant.

7 Sometimes a topic includes a hyperlink or a button to another topic. When you hover the mouse pointer over a hyperlink or a button, it changes to a hand. Click the hyperlink or button to display the target topic.

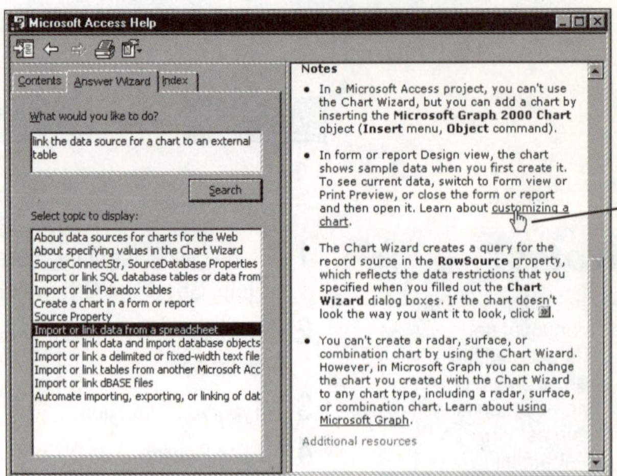

8 To return to the last topic that you read, click **Back**  in the toolbar. To go forward again, click **Forward** .

9 Repeat from step 3 to ask a different question if desired.

10 Click ☒ to close the Help window.

Get Help Using the Office Assistant

The Office Assistant is a character that stays on the screen while you work. It provides tips about your tasks as you work and you can type questions in the character's balloon to find Help topics.

Notes:

- The Office Assistant is an animated character with a balloon in which you can type questions such as "How do I print a mail message?" (or just "print mail message"). The Office Assistant will respond with a number of topic titles that might be related to your question.
- By default, the Office Assistant pops up automatically as you work and displays help tips on your current tasks or asks you if you want help. You can specify when you want the Assistant to try to give you help or you can disable the character altogether.

1 If the Office Assistant character is not displayed, select **Help**, **Show the Office Assistant**.

2 If the balloon does not appear with the character, click the character.

3 Type your question.

4 Click **Search**. The balloon displays a list of topics related to your question.

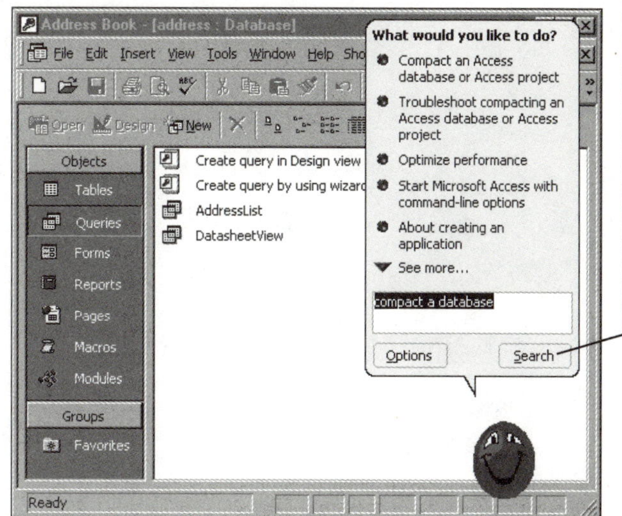

Notes:

- You can also use the Answer Wizard to get help by asking questions (see **Get Help Using the Answer Wizard**).
- If you cannot find the topic you are looking for, you can connect to the Web (provided you have Internet access). The phrase that you entered in the Office Assistant balloon is submitted at the Microsoft Office Web site.

5 To view a particular topic, click the topic title. The topic displays in the Microsoft Access Help dialog box.

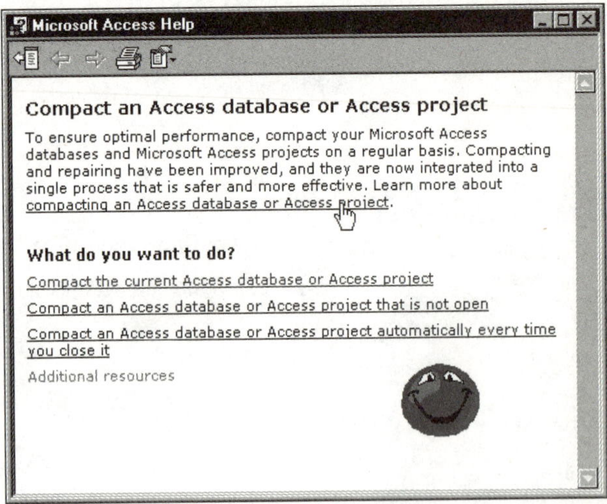

Note: You can drag the Office Assistant anywhere on the screen if it is in your way.

6 Repeat from step 3 to enter a different search phrase if desired.

Customize the Office Assistant

The Office Assistant stays on the screen and offers tips related to your current task as you work. You can change the behavior of the Assistant by setting options that determine when it offers help.

Notes:

- You can have Access display a tip every time Access starts. This feature is called the Tip of the Day.
- Tip options determine when the Office Assistant will automatically display a tip (without your requesting help). Once you are familiar with Access, you will probably want the Assistant to be less active.

1 If the Office Assistant character is not displayed, select **Help**, **Show the Office Assistant**.

2 Click the character to display the balloon.

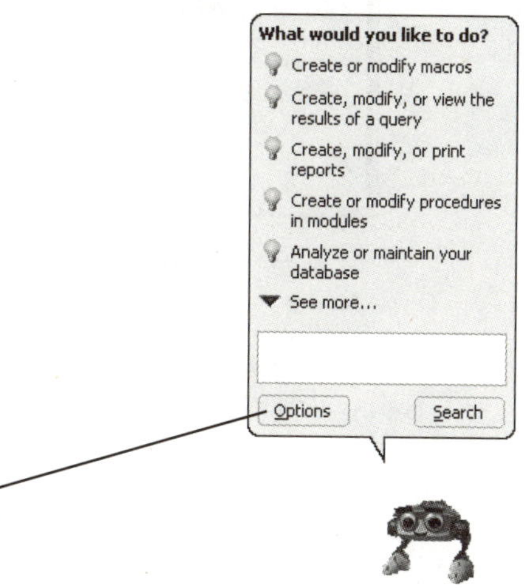

3 Click **Options** in the balloon. The Office Assistant dialog box displays.

4 Click the **Options** tab.

5 Set options as desired:

- **Respond to F1 key**. By default, pressing **F1** displays the Office Assistant if it is hidden or activates the Office Assistant balloon if the Assistant character is displayed.

  If you clear this check box, the Microsoft Access Help dialog box displays instead of the Office Assistant when you press **F1**. If the Office Assistant is not on the screen, you can select **Help**, **Show the Office Assistant** to display it.

  Clearing this check box also changes the action of the **Microsoft Access Help** toolbar button ( ) so that it opens the Help dialog box rather than the Office Assistant. Clearing the check box allows you to access the Answer Wizard, Contents, and Index methods of getting help. You can still access the Office Assistant using the **Help**, **Show the Office Assistant** command.

Notes:

- If you want to be able to open the Microsoft Access Help dialog box to find Help topics, clear the **F1** key option so that pressing it opens the dialog box rather than the Office Assistant. If you only want to use the Microsoft Access Help dialog box to find topics and never the Assistant, see **Disable the Office Assistant**.

- **Help with wizards**. When selected, the Office Assistant automatically displays topics that apply to the procedure you are performing whenever you start a wizard (such as the Import Wizard).
- **Display alerts**. Error messages, warning messages, and confirmation prompts are displayed in the Assistant balloon rather than in the standard Office dialog box.
- **Search for both product and programming help when programming**. By default, when you are creating Access applications in Visual Basic, help topics do not include Access user topics. The Office Assistant will search only Visual Basic help topics. If you check the option, topics on using Access are included when you use the Assistant to search for help.
- **Move when in the way**. When checked, the Assistant appears in an area of the screen away from the cursor position or open dialog box so that it does not hide your work.
- **Guess help topics**. The Assistant displays Help topics that it determines are relevant when it decides that you might need help performing a task.
- **Make sounds**. To disable Office Assistant sounds, clear the check box.

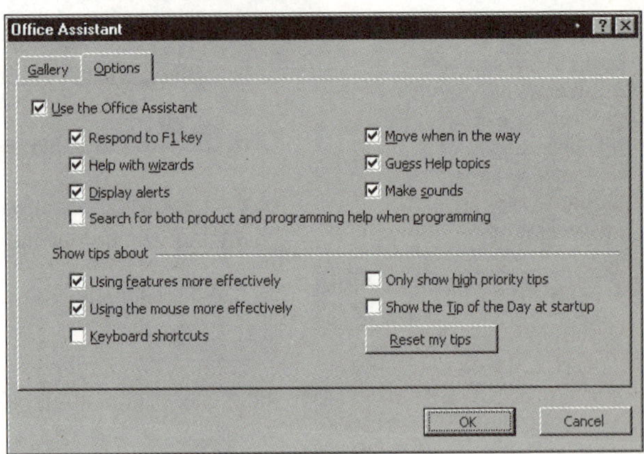

- **Show tips about**. Use this group of options to choose the kinds of information that you are interested in having the Office Assistant display tips about.

  Note: When the Office Assistant has a tip, a light bulb appears above the Assistant character. Click the light bulb to see the tip.

6 Click .

Change the Office Assistant Character

Choose from a number of animated characters displayed in the Office Assistant Gallery.

Notes:

- The gallery shows all of the available characters. However, it is possible that not all characters were installed with Access. If you select an uninstalled character, Access starts the Windows installer and installs it.
- The new Assistant character will be the active character in all Office 2000 programs that you have installed, not just Access.
- Some characters are less distracting than others. For example, the Office Logo does not move, whereas the paper clip character is very active.

1 If the Office Assistant character is not displayed, select **Help**, **Show the Office Assistant**.

2 Right-click the Assistant character and click **Choose Assistant**. The Office Assistant Gallery opens.

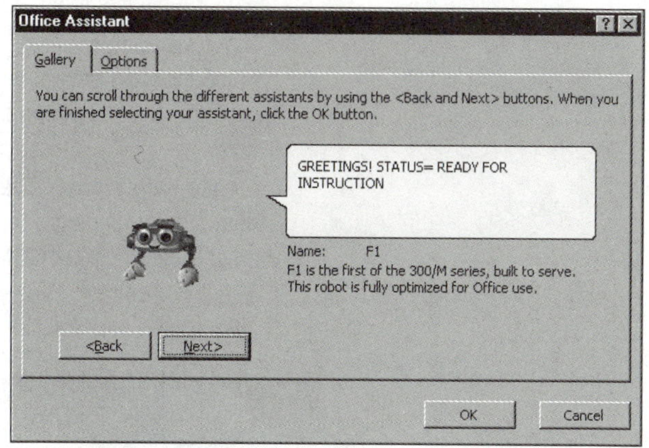

3 Click [Next>] to see a preview of another Assistant character. Click [Next>] and [<Back] to browse characters and display the character to use.

4 To use the character currently displayed, click [OK].

5 If the character is not installed, click **Yes** at the prompt to install it.

Disable the Office Assistant

Temporarily hide the Assistant or else turn it off altogether.

Notes:

- When you temporarily hide the Assistant, it is removed from the screen. It will return again automatically when it is time to display a tip, provide help with a wizard, or display an alert as specified in the Office Assistant options. See **Customize the Office Assistant** to specify when the Assistant should display tips.
- When you disable the Office Assistant, it remains off until you enable it or temporarily show it. When the Assistant is disabled, you can use the Microsoft Access Help dialog box to find help topics. This dialog box includes the Answer Wizard, the Contents tab, and the word list.

1. If the Office Assistant character is not displayed, select **Help**, **Show the Office Assistant**.
2. Right-click the Assistant and select **Options**. The Office Assistant dialog box displays.
3. Clear **Use the Office Assistant** to disable the Assistant.
4. Click OK.

*Note: To enable the Office Assistant, repeat the procedure. To temporarily use the Assistant, select **Help**, **Show the Office Assistant**.*

Temporarily Show/Hide the Assistant

Select **Help**, **Show the Office Assistant** to enable the Assistant. To display the balloon, click the character.

OR

Select **Help**, **Hide the Office Assistant** to disable the Assistant.

Get Help Using the Table of Contents

Browse through the Contents to see help topics organized in a hierarchical structure like the table of contents of a book.

Notes:

- The **Contents** tab contains a list of all the topics in Help organized logically, just as the table of contents appears in a book. Book icons in the **Contents** tab represent levels in the table. Opening a book displays topics and/or books on a particular subject. Opening a topic displays the topic in the right pane of the window.
- Not all topics are listed in the Contents. However, by navigating hyperlinks in topics to view more detailed information, you can access any topic in the Help system.
- The **Contents** tab is on the Microsoft Access Help dialog box. In order to use the **F1** key to open the dialog box, change the action of the **F1** key so that it does not display the Assistant. See **Customize the Office Assistant**.

1 Press **F1**. The Microsoft Access Help dialog box displays.

Note: *If the Office Assistant displays rather than the Microsoft Access Help dialog box, see **Customize the Office Assistant** to change the action of the **F1** key. This also changes the action of the **Microsoft Access Help** toolbar button so that it opens the dialog box rather than the Assistant.*

2 Click the **Contents** tab.

Note: *If the **Contents, Answer Wizard**, and **Index** tabs do not appear in the left pane, click **Options** in the toolbar and select **Show Tabs**.*

3 Scroll in the left pane to view contents.

4 Each book icon represents another level in the table of contents. To open a book to display its contents, click ⊞. To close it, click ⊟.

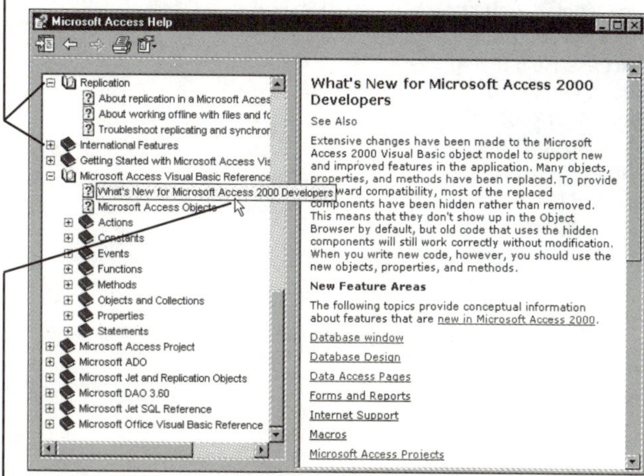

5 If a topic title is hidden, hover the mouse pointer over the title. Access displays the complete title in a pop-up tip.

6 To view a topic, click the topic title. The topic appears in the right pane.

Get Help from Office on the Web

Visit the Office on the Web site to see the latest software developments, download add-ins and patches, and get Help on using Access and other Office 2000 applications.

Notes:

- Access starts your default Web Browser and goes to the Web page.
- You might have to register in order to visit some of the pages in the Office on the Web site. When you register, you have to enter a password. You will need the password to return to the site.
- The Office on the Web site changes frequently as Microsoft is constantly improving and updating its pages. The site might contain different information each time you visit.
- Select **Help**, **Office on the Web**. Access starts your Web browser and connects to the Microsoft Office on the Web site.

Select a page to go to in the Access area of the Web site.

Select a different product. Each product has Updates, Downloads, Assistance, and Newsgroups pages just as in the Access page.

Select an area of the Microsoft Office on the Web site to go to.

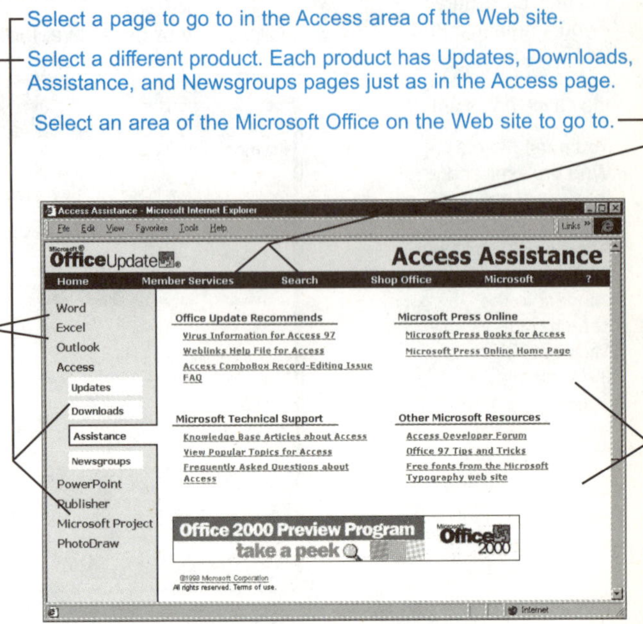

Read an article or browse in these categories.

Get Help in the Office Update Search Page

The Office Update search page is part of the Microsoft Office on the Web site. If the Office Assistant does not find a relevant help topic, you can search the Web.

Notes:

- Use this procedure if you are unable to find help on a particular topic using the Office Assistant.
- You must have a Web browser and an Internet account to use this procedure. Access will start your Web browser and connect to the search page for the Microsoft Office on the Web site.

1 Use the Office Assistant to search for a Help topic (see **Get Help Using the Office Assistant**).

2 Click **None of the above, look for more help on the Web.**

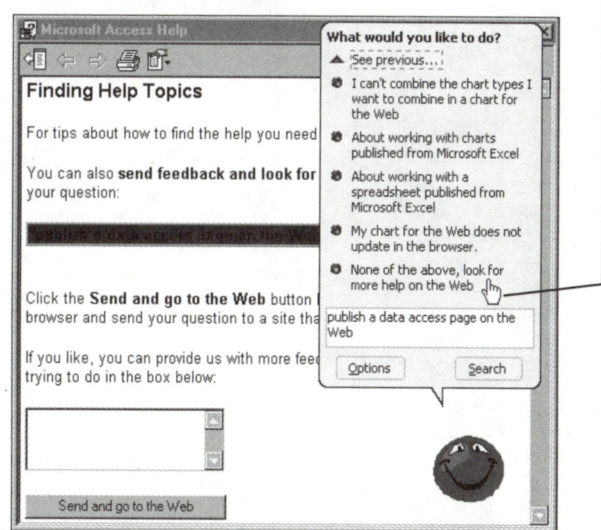

Note: *The phrase that you typed in the Office Assistant balloon will be the search phrase used to find topics on the Web. You can change the search phrase by typing a new phrase in the Assistant balloon.*

Notes:

- Access will search the Office Web site using the search phrase that you entered in the Office Assistant balloon. You are given an opportunity to modify the phrase before submitting it at the Web site.

3 Click Send and go to the Web. Your Web browser starts and connects to the Microsoft Office Update search page.

4 Modify the search phrase if desired.

5 Click the **Search** button.

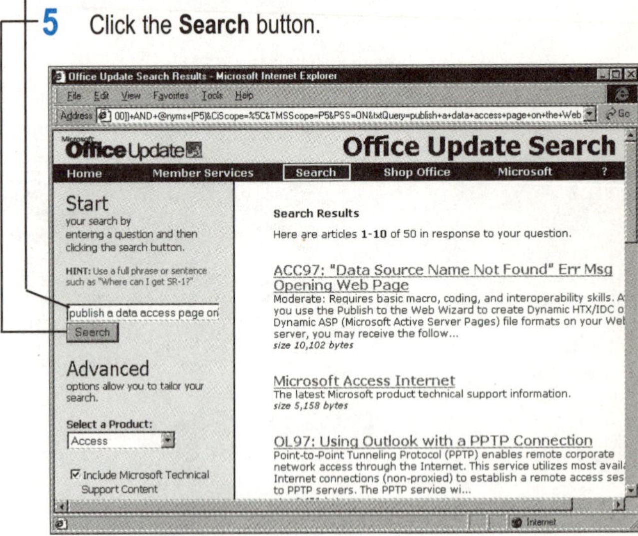

Glossary

AutoNumber

An Access field type that automatically places a sequentially numbered value in each record. AutoNumber fields are typically used to assign a unique number to each record in order to identify it. For example, every part should have a unique number that identifies it.

Calculated control

A control on a form, report, or data access page that displays the result of an expression.

Check box

A control that displays a check for a yes (true) condition or that is blank for a no (false) condition.

Clipboard

An area in memory where Access places data that you cut or copy. You can paste the data from the Clipboard into a field.

Combo box

A control that displays a drop-down list from which you can select the data you want to enter. The combo box can also accept data that you type into the control.

Command button

A control on a form or report that can be set to run a macro or event procedure when it is clicked.

Control

An object that you add to a form, report, or data access page in Design view. Controls are used for a variety of purposes. For example, field controls, list box controls, and combo box controls on forms are used to enter data into the underlying table or query. A field control on a report displays data. A command button on a form usually runs a macro or Visual Basic procedure when it is clicked. An image control displays a picture on a data access page, form, or report.

Criteria

Instructions that you enter in order to limit the records that will be included in a query, form, or report. For example, you can enter criteria in a filter to specify that only those clients located in the state of Florida will be displayed in a table. Clients located in any other state do not appear in the list of records in the table when the filter is applied.

Data

Information stored in a table in the database.

Database object

A form, report, query, table, data access page, or module.

Datasheet

Data from a table or query displayed in columns and rows, similar to the way a spreadsheet is displayed. Each column in the datasheet is a field and each row is a record.

Design view

An Access mode that you switch to in order to modify the structure of a form, report, query, table, or data access page.

Export

To copy an object or data to a separate file (usually in another file format) that you can use in another application. For example, you can export the data in an Access table to an Excel worksheet.

Filter

Criteria applied to a table to limit which records will be displayed or printed. For example, you could create a filter that, when applied to a table, showed only orders for the current year. Orders from previous years would not be displayed.

Form

A database object used to enter and/or display data in a table or query.

Index

A sort order that stores table data in a particular order. Indexes can decrease the amount of time it takes to search tables.

Label

A control that displays text such as a title on a form, report, or data access page.

Link

A reference to data stored in another file. For example, you can link the current database to the data in a table in another Access database or to an external SQL Server database.

List box

A control on a form, datasheet, or data access page that displays a list of values for a particular field. You create a list box in Design view. When you edit the data in a form, datasheet, or page, you can select from the list of values in order to enter data in the field.

Module

Database object that contains macros and Visual Basic procedures.

Orientation

The position of text on a printed page. Landscape orientation places the text horizontally (lengthwise) on the page. Portrait orientation places text vertically on the page.

Primary key

A field or combination of fields that uniquely identifies a record. For example, an AutoNumber field might be a primary key field because no two records in the table can have the same number in an AutoNumber field.

Property

An object attribute. For example, size, color, and font are all properties of a label control. The text displayed in the window title of a form is one of the properties of a form. The default value for a field is a field property.

Query

A stored set of instructions that display or change the data in one or more tables.

Relationship

A link between common fields in different tables in a database.

Sort

To alphabetize or sequentially order the records in a table or query based on the values in one or more fields. For example, you can sort (alphabetize) employee records by last name. You can sort in either ascending (a–z, 1–9) or descending (z–a, 9–1) order.

SQL

Structured Query Language, a programming language developed to query databases.

Subform

A form within a form that can display fields from an additional table or query.

Subreport

A report within a report that can display fields from an additional table or query.

Table

The basic structure of a relational database. A table contains data organized in rows (records) and columns (fields).

Template

A design that you can use to create a new database for a particular application, such as an Order Entry or a Time and Billing system. Use the Database Wizard in Access to use a template to create a new database.

Toolbox

A group of buttons visible in Design view that you use to create controls on a form, report, or data access page.

Wildcards

Characters that you use in an expression to stand for other character(s) or number(s). For example, the **?** wildcard stands for any single character or number.

Wizard

A Microsoft tool that automates many database tasks.

Zoom box

A window that gives a larger view of the data in a cell or field.

Index

A

Add a Command Button to a Form 176
Add a Field to a Form or Report 120
Add a Field to a Table 32
Add a Form Header and Footer 114
Add a Graphic to a Form or Report 180
Add a Header and Footer to a Report 134
Add a Label to a Form, Report, or Page 178
Add a Lookup Field to a Table 34
Add a Toolbar Button That Opens a Web Page 12
Add Borders to a Form, Report, or Page 174
Add or Edit Table Relationships ..20
Add or Remove a Field in a Query 68
Add or Remove a Table in a Query 66
Add Page Numbers to a Report 136
Adjust Datasheet Column Width and Row Height 74
Apply an AutoFormat to a Form 106
Apply an AutoFormat to a Report 127
Apply an Input Mask to a Field on a Form 118
Apply a Theme to a Data Access Page 154
Apply a Validation Rule to a Field 38

C

Change the Default Database Folder 7
Change the Font of Text in a Label 179
Change the Form Window Title..116
Change the Office Assistant Character 200
Change the Record Source for a Form or Report 184
Control Basics 162
Copy and Move Data in Forms, Datasheets, and Pages 82
Copy Control Formatting 166
Create a Crosstab Query Using a Wizard 54
Create a Data Access Page Using AutoPage 152
Create a Data Access Page Using a Wizard 150
Create a Database Using a Wizard 14
Create a Find Duplicates Query Using a Wizard 50
Create a Find Unmatched Query Using a Wizard 52
Create a Form Using AutoForm 100
Create a Form Using a Wizard 98
Create a Group in the Database Window 4
Create a Hotspot Control That Opens a Web Page 156
Create a Make-Table Query 56
Create a Multiple-Tab Form 102
Create an Append Query 60
Create an AutoReport 126
Create an Update Query 58
Create a Report Snapshot 146

Create a Report Using a Wizard 124
Create a Simple Select Query 64
Create a Subform and Add It to a Form 108
Create a Table Using a Wizard 28
Create a Tip for a Control 182
Create Mailing Labels Using a Wizard 128
Customize the Office Assistant ..198

D

Delete a Field from a Table 42
Disable the Office Assistant 201
Disable the Startup Dialog Box 6
Display All Fields in Query Results 70
Display Objects in the Database Window 2
Draw a Line on a Form, Report, or Page 172

E

Edit a Subform 110
Enter Data in a Datasheet, Form, or Page 80
Exclude Duplicate Records in a Query 72
Export to a Word Mail Merge Data Source 190
Expressions 168

F

Filter Records in a Datasheet or Form 90
Find Data in a Form or Datasheet 86

G

Get Help from Office on the Web 203
Get Help in the Office Update Search Page 204
Get Help Using the Answer Wizard 194
Get Help Using the Office Assistant 196
Get Help Using the Table of Contents 202
Group a Report 140

H

Hide a Column in a Datasheet 78
Hide or Show Datasheet Gridlines 76

I

Import Data from a Non-Access Database 188
Import from Another Access Database 186
Index a Table 46
Insert the Date/Time in a Report 138

L

Link to a Table in Another Access Database 24

M

Move a Field in a Table 40

N

Navigate in a Datasheet, Form, or Page 84

O

Open a Data Access Page 158
Open a Database 18
Open a Form 104
Open a Report 130
Open a Table 30
Output Report Data to Microsoft Excel 191

P

Personalized Menus 8
Preview a Report 142
Print a Report 144
Properties 164

R

Replace Data in a Form or
Datasheet 88
Require a Field Value 37

S

Set Default Properties for
Controls 167
Set Report Page Margins and
Orientation 132
Set the Default Field Value 36
Set the Primary Key for a Table ..44
Set the Tab Order in a Form 112
Show or Hide a Toolbar................10
Show the Result of a Calculation
on a Form 117
Sort the Data in a Datasheet
or Form 94

U

Use the Grid in Design View......170